A WORLD OF
INEQUALITIES

PREVIOUSLY PUBLISHED RECORDS OF
BUILDING BRIDGES SEMINARS

The Road Ahead: A Christian–Muslim Dialogue, Michael Ipgrave, editor (London: Church House, 2002)

Scriptures in Dialogue: Christians and Muslims Studying the Bible and the Qurʾān Together, Michael Ipgrave, editor (London: Church House, 2004)

Bearing the Word: Prophecy in Biblical and Qurʾānic Perspective, Michael Ipgrave, editor (London: Church House, 2005)

Building a Better Bridge: Muslims, Christians, and the Common Good, Michael Ipgrave, editor (Washington, DC: Georgetown University Press, 2008)

Justice and Rights: Christian and Muslim Perspectives, Michael Ipgrave, editor (Washington, DC: Georgetown University Press, 2009)

Humanity: Texts and Contexts: Christian and Muslim Perspectives, Michael Ipgrave and David Marshall, editors (Washington, DC: Georgetown University Press, 2011)

Communicating the Word: Revelation, Translation, and Interpretation in Christianity and Islam, David Marshall, editor (Washington, DC: Georgetown University Press, 2011)

Science and Religion: Christian and Muslim Perspectives, David Marshall, editor (Washington, DC: Georgetown University Press, 2012)

Tradition and Modernity: Christian and Muslim Perspectives, David Marshall, editor (Washington, DC: Georgetown University Press, 2012)

Prayer: Christian and Muslim Perspectives, David Marshall and Lucinda Mosher, editors (Washington, DC: Georgetown University Press, 2013)

Death, Resurrection, and Human Destiny: Christian and Muslim Perspectives, David Marshall and Lucinda Mosher, editors (Washington, DC: Georgetown University Press, 2014)

The Community of Believers: Christian and Muslim Perspectives, Lucinda Mosher and David Marshall, editors (Washington, DC: Georgetown University Press, 2015)

Sin, Forgiveness, and Reconciliation: Christian and Muslim Perspectives, Lucinda Mosher and David Marshall, editors (Washington, DC: Georgetown University Press, 2016)

God's Creativity and Human Action: Christian and Muslim Perspectives, Lucinda Mosher and David Marshall, editors (Washington, DC: Georgetown University Press, 2017)

Monotheism and Its Complexities: Christian and Muslim Perspectives, Lucinda Mosher and David Marshall, editors (Washington, DC: Georgetown University Press, 2018)

Power—Divine and Human: Christian and Muslim Perspectives, Lucinda Mosher and David Marshall, editors (Washington, DC: Georgetown University Press, 2020)

A WORLD OF INEQUALITIES

CHRISTIAN AND MUSLIM PERSPECTIVES

A Record of the Seventeenth
Building Bridges Seminar

Hosted by
The Faculty of Islamic Studies in Sarajevo
The Faculty of Catholic Theology
The Faculty of Orthodox Theology
The Gazi Husrev-beg Library
Sarajevo, Bosnia and Herzegovina
June 18–22, 2018

LUCINDA MOSHER
EDITOR

Georgetown University Press / Washington, DC

The publisher is not responsible for third-party websites or their content. URL links were active at time of publication.

Library of Congress Cataloging-in-Publication Data
Names: Building Bridges Seminar (17th : 2018 : Sarajevo, Bosnia and Herzegovina), author. | Mosher, Lucinda, editor.
Title: A world of inequalities : Christian and Muslim perspectives : a record of the seventeenth Building Bridges Seminar / Lucinda Mosher, editor
Other titles: Seventeenth Building Bridges Seminar
Description: Washington, DC : Georgetown University Press, 2021. | Hosted by the Faculty of Islamic Studies in Sarajevo, the Faculty of Catholic Theology, the Faculty of Orthodox Theology, the Gazi Husrev-beg Library, Sarajevo, Bosnia and Hercegovina, June 18-22, 2018—Title page. | Includes bibliographical references.
Identifiers: LCCN 2020008159 | ISBN 9781626168084 (hardcover) | ISBN 9781626168091 (paperback) | ISBN 9781626168107 (ebook)
Subjects: LCSH: Equality—Religious aspects—Christianity—Congresses. | Equality—Religious aspects—Islam—Congresses.
Classification: LCC BL65.E68 B85 2018 | DDC 261.7—dc23
LC record available at https://lccn.loc.gov/2020008159

♾ This book is printed on acid-free paper meeting the requirements of the American National Standard for Permanence in Paper for Printed Library Materials.

22 21   9 8 7 6 5 4 3 2   First printing

Printed in the United States of America
Cover design by Debra Naylor

Contents

Participants   vii

Introduction   1

PART ONE: OVERVIEWS

Unjust Inequality as a Challenge for Contemporary Islam   7
Ovamir Anjum

The Challenges of a World of Inequalities for Christians Today   21
David Hollenbach, SJ

PART TWO: MUSLIMS AND CHRISTIANS
FACING THE REALITY OF INEQUALITY

Gender and Islam: Obstacles and Possibilities   39
Samia Huq

The Problem of Race in Christianity   53
Elizabeth Phillips

Nationality and Ethnicity in West Africa: An Economic
and Religious Perspective on Inequalities   59
François Pazisnewende Kaboré, SJ

Islam and the Challenge of Sociopolitical Equality:
The Contribution of Religious Creed   69
Sherman A. Jackson

Caste and Social Class in the Christian and Islamic
Communities of South Asia   77
Sunil Caleb

Slavery: Source of Theological Tension   83
Jonathan Brown

PART THREE: INEQUALITY, THE BIBLE, AND THE CHRISTIAN TRADITION

Inequality in the Old Testament   93
  Leslie J. Hoppe, OFM

Old Testament Texts for Dialogue on Inequalities   107

For All of You Are One in Christ Jesus? The New Testament
Witnesses on Ethnic, Economic, Social, Religious, Racial,
and Gender Inequality   117
  Christopher M. Hays

New Testament Texts for Dialogue on Inequalities   139

PART FOUR: INEQUALITY, THE QUR'AN, AND THE HADITH

Racial, Religious, and Gender Equality: Reflections
on Qur'anic Texts   151
  Abdullah Saeed

Qur'an and Hadith Texts for Dialogue on Human Nature,
Gender, Ethnicity, Religion, and Inequality   163

Economic Equality and Inequality: An Introduction
to Selected Qur'anic Texts   171
  Abdullah Saeed

Qur'an and Hadith Texts for Dialogue on Economic Inequality   193

PART FIVE: POSSIBILITIES AND OBSTACLES TOWARD A COMMON ETHIC OF EQUALITY

Three Strands Leading to the Edge: Considering the Possibility
of a Common Ethic of Equality   201
  C. Rosalee Velloso Ewell

Muslim-Christian Bridges: Toward a Shared Theology
of Human Development?   207
  Azza Karam

PART SIX: REFLECTIONS

Considering Inequalities as Scholars of Faith:
Reflections on Bridge-Building in Sarajevo   217
  Lucinda Mosher

Subject Index   227

Scriptural Citation Index   239

About the Editor   245

Participants in
Building Bridges Seminar 2018

Amir Akrami, Institute for Humanities and Cultural Studies, Tehran, Iran

Ahmet Alibašić, University of Sarajevo, Bosnia and Herzegovina

Ovamir Anjum, University of Toledo, USA

Waleed El-Ansary, Xavier University, USA

Jonathan Brown, Georgetown University, USA

Sunil Caleb, Bishop's College, Kolkata, India

Jonathan Chaplin, Divinity Faculty, Cambridge, UK

Susan Eastman, Duke University Divinity School, USA

C. Rosalee Velloso Ewell, Redcliffe College, UK

Mahmoud Amin el-Gamal, Rice University, USA

Christopher M. Hays, Biblical Seminary of Colombia, Colombia

David Hollenbach, SJ, Georgetown University, USA

Leslie J. Hoppe, OFM, Catholic Theological Union, USA

Samia Huq, BRAC University, Dhaka, Bangladesh

Sherman Jackson, University of Southern California, USA

François Pazisnewende Kaboré, SJ, Kosyam Jesuit University of Science,
   Burkina Faso

Azza Karam, Religions for Peace, International

Sivin Kit, Malaysia Theological Seminary, Malaysia

Daniel Madigan, SJ, Georgetown University, USA

Zorica Maros, University of Sarajevo, Bosnia and Herzegovina

David Marshall, Georgetown University, USA

Katherine Marshall, Georgetown University, USA

Pavle Mijović, University of Sarajevo, Bosnia and Herzegovina

Mahan Mirza, University of Notre Dame, USA

Lucinda Mosher, Hartford Seminary, USA

Kenan Musić, University of Sarajevo, Bosnia and Herzegovina

Elizabeth Phillips, Margaret Beaufort Institute of Theology, UK

Samer Rashwani, University of Tübingen, Germany

Shirin Shafaie, Centre for Muslim-Christian Studies (CMCS), Oxford, UK

Asim Zubčević, University of Sarajevo, Bosnia and Herzegovina

Introduction

"We agree that 'inequality' is rampant in our world; we agree less so as to whether there should be 'equality.'" So spoke a Building Bridges Seminar veteran as this project's examination of Christian and Muslim perspectives on "a world of inequalities" got under way. Founded in 2002 as an initiative of the archbishop of Canterbury and under the stewardship of Georgetown University since 2012, the Building Bridges Seminar is believed to be the longest-running dialogue of Christian and Muslim scholar-practitioners. Meetings have been held in both Muslim- and Christian-majority locales—among them, Qatar, Singapore, Italy, and the United Kingdom. This book presents the proceedings of the seventeenth Building Bridges Seminar, convened June 18–22, 2018, in Sarajevo, Bosnia-Herzegovina. Chaired by Daniel A. Madigan, SJ, the Jeanette W. and Otto J. Ruesch Family Associate Professor in Georgetown's Department of Theology, most sessions took place in Sarajevo's Gazi Husrev-bey Library. In fact, in 2005, Sarajevo had provided the venue for the fourth seminar. It has been remarked many times since that the city itself—its physical location and history—bore palpably and uniquely on the seminar's conversations.[1] Longtime participants in this project were delighted to be back. The Building Bridges Seminar is always an exercise in extending theological hospitality to each other as Christian and Muslim scholars. In 2018 this was only enhanced by the warmth of the Bosnian welcome.

Under this project's auspices, a conversation circle comprising some thirty scholars is created annually (by invitation only) for the purpose of deep dialogical study of texts—scriptural and otherwise. In constructing the circle, balance is always the goal. Thus, Christians and Muslims are always nearly equal number, with women well represented in both cohorts. While most Christian participants have been Anglican or Roman Catholic, Orthodox and Protestants have also been included. Similarly, while most Muslim participants have been Sunni,

Shi'a have always taken part. The material to be read, analyzed, and commented upon is chosen to provoke deep discussion of a carefully framed, multilayered theme, such as revelation, prophethood, prayer, human destiny, forgiveness, power, or—as in 2018—inequality.

As an ongoing dialogue, the Building Bridges Seminar's goals are to gain better understanding of each other's tradition, to wrestle with theological complexities, and to improve the quality of our disagreements. Its structure facilitates this by conducting almost all of its work in closed session, by organizing the participants into four discussion groups (usually composed of eight individuals) that remain consistent throughout the meeting, and by opening and closing each day with a robust plenary conversation. Over the years it has become customary to offer a public session featuring overviews of the topic at hand. Each day thereafter, morning and afternoon plenaries feature brief lectures exegeting or otherwise introducing texts to be subjected to close reading and discussion in the ninety-minute "small-group" session to come. Hour-long evening plenaries are for reflection and synthesis. The purpose of the present volume is to bring together material for further study or for use in the reader's own dialogical endeavors.[2]

Thus, part 1, "Overviews," offers a pair of essays: "Unjust Inequality as a Challenge for Contemporary Islam" by Ovamir Anjum and "The Challenges of a World of Inequalities for Christians Today," by David Hollenbach, SJ, originally presented as lectures at the public forum that opened the 2018 meeting. Given the complexity of *inequality* as an overarching topic, the first full day of the seminar was dedicated to taking stock. Six sessions featured a speaker presenting on one aspect of the reality of global inequality. These brief lectures were crafted to open up the issue of the ways in which our religions often collude in the maintenance and perpetuation of these inequalities in our religious structures, offering readings of our scriptures that justify and give a religious patina to various kinds of division, exclusion, and domination that have their origins not in God's desire for us but in the human will to power. In this volume's part 2, "Muslims and Christians Facing the Reality of Inequality," the reader will find six essays: "Gender and Islam: Obstacles and Possibilities" by Samia Huq; "The Problem of Race in Christianity" by Elizabeth Phillips; "Nationality and Ethnicity in West Africa: An Economic and Religious Perspective on Inequalities" by François Pazisnewende Kaboré, SJ; "Islam and the Challenge of Sociopolitical Equality: The Contribution of Religious Creed" by Sherman A. Jackson; "Caste and Social Class in the Christian and Islamic Communities of South Asia" by Sunil Caleb; and "Slavery: Source of Theological Tension" by Jonathan Brown.

"The Building Bridges Seminar is deliberately centered on texts and theology, with an admirable scholarly tone and tenor," explained one participant in the 2018 convening. "This focus on texts highlights common themes that can link different communities. It also brings out the complexities around interpretations of both words and ideas that were set down in very different eras, however divinely inspired." In Sarajevo, the second and third full seminar days were devoted to giving close attention to a selection of passages from the Bible and the Qur'an that offer a vision of human living beyond inequality as well as to scripture passages that at least some people in each tradition believe require adherents to perpetuate inequalities. Four scholars who had been instrumental in choosing this material provided exegetical overviews. Thus, in this volume's part 3, "Inequality, the Bible, and the Christian Tradition," we have essays by Leslie J. Hoppe, OFM ("Inequality in the Old Testament"), and Christopher M. Hays ("For All of You Are One in Christ Jesus? The New Testament Witnesses on Ethnic, Economic, Social, Religious, Racial, and Gender Inequality") plus sets of Old Testament and New Testament texts; in part 4, "Inequality, the Qur'an, and Hadith," are two essays by Abdullah Saeed—"Racial, Religious, and Gender Equality: Reflections on Qur'anic Texts" and "Economic Equality and Inequality: An Introduction to Selected Qur'anic Texts"—plus sets of Qur'an verses and hadiths aimed at encouraging dialogue about gender, ethnic, and religious inequality, on the one hand, and economic inequality, on the other.

Plenary and small-group work on the morning of the 2018 seminar's final day focused on the possibilities for and the obstacles to a common ethic of equality, the topic of the present volume's part 5. In anticipation, several complex questions had been posed: Do fundamental theological differences preclude a shared ethic? Does error have rights? Is one vision of human society as good as another? Might there be kinds of inequality that are acceptable, even necessary? The creative reflections that launched discussion of these issues during plenary and small-group sessions appear here in essay form: "Three Strands Leading to the Edge: Considering the Possibility of a Common Ethic of Equality" by C. Rosalee Velloso Ewell and "Muslim-Christian Bridges: Toward a Shared Theology of Human Development?" by Azza Karam. Completing this book is "Considering Inequalities as Scholars of Faith: Reflections on Bridge-Building in Sarajevo," an essay by the seminar's rapporteur, meant to enable the reader to "overhear" some of the various levels of conversation during the seventeenth convening.

Our purpose in providing exegetical essays and collections of texts for study organized as the seminar itself took them up is to encourage others to consider these same topics and questions—either as individuals, as students in a university course, or as members of an ongoing dialogue, which, as its name implies, requires time, patience, and ongoing commitment. Readers may wish to undertake further exploration of topics central to this book. However, one is unlikely to find a single resource addressing all six distinct forms of inequality on our agenda. While a lengthy list of suggestions for supplemental reading could quite easily be developed for each of those categories, we have limited our recommendations here to just five titles: Walter Scheidel, *The Great Leveler: Violence and the History of Inequality from the Stone Age to the Twenty-First Century* (Princeton University Press, 2017); Anthony B. Atkinson, *Inequality: What Can Be Done?* (Harvard University Press, 2015); Mahmoud El-Gamal, *Islamic Finance: Law, Economics, and Practice* (Cambridge University Press, 2006); Glenn C. Loury,

The Anatomy of Racial Inequality (Harvard University Press, 2002); and Judith Lorber, *Gender Inequality: Feminist Theories and Politics*, 5th ed. (Oxford University Press, 2012).

In the main text of this volume, diacritics have been kept to a minimum. Dates are "CE" unless otherwise noted. Gratitude is owed to many publishers for permission to use the material excerpted in this volume. All are credited in due course. Unless otherwise noted, Qur'an quotations are according to M. A. S. Abdel Haleem, trans., *The Qur'an: English Translation and Parallel Arabic Text* (Oxford University Press, 2010, used by permission; all rights reserved); Bible passages are from the New Revised Standard Version of the Bible, copyright 1989 by the Division of Christian Education of the National Council of the Churches of Christ in the USA (used by permission; all rights reserved). Deep appreciation is extended to Georgetown University president John J. DeGioia for his ongoing support of the Building Bridges Seminar. As has been the case for many years, the Seminar's academic director, David Marshall (World Council of Churches), and its chair, Daniel Madigan (Georgetown University), were instrumental in setting the 2018 theme, organizing the roster of scholars, and—in careful conversation with those designated as presenters—choosing the texts to be studied. Others with strategic roles in the 2018 gathering include Lucinda Mosher (Hartford Seminary), the Seminar's rapporteur; Samuel Wagner, who, as director of dialogue and Catholic identity in the Office of the President, provided logistical support; Samedin Kadić, a graduate student at the University of Sarajevo, Bosnia-Herzegovina, who assisted with note taking during all sessions; and Georgetown University's Berkley Center for Religion, Peace, and World Affairs— which also provides an ongoing base of operations and online presence for the Seminar and has made the publication of this book possible. Finally, gratitude is extended to Al Bertrand and the staff of Georgetown University Press for their patient assistance with this project.

Notes

1. For the proceedings of the Fourth Building Bridges Seminar, see Michael Ipgrave, ed., *Building a Better Bridge: Muslims, Christians, and the Common Good* (Washington, DC: Georgetown University Press, 2008).

2. With few exceptions, the essays herein are substantial revisions—or even replacements—of the original seminar presentations.

PART ONE

Overviews

Unjust Inequality as a Challenge for Contemporary Islam

OVAMIR ANJUM

I have been asked to offer as a Muslim a diagnosis of the challenge of the many inequalities that afflict our world. I shall, therefore, reflect on the challenges and paradoxes rather than attempting to articulate cures. Let me begin by stating that Muslims have often failed to uphold the teachings of justice and compassion to which God has called us through the teachings of his beloved Prophet Muhammad, upon him be peace and blessings. God sent the Prophet as nothing but "Rahma to all the worlds." One of my students taught me that *Rahma* is not fully captured by its common English translation, *mercy*, as the latter connotes primarily forgiveness for the guilty; a better alternative is *compassion*, which emphasizes the concern for the weak. As a community of God called to compassion and justice, we have a long way to go. It goes without saying that Muslim states in the world today suffer from most grievous injustices, many of which are self-inflicted. My relevant claim here is that these injustices are inflicted and sustained not in spite of the normative culture but as a result of it; these normative cultures, diverse as they may be, are in varying degrees informed by Islamic tradition.

Equally evident, however, is the fact that as economically peripheral peoples of the world, the biggest sin of Muslims as a whole appears to be weakness. From colonialism to neoliberalism, foreign forces have contributed to the destruction of traditional Muslim institutions, which has wrought incalculable damage to the Muslims' ability to confront the tremendously rapid economic and social transformations that have ensued—and those transformations have left them with a deeply defensive posture of fearful conservatism rather than having encouraged a principled critique of and engagement with them. But this material and structural analysis offers only a partial explanation to us believers, to whom God can do all things if we keep our promise to Him; therefore, we see all problems ultimately in moral terms as part of our faith. Yet often this recognition of our own failure turns into spiritualized fatalism and abdication of responsibility—which, I believe, can be averted through a critical appraisal of the problem at hand.

Let me proceed by sharing a couple of profound paradoxes of our time that should concern any thinking about religion and inequality. First, there is the obvious paradox of religion and inequality in the modern world—one that is not unique to Islam. The data show, and it does not take too much imagination to heuristically confirm, what the opening line of a recent volume on the subject declaims: "Religion is one of the strongest and most persistent correlates of social and economic inequalities."[1] Research in Western Christianity (and Indian Hinduism, for instance) shows the rise in religiosity as neoliberalism increases inequality.

Although I am not aware of research focusing on Muslim-majority countries, I suspect that the conclusions would be comparable. This phenomenon is explained either through the relative power theory (the rich support religion for a number of reasons, and their support for it attracts the poor; religion may also contribute by deflating pressures for redistribution) or the less-favored deprivation theory (religion provides comfort to the economically disadvantaged). An alternative explanation may be that the success of the modern state as the agency of redistribution and management leads to decline in the role of religion in small, modernized, homogeneous societies. This dovetails well with the notion many anthropologists have posited: that the modern state is a secular and secularizing agent. Regardless, it seems clear that religious intelligentsia have much to worry about: whereas our normative teachings call for renunciation and otherworldliness that should presumably mitigate inequalities, their effective impact in the modern world may be quite the opposite.

The second paradox is the curious relationship between the Left liberal demand for total and uncompromising equality in exactly the same age and encouraged by the same forces of neoliberalism that have generated some of the greatest inequalities and injustices of our time and have resurrected the radical right.

A third paradox is one of defining justice, as Muslims are often called to hurry up and imitate before the next wave of conceptual transformation and a new set of definitions hits. Injustice or unjust inequality, no doubt, is at the heart of some of the key issues the world is facing today—crises where Muslims are in the eye of the storm. As victims as well as perpetrators, Muslims are violently confronted with the question of justice. Yet a settlement of what constitutes justice remains elusive, as modern aspirations are deeply chimerical. How radically these definitions and aspirations change from one decade to the next in our age of accelerated change can be appreciated if we trace the transformation of justice debates over the last couple of decades: from the equality versus freedom debate of the Cold War to the near triumph of individualism and capitalism in the neoliberal age, when the crucial questions become those of personal sexual choice, gender pronouns, and gender pay gap. These changing norms are not primarily the result of some nefarious conspiracy. Nevertheless, in this drama, the Anglo-American economic and political swings have been inordinately influential in deciding for the global cosmopolitan culture what justice ought to mean and what kind of inequalities are worth opposing and which ones are inevitable, tolerable, even desirable. More precisely, even as the notion of justice has in the modern period been equated to the notion of equality, still the progressive liberals possess no moral criterion to differentiate between tolerable and intolerable inequalities, thus letting the market force and brute power to silently draw lines in the sand. Like hierarchy, equality comes with costs. The rise of liberal democratic equality has been accompanied by if not facilitated by modern individualism and has greatly eroded familial and communal forms of life—institutions our religious traditions consider crucial for righteous life. The resurrection of the new Far Right to prominence across the West indicates the anemic state of these institutions.

Justice and Mercy

Allow me now to turn to the Islamic scripture. The Qur'an call us to be *just*—first and foremost—in the most intimate sense, even against ourselves and our kith and kin:

> O you who believe! Be staunch in justice, witnesses for God, even though it be against yourselves or [your] parents or [your] kindred, whether [the case be of] a rich man or a poor man, for God is nearer unto both [them ye are]. So follow not passion lest you lapse [from truth] and if you lapse or fall away, then lo! God is ever informed of what ye do. (Q. 4:135)[2]

Elsewhere, a similar verse emphasizes justice even against your enemy, and not just any enemy but your religious persecutor. "And let not your hatred of a folk who [once] stopped your going to the holy sanctuary seduce you to transgress" (Q. 5:2).

But justice is still second to the virtue that we are most frequently reminded of in the Qur'an: that of rahma, mercy and compassion. The Qur'an has God saying, "My mercy encompasses all things" (Q. 7:156). A Prophetic tradition has it, "When God created the heavens and the earth, he wrote his slogan on His throne, 'My mercy has overwhelmed my wrath.'"[3] In contrast to justice (al-adl) and fairness or equal distribution (al-qist), plain equality is a concept that does not find direct expression in the Qur'an—nor is it a cardinal virtue in an unqualified sense.

Nobility in Piety and Faith Alone

A basic equality of all humans as humans can be deduced from a number of teachings, such as the verse:

> O people! Lo! We have created you from a male and a female, and have
> made you nations and tribes that ye may know one another. Lo! the noblest
> of you, in the sight of God, is the most pious. Lo! God is All-Knowing,
> Aware. (Q. 49:13)

Here the import is to reject inequality based in race, tribe, and lineage generally.
Yet, even here, a criterion for inequality is posited—namely, *taqwa*: nobility is
not absent, but it comes from piety, being mindful of God, and fear of God.[4]

Gender In/equality

Men and women are, according to the Qur'an, allies and partners of each other,
awliya'. It posits no difference in their religious status, aspirations, and virtues,
and it strongly suggests equality in these respects.

> Lo! For Muslim men and Muslim women, for believing men and believing
> women, for devout men and devout women, for truthful men and truthful
> women, for perseverant men and perseverant women, for men who devoutly
> humble themselves and women who devoutly humble themselves, for men
> who give in charity and women who give in charity, for men who fast and
> women who fast, for men who guard their chastity and women who guard
> their chastity, and for men who praise God abundantly and women who
> praise God abundantly: for them has God prepared forgiveness and great
> reward. (Q. 33:35)

The Qur'an also conspicuously notes that in the story of creation, both Adam and
Eve ate of the tree and both were forgiven; the Qur'an goes out of its way to use
a dual verbal form to emphasize this point (Q. 20:121). Yet some hadith accounts
seem to give a different bent to this story and reproduce the biblical narrative.
One hadith also suggests, at least in an apparent sense, that women are deficient
in religion and intellect.[5]

When discussing the marital institution, however, the Qur'an unequivocally
declares that "they [women] have rights similar to those [of men] over them, and
men are a degree above them" (Q. 2:228), and "men have authority over women,
owing to what they spend on them, and owing to God's grace to some over others" (Q. 4:34). The same verse allows men to discipline their disobedient wives
by warning, abandoning them in beds, and even striking them; the hadith reports
express the Prophet's dislike of striking and qualify that permission by prohibiting the striking of face or striking so hard that it leaves a mark. The Qur'an
also limits polygamy to four wives, if a man can be just among them; if he cannot, then only one. The women's share in inheritance, in itself a radical move—
as women had been often deemed property rather than property owners—is

nonetheless half that of men in most classes of heirs. The Qur'an also deems one man's testimony equivalent to that of two women in certain cases (Q. 2:282).

The juristic tradition received this Qur'anic model more or less faithfully; yet its attempt to formalize and standardize sometimes accentuated the inequality more than what scripture allowed—and on occasion in obvious contradiction to the prophetic teachings.[6] Careful readers of the Qur'an even in the premodern period found this problematic. For instance, Ibn Taymiyya, a particularly close and independent reader of the Qur'an and hadith, argued that women were religious equals of men, that the hadith suggesting deficiency of women was in fact a reference to the particular issue that menstruating women may not pray or fast (the Prophet was using this fact only rhetorically, perhaps to encourage them to be more generous than men), and that their testimony was deemed half only in the special case of certain transactions conducted outside the court. Yet certain obvious differences were undeniable: all prophets, the Qur'an declared, had been men. Some in later tradition did balance that by observing that no women had ever been tyrants or hadith fabricators.

A remarkable verse in the Qur'an, just before 4:34, anticipates the reaction one might have in response to the inequality that is later posited:

And wish not the thing in which God has made some of you excel others. Unto men a share from that which they have earned, and unto women a share from that which they have earned. But ask God of His bounty. Lo! God is ever Knower of all things. (Q. 4:32)

In contrast to these verses that establish a social hierarchy along with spiritual equality, most other Qur'anic verses concerning women are dedicated to warning men against abusing the authority they are given in matters of marriage, divorce, custody, and female children.

Wealth Inequality and Mitigative Measures

Unlike gender inequality at the social level, which is carefully justified and regulated, economic inequality is treated as undesirable but to an extent unavoidable. Moreover, a number of means are devised to mitigate it. Inequality in wealth is tolerated only as a natural result of divinely ordained diversity of human circumstances. God gives some more than others, but *only* to test them, and vehemently denies any superiority on that basis. As earlier prophets had been, the Prophet Muhammad is warned never to let the poverty of his devout early followers be a cause for looking down on them or passing over them in favor of the affluent. Among the believers, the disparity must be mitigated through charity and alms and other means such as most strident prohibition of usury. The inheritance laws of the Qur'an similarly function to distribute the wealth such that it normally becomes split up and redistributed from one generation to the next. These staples of Islamic law were intended to and did in fact historically militate against accumulation of wealth under normal conditions and hence prevented excessive accumulation, a condition that was to be crucial in the later rise of modern capitalism.

Yet, if one posits the human invention of private property as the foundation of all later inequality and even capitalism, as leftist historians often do, then that foundation is remarkably preserved in the Qur'an: the right to own and freely engage in trade is unequivocally preserved, and theft is severely punished. Islamic law thus created a strong free market and private property, which engendered worldwide trade networks spanning in particular the Indian Ocean world yet prevented the rise of modern predatory capitalism.

Inequality in Status: Slavery

The Qur'an offers no justification, unlike in the previous two cases, for slavery, although its tolerance of slavery is comparable to the tolerance of poverty. Slaves are spoken of nearly always in the context of freeing them as expiation of a number of sins. The Prophet required that enslaved people be treated kindly; that one must feed and clothe them from the same kinds of things one consumed and wore oneself; even commanded that, if one hits a slave, the expiation is to free him or her; and discouraged people from calling them *'abd/'abid* (the common term for slaves, which underscores total subservience and lack of claim against the master, reserved now properly for God-human relationship alone) but rather to call them *mamluk* (owned). Free Muslims and protected non-Muslims (*dhimmi* or *musta'min*) could not be enslaved, and enslaving a free person was deemed a major sin. Slaves, the Prophet said, are your brothers, whom God has placed under your authority. Yet there was no general prohibition of owning slaves, and slavery continued in the Muslim lands until its abolition in the modern period.

In summary, two observations can be made about the Qur'anic responses to these various kinds of inequality. First, in the five categories of inequality that I have mentioned in a deliberate order, we can note a gradation: faith (inequality is imperative, accentuated), gender (legally mandated but mitigated), property and status (tolerated but highly mitigated), and race/ethnicity/tribe (categorically rejected).

Second, in responding to nearly all types of inequality within the community of the faithful, gender, wealth, and status, the Qur'anic response follows a pattern. The baseline of the Qur'an seems to be to accept the form of life that had emerged in nearly all major civilizations and the Near East in particular over millennia. This included ascriptive and social institutions: family, clan, tribe, private property, and patriarchy were adopted in a more or less modified form. Depending on one's focus, one may emphasize one or the other, but both elements of acceptance and modification are undeniable: there was neither a radical rejection nor a total acceptance.

Finally, in all these dimensions, it is Islamic law (*sharia*) that emerged as the site of management and mitigation of hierarchy and inequality.

Inequality as a Concept

Note that I have qualified the kind of inequality maintained in Islamic law as hierarchical inequality. This suggests the question: What other kinds may I be presupposing, and how might we better understand this loaded concept? At a very rudimentary level, we can identify three kinds of inequality:

1. *Hierarchical inequality* serves a social function and is justified by the normative order; it is here that the tensions between Islam and the liberal discourse on human rights lie, which I shall accept as the point of reference dominant in our time.
2. The prohibition against *might is right inequality*—that is, against accepted legal norms; for example, when certain groups are above the law—happens to be an area of overall agreement between the two traditions.
3. *Outcome inequality* is seen as a necessary result of liberty in classical liberalism and its contemporary republican version. But in both Left liberalism and Islam, it is seen as the object of mitigative action. The site and nature of these actions differ: Left liberalism functions largely through the secular redistributive state in a top-down fashion; Islam functions largely through family, community, and religious law in a bottom-up fashion.

Another underlying (one could say metaphysical) difference between Islamic scriptural and liberal prescriptions and aspirations while mitigating inequality is in their respective attitude toward nature: the natural order is seen as divine, and the Qur'an requires respecting it, whereas contemporary Left liberalism demands the intervention of states, court decisions, and technology to mitigate the natural differences. This is evident in economic as well as gender inequality.

Unable to offer a satisfactory history or genealogy of the concept of inequality here, I only broach some important questions that must be kept in mind when confronting scripture or tradition with this challenge. What are the origins of the fact of inequality, and, relatedly, what are the origins of inequality as a problem to be overcome? First, in nature and human society, inequality is the norm. Whether it is the prides of lions, packs of wolves, or gangs of primates, the struggle for dominance is part of the animal kingdom; among humans, similarly, no civilized society has survived without hierarchy. Even the precious few human groups that the anthropologists first thought lacked social hierarchy—such as primitive tribes of the Andamanese in the Indian Ocean or the Sudanese

Nuer—live as clans with hierarchy of gender and age. The remarkable idea of the equality of all humans can be credited in the known history to the Abrahamic tradition, in which God made life sacred and human beings special. Ironically, then, Christians and Muslims are gathered today to address a problem that is entirely the creation of their belief in God. However, in its secularized popular form, it appears as a self-evident belief in no need for a justification. Yet if it is not God who created us as special and equal, there is nothing in nature that indicates that we are either special or equal to each other in any way. The Qur'an says,

> For that cause We decreed for the Children of Israel that whoever kills a human being for other than manslaughter or corruption in the earth, it shall be as if he had killed all humankind, and whoever saves the life of one, it shall be as if he had saved the life of all humankind. (Q. 5:32)

Political equality of the free, propertied males was thought to be the invention of the Greeks, although it has been now shown that that qualified kind of equality was not strange to the Mesopotamian civilizations to the east. To not wander too far afield, I wish to stress that equality of humans at the abstract, spiritual level is a relatively rare concept in human history, one whose metaphysical roots lie in Abrahamic monotheism.

Second, the concern for sociopolitical equality in its current form as being among the highest moral goods is a distinctively modern, in particular, liberal concern, and is difficult to imagine without the prior rise and establishment of a few fundamental beliefs—one being individualism and another being secularism—because such a conception requires discounting the settling of scores and righting of wrongs in an afterlife as well as any religious fatalism. In other words, liberalism had to disavow or deny its religious roots in order to arrive at the current form of individual equality as a good in need neither of justification nor of balancing with other, potentially more important goods.

We would also have to ask how it is that modern liberal political and economic systems have produced and entrenched such tremendous inequality in the world. Might there be something profoundly questionable about the Pollyanna-ish demand for equality at the expense of all other goods, and might the concept of equality itself need rethinking? Such an inquiry would have to confront the fact that different moral traditions respond to different classes of inequality differently, as Catholic philosopher Alasdair MacIntyre's classic *Whose Justice? Which Rationality?* reminds us.[7] Such an inquiry would have to confront the kinds of questions Lila Abu-Lughod does in her book *Do Muslim Women Need Saving?* when she demonstrates the colonialist and imperialist underpinnings of even the seemingly most well-meaning liberal demands for gender equality in Muslim countries.[8]

Islamic history has had its own complex history of toying with radical egalitarianism. The early Islamic egalitarians, the Kharijites, violently sought equality at a political and religious level, and their anarchism and violence led to their extinction and predictably cooled the ardor for their ideas among the Muslim mainstream. Another early movement that did succeed, the Abbasids, was fueled largely by the non-Arabs desire for equality with the Arab Muslims. Both of these movements for relative equality were violent, like the French Revolution; equality is a powerful idea that has often unleashed carnage. The American Revolution, with its noble, self-evident truth that "all men are created equal" and are possessed of certain inalienable rights—those of life, liberty, and pursuit of happiness—while successful in avoiding the immediate carnage, was in fact part of a colonial project enabled by mass killings and perhaps the worst kind of enslavement in recent history, and one that sought to protect the propertied class of men. We may cautiously venture, therefore, that no instance of the demand or granting of equality has been innocent, and none has been total.

Modern Muslim Responses

Muslims confronted by the challenge of the modern emphasis on human equality respond in various ways. Progressivists, on the whole, reject the traditional answers. I propose to divide their approach into two kinds. Soft progressivists (some may call them reformists) reinterpret the scriptural texts to arrive at more or less liberal solutions and, in the process, recruit classical tradition without being bound by it. Their critics see them as quietly accepting the prevailing Left liberal norms as self-evident, as "the end of history," and their method as starting with the desired results and reverse-engineering their way to the scriptural texts and interpretive methodologies.

Hard progressivists, in contrast, reject parts of the scripture explicitly, using different strategies. Some reject Medinan suras that spoke of laws and norms in favor of Meccan suras that generally emphasized beliefs and ethics. Others abstract general principles, such as monotheism and justice, and argue that these require the rejection of the particular teachings of the Qur'an and the hadith. The attempts that can be characterized as hard progressivist can be seen as early as the nineteenth century, but they have generally struggled with philosophical grounding as well as cultural authority. They assume the universal existence of a standard strong enough to oppose and replace scripture and tradition, yet in a rapidly changing world of epistemic anarchy, they are left with no authoritative foundations on which to build their critique and to decide which inequalities to reject and which to accept, or on what ground to prioritize between competing values, such as survival, identity, solidarity, good order, freedom, and God. Thus theoretically challenged, they often turn to social activism or help from Western power institutions, which leaves them heavily reliant on current trends and exposed to charges of insincerity and worse.

The traditionalists—namely, those who take Islamic discursive tradition as largely probative and authoritative—are a camp too large and internally diverse to adequately characterize through a single hermeneutic. They have often rejected the absolute imperative of equality and have reformulated it as the question of equity and justice, not equality. Some adopt a theology of antimodernity; others embrace obscurantism (that is, sanctification of tradition and unwillingness to systematically reevaluate it); and yet others, fideism.

Even though my own sympathies lie in the traditionalist camp, as I see in it seeds of the most compelling scriptural and moral reasoning, traditionalists have yet to offer a widely persuasive account of old and new structural injustices—let alone inequalities. Part of the reason, I suppose, is that the premodern tradition saw injustice as primarily an individual sin or its accumulated result. The social and political institutions of premodern Islam had been largely those of the agrarianate empires that gradually evolved in the region over millennia, and medieval jurisprudence largely took them for granted. In contrast to the rapid structural ruptures introduced by modern revolutions, the development of large-scale associations of bureaucracy, professional military, and business corporation has introduced enormous forms of power. Modern injustices and inequalities imminent in such structures, therefore, cannot easily be arrested through premodern traditional ethics.

On the one hand, as Alasdair MacIntyre powerfully observes, modern secular ideologies have produced no epistemic or ethical consensus, making our ethical language as well as aspirations little more than hangovers from an earlier age. So while there are no compelling reasons for why we ought to seek equality or justice or virtue if there is no God, we continue to speak as if we ought to. This is why reinvigorating tradition may be the only viable alternative for ethical thinking and practices. On the other hand, traditionalism can be an escape from responsibility. To Muslims, this imposes the enormous challenge of sifting through competing strands of tradition as well as varying accounts of modernity, reconciling the will of God as revealed in scripture with that as revealed in history and contemporary moral dilemmas.

Looking Ahead

If inequality in itself is not an absolute injustice or one that is exorable, we must focus our attention to kinds of inequalities that are unjust and that are curable. The vast majority of gratuitous suffering that humans inflict on others is of this kind.

Among the kinds of injustices that can no longer be mitigated—yet they invite reflection on God's infinite wisdom, even anticipation of miraculous redemption—is environmental degradation. Over the last two centuries, all the fruits of industrialization—the phenomenon that is singlehandedly responsible for the coming apocalypse—have been reaped by the Atlantic world. Yet its most devastating consequences are being visited upon those poor who barely ever enjoyed a bite of that apple, who have been at the receiving end of colonialism and imperialism, and whose carbon footprint is invisible among the giants. Yet, if you look at the map, the areas with the least carbon footprint are also the first ones to be rendered uninhabitable by global warming and flooding and rising sea levels. These include nearly a billion people in low-lying coastal areas of Pakistan, Egypt, Indonesia, Bangladesh, India, and the like. God has put the fate of most densely populated areas of Muslim majorities in the hands of those who have consumed the oceans and scorched the earth. Yet they deny not only their guilt but that there has been a murder of God's green earth.

I will now mention some of the ways in which deep and unjust inequalities have been tolerated or celebrated for "Islamic reasons," and where Islamic critiques of inequality have either been unavailable or successfully suppressed. Rather than list any recommendations, I want to point out some tough paradoxes that suppress what I believe to be the true Islamic egalitarian spirit.

The Muslim moneyed class has welcomed neoliberalism, and the religious establishment has gladly embraced a Muslim version of the prosperity gospel. One pundit has even argued that the only way to keep Muslim youth from falling prey to terrorism is to turn them into capitalists.[9] The imperative of even minimal justice and dignity is rudely confronted by the desire for survival or containment and, among the faithful, for power to preach and missionize. Let me offer a few examples.

Modern Turkey is a neoliberal miracle that has used pious wealth to bolster an Islamist democracy to push back against half a century of despotic secular chauvinism. Turkey has also taken a new role as the only power speaking for the masses of oppressed Muslims across the Muslim world. Even before the current wave of political suppression, leftist critics had pointed out the growing inequality in the country, along with the corruption of morals brought by new wealth. Thoughtful Muslims find themselves torn between Islamic objections to neoliberalism and the growing potential for inequality and the empowerment of a strong (if not the only Muslim) ally in places like Palestine, Myanmar, and elsewhere.

In a similar vein, the Saudi Arabian oil wealth has long been interpreted as a sign of divine favor for the "true monotheists," the Wahhabis, where a culture of puritan piety long concealed the deep-seated and largely unjust inequalities between men and women, between tribals and nontribals, between various tribes and regions, and between Gulf citizens and the rest of the Muslims. Religious piety served effectively as cover for a culture that was becoming deeply bigoted by any interpretation of Islamic standards. My parents' generation of Pakistani expatriates felt extremely loyal and grateful to the Saudis; they prayed for the kings for building such stupendous facilities around the two holy mosques. It is easy to demonize the illiberal Saudi policies, so I will avoid scoring cheap shots, but I cannot help mentioning that as a high school student in Saudi Arabia myself,

I often wondered why even the enlightened Saudi preachers rarely spoke of the problems of injustice against foreigners and other such elephants in the room.

Finally, let us consider the somber fact that the most ardent opposition to social and political justice today comes from a group of clerics associated with the Muslim states in the Saudi-UAE-Egypt camp that has been formed against the 2011 Arab uprisings for dignity and justice, and from the very same ulama who wrote strongly worded condemnations of ISIS. "Justice," "accountability," and "rights" are dangerous words in much of the Middle East; their only advocate is the small alliance of countries led by Turkey.

These dilemmas call for a renewed and thorough reevaluation of Islamic tradition with an eye for justice as a first-order commitment and without losing sight of the complex hegemonic structures that function precisely by imposing their own definitions of justice.

Notes

1. Lisa A. Keister and Darren E. Sherkat, eds., *Religion and Inequality in America: Research and Theory on Religion's Role in Stratification* (Cambridge: Cambridge University Press, 2014), 1.

2. Here and throughout this chapter, Qur'an quotations are according to Marmaduke Pickthall, *The Meaning of the Glorious Qur'an: An Explanatory Translation* (London: Knopf, 1930), modified slightly.

3. Al-Bukhari #3194, Muslim #2751. Translation mine.

4. This inequality of piety may have only a highly qualified social or political consequence, as the Qur'an emphasizes, "Do not claim your purity, only God knows who is pure" (Q. 53:32, translation mine). The Prophet's teaching that "Piety is in the heart" makes a similar point. So does his own practice of behaving as an equal of his companions—as in the famous incident when he accidentally prodded a soldier while straightening the rows in a battle; when the soldier demanded retribution, the Prophet immediately offered it, and the soldier took the opportunity to kiss the Prophet's abdomen for blessing. Those who have knowledge, similarly, are to be given mild preference in terms of social ordering but only inasmuch as it facilitates learning—one verse instructs believers to give room to senior companions "who have been given knowledge" so they may sit next to the Prophet and learn.

The real inequality pertains to the knowledge of God. The Qur'an is emphatic that the pious and the impious, those who know God and respond to God's message and those who do not, those who see God's signs and those who do not, are unequal; to neglect that inequality is most loathsome. Apart from this normative dichotomy, there is divinely ordained hierarchy: even the prophets are unequal in status, for God places some above others, even though all equally true (Q. 2:253).

5. Bukhari #304. Translation mine.

6. One recent study concludes, for instance, that the Hanafi jurisprudence settled on prohibiting or discouraging women from attending mosques against an explicit hadith that prohibited men from preventing women from mosques, and even when challenged, the

fiqh tradition did not revert to the hadith. See Behnam Sadeghi, *The Logic of Law Making in Islam: Women and Prayer in the Legal Tradition* (Cambridge: Cambridge University Press, 2013).

7. Alasdair MacIntyre, *Whose Justice? Which Rationality?* (Notre Dame, IN: University of Notre Dame Press, 1989).

8. Lila Abu-Lughod, *Do Muslim Women Need Saving?* (Cambridge, MA: Harvard University Press, 2015).

9. Vali Nasr, *The Rise of Islamic Capitalism: Why the New Muslim Middle Class Is the Key to Defeating Extremism* (New York: Free Press, 2010).

The Challenges of a World
of Inequalities for Christians Today

DAVID HOLLENBACH, SJ

This essay highlights several aspects of the Christian tradition that are relevant in efforts to respond to the inequalities present in the world today. Although what is said here highlights questions that seem important for interreligious dialogue concerning equality, the essay deals exclusively with Christian approaches. It leaves the consideration of Islamic approaches to other authors. Because the author is Roman Catholic, the essay gives particular, though not exclusive, attention to approaches to equality by the Catholic community. These Catholic approaches, of course, have analogies in other Christian communities. What is said here is neither a full history nor a systematic overview of the Christian stance toward equality and inequality. Rather, the essay provides one possible starting point for Christian contributions to interfaith dialogue about responses to the inequalities of the world today.

The essay has five parts. First, it sketches some of the inequalities in today's social life, particularly in the economic domain. Second, it presents some important theological and philosophical reasons why Christians affirm the basic equality of all persons. Third, it notes how the moral standard of justice can help specify when strict equality is required and when certain forms of inequality may be acceptable. Fourth, a brief discussion of Christian stances on the issues of slavery and the religious freedom of those who are not Christian suggests that Christians must acknowledge that their faith community has in the past supported forms of inequality that most people regard as morally objectionable today. Finally, it considers the issue of how a religious tradition can change and develop. Such development in fact enabled Christianity, especially Catholicism, to move from a stance of opposition to human rights and democracy to a position of leadership in the promotion of equal human rights and democracy today. This shift raises the question of what new developments in the stance of believers toward contemporary inequalities may be required today. It is hoped that the dialogue of this conference can produce some helpful answers to that question.

Inequality Today

Several forms of inequality mark our world today. Among these are the inequalities in the distribution of income and wealth. We cannot, of course, measure human well-being simply in dollars, euros, dinars, or convertible marks. Income and wealth are means, not ends. If these means are pursued for their own sakes, this can distort the quest for higher values, such as greater care for one's fellow humans, support for a sustainable environment, and the deepening of one's relation to God. Nevertheless, money very often helps people obtain goods that are valuable in themselves, such as health, longevity, and education. A lack of income or wealth is today preventing many people from attaining the health or education they need to live with basic human dignity. Inequalities in the distribution of income or wealth are among the sources of severe human deprivation. Distorted distributions of these goods can impede the moral and spiritual growth of those it affects. It is useful, therefore, to begin our discussion of the inequalities that mar the world today with some facts about inequalities of income and wealth.

There has been an encouraging decline in the worldwide number of poor people over recent decades. Recent figures from the World Bank tell us that the number of extremely poor people—those living on less than $1.90 per day—declined from 1.89 billion people in 1990 to 735 million in 2015. This is a decline in extreme poverty from 35.9 percent of the world's population in 1990 to 10 percent in 2015. This is surely genuine progress.[1] It shows that attaining the United Nations' Sustainable Development Goal of ending extreme poverty in our time is a realistic hope. Nevertheless, far too many people continue to face severe deprivation, and poverty has declined in some regions of the world much more than in others. Severe poverty is greatest today in sub-Saharan Africa, where 389 million people, or 41 percent of the African population, are poor. This means there are more severely poor people in sub-Saharan Africa than in all other regions of the world combined. This is a significant change from 1990, when half of the world's poor were living in East Asia and the Pacific, while today only 9.3 percent of the global poor live in that region.[2]

Inequality of income and wealth is one of the causes of continuing poverty. By conventional economic measurements, the inequality among all the people of the world, no matter where they live, has been declining. However, several forms of inequality are moving in opposite directions. The inequality between countries has been declining while the inequalities within most countries has been increasing, again by conventional measures.[3] For example, in 2016 the top 10 percent of earners in Europe took home 37 percent of Europe's total income; in China, 41 percent; in Russia, about 46 percent; in the United States and Canada, 47 percent;

in sub-Saharan Africa, Brazil, and India, around 55 percent. The Middle East is the world's most unequal region, where the top 10 percent of earners gained 61 percent of national income.

Not all is well in the United States and Canada, however. Since 1980, inequality has been increasing rapidly in North America, especially in the United States.[4] The United States and Western Europe are on different tracks. In 1980 in both regions, the people in the top 1 percent income bracket took home about 10 percent of the total income of their country. By 2016 the top 1 percent group in Western Europe increased its share only slightly, to 12 percent of the total, while in the United States the share of the top 1 percent shot up to 20 percent of the country's total income. In the same time period the share of national income going to the bottom 50 percent in the United States declined from 20 to 13 percent. In addition, Nobel Prize–winning economist Angus Deaton concludes from recent data that an unexpectedly large number of people in the United States live in extreme poverty today. At the $1.90 per day used by the World Bank to measure extreme poverty, there are 3.2 million extremely poor persons in the United States and 3.3 million in all other high-income countries combined. If this measure of extreme poverty is adjusted to reflect needs for warm clothing and housing in the United States, Deaton estimates that there are 5.3 million extremely poor people in the United States. The severity of their poverty accounts for the fact that in the US regions of the Mississippi Delta and Appalachia, life expectancy is lower than in Bangladesh and Vietnam.[5]

Whether one is poor is clearly influenced by race, class, and gender. Racial inequality has a significant impact on the well-being of Black Americans—both within the United States and in comparison to some parts of the developing world. Amartya Sen notes that Black Americans are notably poorer than white Americans. Black men live to about age sixty-seven while white men live to eighty-three; Black women live to age seventy-eight while their white sisters live to age ninety. Surprisingly, both Black men and women in the United States have shorter lives than do all people in India's Kerala state, and Black men in the United States do not live as long as men in China.[6]

Class inequalities are also important. In the United States today, class, as measured by the level of education attained, influences survival in a significant way. Economists Anne Case and Angus Deaton have shown that white US citizens with no more than secondary level education have declining lifespans and increased mortality due to drug and alcohol abuse and rising suicide rates. Many of these people have given up hope because of the barriers to well-being their lack of education creates. They end up living in ways that cause them to succumb to what Case and Deaton call "deaths of despair."[7]

Sen has also shown that gender inequalities have a significant influence on who is poor and even on who survives in the world today. He vividly illustrates the inequalities between men and women through his discussion of "missing women," women who have perished because they are not treated equally to men.

Drawing on biologically determinable predictions of male and female birth rates and on ordinary survival rates in regions where gender equality seems present, Sen concludes that there are about 100 million fewer women alive today than would have been predicted in the absence of female disadvantages. These millions of women are "missing" chiefly because of the neglect of female nutrition and health, especially in childhood. In South and East Asia, many young girls receive less food and less health care than their brothers, so their survival rates are lower and their lives are shorter.[8]

It could be argued, of course, that the central concern in the economic sphere from a religious and ethical point of view should be the well-being of each person, not inequality as such. Such well-being requires meeting the basic needs, respecting the central freedoms, and protecting the supportive relationships, including their relation with God, that persons need to live with dignity. This might suggest that the issue of inequality is a distraction from the more basic task of overcoming poverty, oppression, isolation, or other conditions that make attaining more important values difficult. Indeed, it has occasionally been argued that concern with inequality is a sign that one has succumbed to the vice of envy.[9] Some data on recent economic trends, however, suggest that this worry is quite misdirected. A growing body of research shows that reducing inequalities and overcoming poverty go hand in hand. Reducing inequalities in income and wealth contributes to economic growth, helps reduce poverty, and enables more people to attain stronger education and fuller human development.[10] High inequality undermines sustained economic growth, which in turn makes it more difficult to reduce poverty. In addition, higher initial levels of inequality make it more difficult for poor people to share the benefits that economic growth can bring. A rising tide often does not raise all boats; the poor are frequently left out. Inequalities in income have particularly bad effects on the availability of goods such as education, health care, and social protection. Low levels of education, health care, and social protection are among the defining elements of poverty, and they prevent people from contributing to society in ways that both promote growth and enable people to share the benefits of growth. Thus, there can be a vicious circle in which inequality, poverty, and low growth are reinforcing phenomena.

These considerations lead us to consider the values that should shape our response to the inequalities of our world today. Religious traditions play important roles in shaping these values. We now turn to a consideration of the contributions Christianity can make to overcoming these inequalities.

Basic Equality in Christian Tradition

The Christian tradition is strongly supportive of the equality of all persons. The first book of the Bible, Genesis, affirms that "God created humankind in his image, in the image of God he created them; male and female he created them" (Gen.

1: 27).[11] Thus, every human being possesses a sacredness and dignity that requires respect and social support. There are, of course, differences in human capacities and different levels of merit and achievement among people. But no person lacks the sacredness of being created in the image and likeness of God. Human beings have a worth that deserves to be treated with the kind of reverence shown to that which is holy. In the thirteenth century, Thomas Aquinas expressed this biblical perspective in a way that has notable parallels to Immanuel Kant's eighteenth-century affirmation that persons are ends in themselves. Aquinas wrote that of all the creatures in the universe, only humans are "governed by divine providence for their own sakes."[12] Creation in the image of God confers on each person what can be called basic equality—a worth or dignity that demands equal respect despite secondary differences in talents or levels of achievement.[13] On the most basic or fundamental level, all persons are deserving of the respect and care required for them to live in accord with the dignity God has given them. Since God has given this worth to all persons equally, all persons are equal in this basic way, no matter what other differences there may be among them.

This basic equality is also supported by the Christian conviction that each person is called to an eternal destiny with God, a destiny that goes beyond historical and earthly realities and that has transcendent significance. The transcendent worth of persons as images of God is reinforced by this vocation to union with God, a union they can attain with the help of God's grace. Christianity also draws on the further belief that, despite failures and sin, God offers humans redemption and re-creation in Christ.[14] The grace of redemption is offered to all because of God's love for them, and this love gives them a worth that transcends even the sacredness of being created in God's own image. It is not surprising, therefore, that the Second Vatican Council taught that a commitment to defend the equal human dignity of all persons flows from the gospel itself and from the heart of Christian faith.[15]

These explicitly religious bases for Christian support for basic equality are reinforced by the way many branches of Christianity also support equality by drawing on more secular, philosophical reflection. The Catholic tradition, for example, holds that human dignity can be recognized by all human beings and makes claims on all, both Christian and non-Christian. This is in line with Catholicism's long-standing, natural law–based conviction that ethical responsibilities can be grasped by human reason and by philosophical reflection on what it is to be human. Thus, in addition to its explicitly theological grounding for human dignity, the Catholic tradition recognizes that there are secular warrants for its affirmation of human dignity and basic equality. For example, the Second Vatican Council (1962–65) not only invoked the theological theme of creation in the image of God as the basis of dignity but the Council also argued that this dignity can be seen in the transcendent power of the human mind. Through their intellects, human beings transcend the material universe. The mind's capacity for wisdom gives humans a worth that reflects the presence of God's wisdom within them.

For the Council, human dignity is also manifest in the capacity of the human conscience to search for moral truth and to adhere to it when it has been found. The Council called conscience the deepest core and sanctuary of a person. Thus, it affirmed that obedience to the dictates of conscience "is the very dignity of the human person." The Council further held that dignity is evident in the excellence of human liberty. Freedom is "an exceptional sign of the divine image within the human person." The dignity of freedom requires that persons act with free choice and that they seek to direct their freedom through knowledge of the true good.[16] These three secular warrants for human dignity—the transcendence of the mind, the sacredness of conscience, and the excellence of liberty—are all manifestations of the likeness of human beings to God. At the same time, because the transcendent orientation of intellect, conscience, and liberty is rationally knowable through reflection on experience, appreciation of the reality of human dignity has a certain autonomy from the explicitly religious and doctrinal beliefs of Christianity. This opens the way for Christians to work together with those who are not Christian in the effort to promote greater respect for equal human dignity.

Although all persons are equal on this most basic level, it is clear that not all persons can or should be treated identically in all domains of activity. Equal regard does not require identical treatment, whether equality is considered from a Christian theological standpoint or from a secular philosophical point of view.[17] Therefore, we need to clarify when basic equality requires treating people the same way and when it calls for treating them differently. The question of when equal treatment is required and when differential treatment is acceptable is frequently a matter of justice. It will therefore be helpful to consider what the norm of justice calls for in Christian response to today's inequalities.

Equality and Justice

Christian thinkers have long recognized that there is a close relation between equality and the moral standard of justice. Thomas Aquinas, for example, observed that justice "denotes a kind of equality."[18] Following Aristotle, Aquinas distinguished two types of equality. The first he called arithmetic equality, in which the shares of the good being distributed are numerically or arithmetically equal. Arithmetic equality exists when a pie is divided into identical size pieces and each person at the table is given one slice. Aquinas does not hold that justice requires arithmetically equal shares for everyone in all areas of life.[19] For example, neither Aquinas nor most others in the Christian tradition would argue that justice requires that everybody's income should be of the same amount. However, many Christians do hold that this kind of strict arithmetic equality is required by justice in other spheres of life. For example, "one person, one vote" is a form of arithmetical equality that was strongly advocated by the Christians who resisted apartheid in South Africa and who advocated that no one should be excluded from voting because of their race, ethnicity, or gender. Democratic societies hold that this kind of strict, numerical equality among all citizens in their voting is necessary for political participation to be just.

Aquinas, again following Aristotle, called a second type of equality proportional. As Aquinas put it, there should be a proportion between the thing being distributed and the person to whom it is distributed.[20] In Aristotle's words, "The ratio between the shares will be the same as that between the persons. If the persons are not equal the shares will not be equal."[21] A maxim that illustrates this kind of proportional equality calls for "equal pay for equal work." The pay should correspond to the amount or difficulty of the labor undertaken. If one person works twice as many hours at the same job as another does, the first person's pay should be double that of the second, thus maintaining an equality in the proportion between wage and work for the two. Similarly, one could maintain that a person's share of some other good should be proportional to need. For example, Catholic social thought and a number of other ethical traditions hold that every person's access to basic health care should be proportionate to that person's need for such care when society has the resources to meet these needs. Still other goods, such as praise for one's achievements or punishment for one's crimes, should be proportionate to what one has actually done.

The key question, of course, is what standards of proportionality should determine what justice requires in a particular situation. Michael Walzer persuasively argues that the criterion of proportionality will be different for different kinds of goods.[22] For a democracy, justice in the distribution of votes in the election of government officials should be governed by arithmetic equality. On the other hand, sentences handed down in criminal court should be proportioned to the severity of the crime committed, not to the size of the payment the defendant is willing to offer the judge as a bribe. Justice in the courtroom should not be for sale. Similarly, although the wages paid to a worker should be proportional to the hours worked and the contribution made by the work done, the justice of income and wages cannot be measured solely by the agreement the worker has made in accepting a certain wage. If a worker has no alternative but to accept the wage offered, the need for at least some income can lead to what Walzer has called an "exchange born of desperation."[23] Workers should not be driven by desperation to accept a wage so low that is does not even enable them to live with basic human dignity. Similarly, justice in the distribution of health care ought to be proportional to need, not to the ability to pay for care. Health care is not simply a commodity to be bought and sold in the market; it can be a matter of life or death.[24]

The question of what standard of proportionality should be invoked in determining what is just thus becomes very important. The standard of proportionality that one relies on will determine whether one sees an inequality as either just or unjust in many domains.

Regrettable Inequalities in Christian Tradition

Despite strong support for the basic equality of all persons, Christian tradition has sometimes supported inequalities that many see as objectionable today. To illustrate the need for humility in our approach to what basic equality requires today, it will be useful to note several forms of inequality seen as legitimate in past periods of the Christian tradition that are recognized to be seriously unjust today. Seminal writings of John T. Noonan, a distinguished historian of Christian and especially Catholic moral thought, provide useful reminders of past Christian support for inequalities that Christians now see as moral deviations.[25] Noonan indicates the nature of the problem by sketching how the Christian tradition has changed its moral teachings on several questions related to inequality. These include slavery and the denial of religious freedom to those who are not Christian.

On slavery Noonan is blunt: "Once upon a time, certainly as late as 1860, the church taught that it was no sin for a Catholic to own another human being." The belief was that enslaved people should be treated humanely; manumission was regarded as good. However, from St. Paul through St. Augustine, Henry de Bracton, and Juan de Lugo down to the American bishop Francis Kenrick in 1841, many of the practices associated with chattel slavery went unchallenged by ecclesiastical authority. More recently, however, "all that has changed. . . . In the light of the teachings of modern popes and the Second Vatican Council on the dignity of the human person, it is morally unthinkable that one person be allowed to buy, sell, hypothecate, or lease another or dispose of that person's children."[26] It should be noted that Pope John Paul II reiterates this condemnation of slavery, citing the Second Vatican Council. The pope, however, made no mention of the eighteen centuries during which slavery was tolerated if not endorsed by the Church. The reality of slavery was seen as compatible with the creation of all in the image of God. This was because the equality called for was judged to be a proportional equality. People could have their freedom limited in proportion to certain qualities, such as being members of "lesser races" with lesser capacities for freedom, or having been legitimately defeated in war.

Equality of the proportional type was also invoked to justify limitations on religious freedom. One's right to religious freedom was seen as proportional to the truth of one's religious belief. In Noonan's words, "Once upon a time, no later than the time of St. Augustine, it was considered virtuous for bishops to invoke imperial force to compel heretics to return to the Church." For a period of more than 1,200 years, "the vast institutional apparatus of the Church was put at the service of detecting heretics, who, if they persevered in their heresy or relapsed into it, would be executed at the stake. Hand in glove, Church and State collaborated in the terror by which heretics were purged."[27] As late as 1832, for example, Pope Gregory XVI declared that the right to freedom of conscience is an "insanity" (dileramentum).[28] Gradually, however, the religious wars in post-Reformation

Europe and, definitively, the persecution of Jews, Christians, and others by fascist and communist regimes in the twentieth century led to a shift in this teaching.

Dramatic change on this issue is evident if one juxtaposes Gregory XVI's condemnation of freedom of conscience with the Second Vatican Council's declaration that "the right to religious freedom has its foundation in the very dignity of the human person, as this dignity is known through the revealed word of God and by reason itself."[29] Indeed, Vatican II linked its support for human rights with the very core of Christian faith when it declared that "by virtue of the gospel committed to it, the Church proclaims the rights of the human person."[30] The basic equality of all persons, and the fact that freedom of belief is now seen as an essential dimension of human dignity, replaces the idea that freedom should be proportioned to the truth of one's beliefs. Indeed, Pope John Paul II saw religious freedom as the "foundation" of all human rights.[31] Regrettably, the fact that the Church had denied the fullness of the right to religious freedom through much of its history, in both solemn teaching and institutional practice, was passed over in silence by John Paul II.

Noonan's account of these dramatic shifts provides a sobering perspective on some aspects of the Christian understanding of the meaning of equality that we cannot accept today. The historical Christian responses to slavery and religious freedom call us to reflect on whether further shifts in our approach to inequality may be called for today, both in Christianity and in other religious-moral traditions as well.

Development of Tradition and Equality Today

These dramatic shifts raise the question of the conditions and limits of legitimate change in a religious tradition, both within Christianity and perhaps in Islam also. Noonan addresses this issue with the help of ideas he draws from John Henry Newman's influential *Essay on Development of Christian Doctrine.* For Newman, in a living tradition, the process of "tradition-ing" is not simply a matter of citing and applying classic texts and authorities from the past. These texts and authorities must certainly be central in any tradition that expects to remain intact. Thus, Newman proposed "conservative action upon its past" as one of the criteria that distinguish authentic developments of the Christian tradition from corruptions of it.[32] But he held that a living tradition is also marked by its power to assimilate ideas originally discovered elsewhere. In Newman's words, ideas about human existence "are not placed in a void, but in the crowded world, and make way for themselves by interpenetration, and develop by absorption."[33]

Hence, living traditions can learn what fidelity to their own identity requires not only by looking to texts and examples from the past but also by attending to new experiences and to the ideas they learn from encounter with those who are different from themselves. It was in this way that Catholicism learned that its conviction that persons are created in God's image requires the abolition of slavery and a new commitment to the religious freedom of all persons. New experiences and encounters with other traditions helped Catholic thinkers recognize that the biblical and doctrinal belief that all persons possess an equal dignity as images of God means they must be granted full equality in all their fundamental rights. These new experiences and encounters led to the recognition that the gospel itself implies that persons have equal rights to religious freedom and rights not to be discriminated against because of religion, race, nationality, ethnicity, or gender. Equal dignity before God was thus seen to require equal human rights in social, political, and economic life.

The examples of slavery and of past limits on religious freedom show that religious communities and their traditions can have negative effects on basic human equality. Vatican II was well aware of the ways that faith communities, including Catholicism, have engaged in behavior that has led some to see religion as a threat to human well-being, including the equality needed to sustain such well-being. The Council acknowledged that this behavior has sometimes led to a distorted picture of religion and indeed of God.[34]

Fortunately, public activity by religious communities also has very positive results in the advancement of equality. Religious leaders such as Mohandas Gandhi, Martin Luther King Jr., the Dalai Lama, Pope John Paul II, and Archbishop Desmond Tutu have played significant roles in the pursuit of peace, justice, and greater respect for human equality. Since we have taken note of some ways that Catholic Christianity has limited and threatened human equality in the past, it will be helpful to conclude by noting some ways that the Christian tradition has made important contributions to the equal dignity of all persons in recent years.

The Catholic community's contributions to the protection of human rights and the promotion of democratic equality have been particularly notable. There is substantial evidence that the post-Vatican II Catholic Church has become one of the strongest worldwide forces for the protection of equal human dignity, human rights, and democracy.[35] Catholicism has played an important role in the global advance of democracy since the Council concluded in 1965, beginning with Portugal and Spain in the late 1960s, in numerous countries in Latin America as well as the Philippines and South Korea in the 1970s and 1980s, and through the role played by the Church in Poland, which contributed to the collapse of the Soviet Union in the late 1980s and early 1990s. It can be argued, therefore, that since Vatican II the Roman Catholic Church has become one of the most effective global bodies contributing to the advancement of democracy. Between the years 1972 and 2009, seventy-eight countries around the world experienced substantial democratization. Monica Duffy Toft, Daniel Philpott, and Timothy Shah have carefully studied the role of religion in these democratic transitions. They conclude that the Catholic community played a role in advancing democracy in thirty-six of the seventy-eight countries that made substantial democratic advances during this period, and it was a leader in the democratization of twenty-two of these countries.[36] Other religious communities also contributed to the advancement of democracy in some regions. Islam was a leader in support of democracy in India, Indonesia, and Kuwait; Hinduism was a leader in India; Orthodoxy, in Serbia; and Protestantism played a leading role in several African countries as well as in South Korea and Romania. Catholicism's contribution, however, was particularly strong.

The move of Catholicism from its more traditional alignment with authoritarian modes of political organization to support for democratic equality was certainly dramatic, perhaps even revolutionary. There seems little doubt that the shift of the Catholic stance from a tendency to support authoritarian government to a quite unambiguous commitment to democracy can be attributed to the innovations of Second Vatican Council, and especially to Vatican II's strong support for human rights, including the right to religious freedom. This shift was brought about by recognition of the dangers of authoritarian regimes such as Nazism and Stalinism in the several decades before the Council. These dangers threatened the Church's own freedom, so the deep Catholic tradition of commitment to the freedom of the Church itself led the bishops at Vatican II to recognize that the right to religious freedom was in continuity with important dimensions of Catholic tradition.[37] At the same time, the broad range of the violations of human dignity by Adolf Hitler and Joseph Stalin showed that more than the Church's own well-being and freedom was a stake. The experience of the multiple kinds of abuse by authoritarian rule led Pope John XXIII, in his 1963 encyclical *Pacem in terris*, to strongly support the equal human rights for all persons, including the equal right to religious freedom.[38] When Vatican II followed the lead of *Pacem in terris* in its endorsement of the full range of human rights articulated by the United Nations, the Council moved the Church to the forefront of the struggle for equal human rights and democratic equality.

We can conclude with a necessarily brief word on the Christian tradition's stance on the economic implications of basic equality today. Once again, the Christian tradition does not hold that a flat arithmetic equality in income or wealth is required by the gospel. However, when inequalities lead to the severe deprivation of those at the bottom, both love of neighbor and the common humanity of all requires challenging such inequalities. The Second Vatican Council affirmed that God wants all people "to live together in one family" as brothers and sisters.[39] Both Christian revelation and secular reason indicate that persons are interdependent and can survive and thrive only with one another's assistance. Thus, we are called to a life that is shared with each another, not divided by inequalities that exclude many from the resources God has created for all. This interdependence is achieved in intimate communities such as families, in larger communities such as the nation, and globally in the human family as a whole. As St. Paul taught, "From one single stock [God] . . . created the whole human race so that they could occupy the entire earth" (Acts 17:26). All men and women have a common origin; all have a common destiny; all are linked together in interdependence on the one earth. Thus, inequalities that create deep divisions in the human community, leaving many millions desperately poor, go against both God's plan for humanity and the very meaning of our common humanity. Indeed, Pope Francis has called such inequalities "the root of social ills." He argues that addressing these ills will require rejection of "the absolute autonomy of markets and financial speculation" and overcoming "the structural causes of inequality."[40]

In light of these teachings and the long tradition on which they are based, the Christian community is challenged to work vigorously to overcome the economic inequalities that wound our world today. When such work is effective, it will both help overcome poverty and strengthen the common good that should be shared among all. On the other hand, when divisions deepen and inequalities grow, the weakest members of society suffer most. In fact, many among the very poor have their lives cut short. Pope Francis is very blunt in his description of the inequalities that mark the world today. In his words, "Just as the commandment 'Thou shalt not kill' sets a clear limit in order to safeguard the value of human life, today we also have to say 'thou shalt not' to an economy of exclusion and inequality. Such an economy kills."[41] Indeed, Pope Francis sees poverty as a sad result of inequalities that exclude far too many people from their rightful share in the goods God has created for the benefit of all.

In a similar way, the US Catholic Bishops see the exclusion of the poor as radically unjust. The US bishops have written that "*basic justice demands the establishment of minimum levels of participation in the life of the human community for all persons*" (emphasis theirs). Negatively put, the US bishops see "the ultimate injustice" in activities that lead to a person or group being "treated actively or abandoned passively as if they were nonmembers of the human race."[42] Inclusion based on equality, therefore, is a mark of justice in society, while exclusion due to inequality is an injustice that mars society deeply.

Conclusion

It is clear from this overview that the Christian tradition supports a strong commitment to the basic equality that requires respect for the dignity of all. It also calls for resistance to those forms of inequality that so divide the human community that some people are deprived of what is required for them to live with basic dignity. Basic human equality should override differences among persons when these differences prevent people from obtaining their most basic needs, restrict their freedoms without justification, or exclude them from essential social relationships. The Christian community has not always lived up to what the central thrust of its tradition requires, and the Christian tradition has not always affirmed what was later discovered to be essential to Christian life. The Christian tradition on equality and inequality remains a living tradition today. We can expect, therefore, that the Christian tradition will continue to develop new insights into what equality requires. Let us hope that the dialogue among the participants in this conference will contribute to this development.

Notes

1. World Bank Group, Poverty and Equity Data Portal, http://povertydata.world bank.org/poverty/home/. For encouraging studies of the reductions in global poverty, see Angus Deaton, *The Great Escape: Health, Wealth, and the Origins of Inequality* (Princeton, NJ: Princeton University Press, 2013); and Steven Radelet, *The Great Surge: The Ascent of the Developing World* (New York: Simon and Schuster, 2015).

2. World Bank Group, *Taking on Inequality: Poverty and Shared Prosperity 2016*, 4, https://openknowledge.worldbank.org/bitstream/handle/10986/25078/9781464809583.pdf.

3. See the website that accompanies Martin Ravaillion's book *The Economics of Poverty: History, Measurement, and Policy* (Oxford: Oxford University Press, 2016), under "Global Inequality," at https://economicsandpoverty.com/read/global-inequality/. Ravaillion is professor of economics at Georgetown University and the former director of research at the World Bank.

4. See Facundo Alvaredo, Lucas Chancel, Thomas Piketty, Emmanuel Saez, and Gabriel Zucman, *World Inequality Report 2018, Executive Summary*, World Inequality Lab, 5–6, https://en.unesco.org/inclusivepolicylab/sites/default/files/publication/document/2018 /7/wir2018-full-report-english.pdf.

5. Angus Deaton, "The U.S. Can No Longer Hide from Its Deep Poverty Problem," *New York Times*, January 24, 2018, https://www.nytimes.com/2018/01/24/opinion/poverty -united-states.html.

6. Amartya Sen, *Development as Freedom* (New York: Knopf, 1999), 22–23.

7. Anne Case and Angus Deaton, "Mortality and Morbidity in the 21st Century," *Brookings Papers on Economic Activity*, Spring 2017, https://www.brookings.edu/wp -content/uploads/2017/08/casetextsp17bpea.pdf.

8. Sen, *Development as Freedom*, 104–7. For Sen's update on his approach to the "missing women," see his "Many Faces of Gender Inequality," *Frontline: India's National Magazine* 18, no. 22 (October 27–November 9, 2001).

9. For a libertarian, free market-oriented critique of Pope Paul VI's argument that inequality has contributed to the lack of development of poorer countries, see P. T. Bauer, "Ecclesiastical Economics: Envy Legitimized," chap. 5 in *Reality and Rhetoric: Studies in the Economics of Development* (Cambridge, MA: Harvard University Press, 1986).

10. Martin Ravaillion, "How Might We Reach a Broad Political Consensus against Inequality," on the website that accompanies Ravaillion's *Economics of Poverty*, https:// economicsandpoverty.com/2017/12/15/how-might-we-reach-a-broad-political-consensus -against-inequality/.

11. New Revised Standard Version.

12. Thomas Aquinas, *Summa contra Gentiles*, part I, chap. 112 and 113, trans. in *Basic Writings of Saint Thomas Aquinas*, vol. 2, ed. Anton C. Pegis (New York: Random House, 1945), 220 and 223.

13. For a discussion of basic equality, see Jeremy Waldron, *One Another's Equals: The Basis of Human Equality* (Cambridge, MA: Harvard University Press, 2017), 2–4 and passim.

14. Pope John XXIII, *Pacem in terris*, no. 10; and Vatican Council II, *Gaudium et spes*, no. 22. Both can be found in David J. O'Brien and Thomas A. Shannon, eds., *Catholic Social Thought: The Documentary Heritage*, exp. ed. (Maryknoll, NY: Orbis, 2010).

15. Vatican Council II, *Gaudium et spes*, no. 41.

16. Vatican Council II, *Gaudium et spes*, nos. 15–17.

17. On the relation between Christian love as equal regard and forms of love that call for different treatment, see Gene Outka, *Agape: An Ethical Analysis* (New Haven, CT: Yale University Press, 1972), esp. chap. 1 and 8.

18. Thomas Aquinas, *Summa theologiae* II–II, q. 57, art. 1., trans. in *St. Thomas Aquinas: Summa Theologica*, vol. III (Allen, TX: 1981: Christian Classics), 1425.

19. Aquinas, II–II, q. 61, arts. 1 and 2.

20. Aquinas, II–II, q. 58, art. 10.

21. Aristotle, *Nicomachean Ethics*, Book V, 1131a, 22–25, trans. Martin Ostwald (Indianapolis, IN: Bobbs-Merrill, 1962).

22. Michael Walzer, *Spheres of Justice: A Defense of Pluralism and Equality* (New York: Basic Books, 1983), 6.

23. Walzer, 100ff. The same position is affirmed in the tradition of Catholic social thought. See Pope Leo XIII's 1891 encyclical, *Rerum Novarum*, no. 34, in O'Brien and Shannon, *Catholic Social Thought*, 31–32.

24. For a classic argument that not all goods ought to be for sale on the market, see Arthur M. Okun, *Equality and Efficiency: The Big Tradeoff* (Washington, DC: Brookings Institution, 1975). Drawing on Okun, Walzer develops this in greater depth in *Spheres of Justice*.

25. John T. Noonan Jr., "Development in Moral Doctrine," *Theological Studies* 54 (1993): 662–77; see also John T. Noonan Jr., *The Church That Can and Cannot Change: The Development of Catholic Moral Teaching* (Notre Dame, IN: University of Notre Dame Press, 2005).

26. Noonan, "Development in Moral Doctrine," 664–67.

27. Noonan, 667.

28. Pope Gregory XVI, *Mirari vos arbitramur*, in *The Christian Faith in the Doctrinal Documents of the Catholic Church*, ed. Josef Neuner and J. Dupuis, rev. ed. (Staten Island, NY: Alba House, 1982), no. 10007.

29. Vatican Council II, *Dignitatis humanae* (Declaration on Religious Freedom), no. 2, http://www.vatican.va/archive/hist_councils/ii_vatican_council/documents/vat-ii_decl_19651207_dignitatis-humanae_en.html.

30. Vatican Council II, *Gaudium et spes*, no. 41.

31. Pope John Paul II, *Veritatis splendor*, encyclical issued August 6, 1993, no. 31, http://w2.vatican.va/content/john-paul-ii/en/encyclicals/documents/hf_jp-ii_enc_06081993_veritatis-splendor.html. There is, unfortunately, ambiguity in John Paul II's discussion of religious freedom. Most of the time it is interpreted in a way that is compatible with Vatican II's statement that this right "continues to exist even in those who do not live up to their obligation of seeking the truth and adhering to it"—that is, the right exists for believers and unbelievers alike. See *Dignitatis humanae*, no. 2. At other times he suggests that religious freedom means the right to hold the truth, as when the

pope says, "In a certain sense, the source and synthesis of these rights [all human rights] is religious freedom, understood as the right to live in the truth of one's faith and in conformity with one's transcendent dignity as a person." *Centesimus annus*, no. 47. I think the ambiguity here is a studied one. I have discussed it in relation to the clear positions of Vatican II and of John Courtney Murray in my "Freedom and Truth: Religious Liberty as Immunity and Empowerment," in *John Courtney Murray and the Growth of Tradition*, ed. J. Leon Hooper and Todd Whitmore (Kansas City, MO: Sheed and Ward, 1996), 129–48.

32. John Henry Newman, *An Essay on the Development of Christian Doctrine* (Garden City, NY: Doubleday Image Books, 1960), 200–204.

33. Newman, 189.

34. Vatican Council II, *Gaudium et spes*, no. 19.

35. For evidence of the strong alliance of Catholicism and democracy that has developed since the Second Vatican Council, see José Casanova, "Civil Society and Religion: Retrospective Reflections on Catholicism and Prospective Reflections on Islam," *Social Research* 68, no. 4 (Winter 2001): 1041–81; Daniel Philpott, "The Catholic Wave," *Journal of Democracy* 15, no. 2 (April 2004): 32–46; and Samuel Huntington, "Religion and the Third Wave," *National Interest* 24 (Summer 1991): 29–42.

36. Monica Duffy Toft, Daniel Philpott, and Timothy Shah, *God's Century: Resurgent Religion and Global Politics* (New York: Norton, 2011), chap. 4, esp. tables 4.1, 4.2, 4.3, and 4.4. On Islam and democracy, see Daniel Philpott, *Religious Freedom in Islam: The Fate of a Universal Right in the Muslim World Today* (Oxford: Oxford University Press, 2019); and Daniel Philpott, "Religious Freedom in Islam: A Global Landscape," *Journal of Law, Religion & State* 2 (2013): 3–21.

37. See John Courtney Murray, "The Tradition," chap. 2 in *The Problem of Religious Freedom* (Westminster, MD: Newman, 1965), esp. his treatment of the "freedom of the church" at pp. 47–64.

38. Pope John XXIII, *Pacem in terris*, encyclical issued in 1963, nos. 8–27, affirms most of the human rights set forth in the Universal Declaration on Human Rights.

39. Vatican Council II, *Gaudium et spes*, no. 24.

40. Pope Francis, *Evangelii gaudium*, apostolic exhortation issued November 24, 2013, n. 202, http://w2.vatican.va/content/francesco/en/apost_exhortations/documents/papa-francesco_esortazione-ap_20131124_evangelii-gaudium.html.

41. Pope Francis, no. 53.

42. US Conference of Catholic Bishops, *Economic Justice for All: Pastoral Letter on Catholic Social Thought and the U.S. Economy*, issued 1986, no. 77, in *Catholic Social Thought: The Documentary Heritage*, by David J. O'Brien and Thomas A. Shannon (Maryknoll, NY: Orbis, 1992), 576–77.

PART TWO

Muslims and Christians Facing the Reality of Inequality

Gender and Islam
Obstacles and Possibilities

SAMIA HUQ

Gender, Religion, and Social Progress

In 2017, when the government of Bangladesh lowered the age of marriage for girls from eighteen to sixteen, there was uproar from secular feminists who considered the move to be detrimental to women's lives.[1] The religious quarters remained mute on the matter—their silence premised on the ambiguity around the correlation between "age of marriage" and what is good for women in their roles in holding up a virtuous community.[2] The government's position seemed to rest on the fact that this move would prevent elopements and would help align the families' wishes with that of the girls. The questions of why a girl elopes, what choices are available to her at that point, the meanings that she ascribes to the options available to her, and—last but not least—a sociological wrestling with whether and how a virtuous and flourishing community is born when the happiest option for an adolescent girl is to undertake the pleasures, pains, and responsibilities that marriage entails are almost absent, or at best very partial, in the decree that allows adolescent girls to marry.

As the example above demonstrates, the relationship between gendered expectations and public religious voices is not straightforward or unique. It is often the case in Muslim-majority countries that state policies and decisions even when under the "secular" banner reflect a certain conservatism that is usually otherwise considered to be the sole preserve of regressive religious quarters. Beyond question of political expediency and strategic alliances, an important issue to consider in policies around women and men is the vision of gendered roles in society that different actors uphold. In that, the sanctity of the family is asserted as very important for religious actors as well as many "secular" policies. While religion has historically been associated with many different forms of family and a wide variety of sexual and gendered relations, it is the heterosexual, joint, and nuclear family that came to dominate the religious as well as the secular imagination under modernity. Official forms of religion and their male leaders played an important role in shaping this ideal.[3] In Islam, while conservative quarters retained the Qur'anic endorsement of a maximum of four marriages, the mainstream, educated norm in most postcolonial Muslim countries had become families based on heterosexual monogamous unions. These ideals of marriage and family were premised on the male breadwinner model, exalting women's domestic responsibilities, and affirming strong parental authority over children. By the late twentieth century, while many Islamic authorities accepted the permissibility of women's paid work outside the home, others continued to endorse in some form a doctrine of the "complementary" of essentially different roles of men and women. It is in the preservation of such a unit and the roles deemed ideal in it that much religious and secular energy is vested in order to create functional and virtuous societies.

Before proceeding further, I need to explain what I mean by "religion" and the "religious" here. In "Religions and Social Progress: Critical Assessments and Creative Partnerships," my colleagues and I approached religion as both the very broad range of institutions, beliefs, and practices that social scientists have typically thought of as religion and the much larger domain of everyday beliefs and practices that constitute lived religion.[4] Conceiving religion this way means that equal weight is given to the ways in which lived realities and everyday practices allow both religious professionals and lay persons to respond to their personal and institutional contexts.[5] Such responses in the everyday renders "Tradition" (with a capital T) a dynamic process that is beyond the pale of revealed and recorded words and legalistic opinions. The fact that religion is practiced differently by different adherents also means that religious ideas and practices are situated, and that every religious tradition, including Islam, is internally diverse and caught in an ongoing process of creation and re-creation.[6] A dynamic approach to "tradition" may be considered a dilution of Tradition (with a capital T)—a dilution that is owed to human whims. However, the sociological reality that tradition has transformed and consequently been transformed means that change is an important and integral part of any religious tradition.[7]

This raises the question, What should be the parameters of change, and who should be authoring it? The example that I began with regarding child marriage and the conservative silence around it demonstrates clearly that identifying and fixing who could be charged to oversee change is a matter that cannot be easily settled. As a social scientist, I contend that a confluence of authorities that determine and decide on change around gender relations or any other matter must do so by seriously engaging the question of what social progress means to communities. By social progress, I do not refer to technological formulas and liner changes but rather moral deliberations and judgments that beg a re-imagining of possibilities and human flourishing. Furthermore, social progress must be disentangled from its Enlightenment assumptions in order to encompass a broader understanding of movements toward freedom, dignity, and relationships of solidarity and mutual well-being. A disentanglement from Enlightenment assumptions means that religion must also be seen in a different relationship to, and according to, an altered definition of secularity. Drawing on recent rethinking of secularism as a process that regulates (through forces of modernity—notably, the modern state) rather than emptying the public and private world's religious content, religion needs to be assessed in its myriad involvements with formal and informal forms of modern power. In this, as the brick wall between the religious and the secular gets broken down, processes of secularization produce particular kinds of embodied religious subjects. How do these religious subjects make sense of religion in general and Islam in particular under conditions of modernity and within their particular contexts to emote, live, and rethink gender roles and expectations? Evidently, lived experiences produce multiple results. In the resultant diversity in thinking about and being men and women in the world, communities adhere to, negotiate, and contest "official" doctrine, which encompasses local religious authority, the authority of particular textual verses, and a privileging of certain kinds of histories. In the absence of a centralized church in the Muslim world, these authorities that constitute the Tradition with a capital "T" are also multiple and fragmented. In the following pages, I highlight some of the ways in which gender is lived by Muslim communities, including the different ways in which social progress is gauged, the partnerships that are formed, and the unanswered questions and unresolved issues vis-à-vis gender that communities are left with as they live their lives in the modern world.[8]

Living Islam Conservatively

When Muslims live conservatively vis-à-vis gender, they do so by promoting particular ideals in gender roles and expectations in family life. These expectations are anchored in a defense of the male-headed "traditional" family. Of course, the nuclear and monogamous version of the family is one that has emerged as ideal under conditions of modernity as other family forms (found in scripture and through history) have receded to the background. While there are many examples from the Islamic tradition that are brought to bear on such defenses, the one verse that stands out as the authority privileging the traditional male-headed family is Q. 4:34, which reads,

> Men are the protectors and maintainers of women, Because God has given the one more [strength] than the other, and because they support them from their means. Therefore the righteous women are obedient. . . . As those women on whose part ye fear disloyalty and ill-conduct, first admonish

them, next, refuse to share their beds, and last beat them. But if they return to obedience, seek not against them means [of annoyance], for God is most high, great.[9]

Many normative statements are packed into this verse that allow for men's superiority as material providers to claim a privileged place in the Muslim psyche in a way that normalizes female obedience and retribution for disobedience, even in the form of striking. Recent research has shown how the term *qawammun* (protectors and maintainers) has traveled through the centuries to acquire a normative, prescriptive status from a descriptive one.[10] This evolution toward normativity reaches a crescendo with the development of the "*qiwamah* postulate," which underscores how Muslim laws in various contexts deal with women and gender relations to authorize unequal treatment of men and women within and outside the home.[11]

However, when Muslims refuse to view the hierarchy enshrined in scripture and exegesis as anything but divinely ordained, they often do so because their particular contexts are amenable to such readings, either due to the fact that local settings are and have always been conservative or as a part and parcel of a "return to Islam" that seeks to redress failings at multiple levels ranging from the geopolitical to the national and domestic. Many conservative Muslims argue that "equality" is a liberal chimera that disrupts the natural balance as divinely ordained. Rather than equality, they prefer gender complementarity, wherein men and women have specific tasks to fulfill and a well-laid-out path to achieving spiritual and worldly gains. As a result, conservative readings are often held close to heart by traditionalists, Islamists, fundamentalists, and even militants. My placing of all the categories together is in no way suggestive of their similar points of origin or worldview and vision of the future. However, I contend that gender hierarchy is considered unproblematic, even beneficial, by most who subscribe to a pietist, traditionalist, and fundamentalist worldview, even if adherents end up treating men and women differently, mobilizing them in different ways in their public and political programs.

Be that as it may, recent anthropological studies on how women live under patriarchal norms highlight not only cultural variations but also negotiations on the part of women so that their lives are not rendered as rigid as critics of conservative religion would like to portray. Saba Mahmood's groundbreaking work on Egypt's piety movement sheds light on liberal blind spots, arguing that feminist notions of desire and agency are inadequate for an understanding of what pious bodily and sensorial cultivation entail for a sense of achievement and self-fulfillment.[12] Mahmood defines women's agency not necessarily against the grain of patriarchy but from within the local context that produces a different notion of desire, enabling different enactments for self-realization. Through such processes and the real mobility that allows women to claim hitherto male-only spaces such as mosques, Egyptian women feel worthy and responsible and in the service of God and community. Lara Deeb argues that, for women in the suburbs of Beirut, joining Islamist groups such as Hizbollah results in a re-enchantment of modernity, where the "Western woman" is invoked both as foil and impetus to create an authentically Islamic and modern way of life.[13] My own study of the cultivation of piety among educated, urban Bangladeshis shows that remaining attached to traditional families headed by men does not foreclose greater individualistic reflection on the part of women. They take on the "failed" promises of modern deliveries of marriage and a wife's role in it to infuse a new meaning of how they would like to become Islamic wives. In doing so, women also end up speaking critically to overarching nationalist ideals that frame the "modern," "secular," Bangladeshi woman.[14]

Needless to say, the idea that living Islam conservatively may also have positive agentive consequences for women has been met with much criticism. Given that women do not take on gender inequality head on, there is suspicion that conservative Islam leaves men and women with a gender narrative that promotes a hypermasculinity. Whether women are able to overcome problems like domestic violence or to access state facilities for legal and other kinds of redress are points on which there is doubt around conservative Islam's potential to deliver gender justice. However, it should be clearly stated that a sense of hypermasculinity and women's inability to seek legal and other community or state redresses are rooted in the cultural-political context, much of which may be more postcolonial and "secular" than Islamic. The extreme example of religiously legitimated male domination and violence against women in fundamentalist groups like ISIS and Boko Haram is now beginning to be studied, but larger patterns and processes are not yet well understood.[15] Thus, the salience of a conservative narrative on gender and religion is linked to contexts—personal or broader—whereby the promises of conservative Islam (as limited as they may seem to critics) appear more appealing than other "secular" alternatives. Therefore, a religious stance—whether conservative, fundamentalist, or militant—has to be understood for its link to the larger context and what that offers for men, women, and a relationship between the two that leads to the flourishing of both.

Challenging Complementarity

Historicizing Islam and its various commands has resulted in a plethora of academic accounts that have placed gender relations on a continuum, viewing equality and not complementarity as the ideal destination that is congruent with the spirit of change and justice that lay at the heart of the prophetic mission. Some of the early academic seeds of this kind of thinking were sewn by scholars such as Leila Ahmed, Fatima Mernissi, and Asma Barlas.[16] With these scholarly accounts as a backdrop, in the wake of the Iranian Revolution, certain movements gained grounds among academic and activist circles that sought feminist teachings in

Islamic scripture, claiming "Islamic Feminism" as an authentically Islamic approach to tackling gender inequalities and eventually amending gender-unequal laws. Some notable examples include groups such as the Malaysia-based Sisters in Islam and Musawah. Musawah aims to reform Muslim family law through its work with legal experts, Islamic clergy and scholars, and anthropologists and historians. In an edited volume titled *Men in Charge: Rethinking Authority in Muslim Legal Tradition*, we read,

> The most pervasive gender-based legal inequalities that confront Muslim women relate to spousal and parental roles and rights. In many Muslim family codes, men can unilaterally repudiate their wives, take four wives, have legal claim to their wives' obedience and have sole guardianship over children. Women's access to divorce is usually restricted; they often cannot have guardianship of their children; and their claim to spousal maintenance is often contingent on their "obedience" to their husbands.[17]

By highlighting the diversity of legitimate Islamic juristic opinion and by engaging in research on the ground, Musawah seeks to shift the construction of marriage and gender relations away from obedience and subjugation to love, mercy, and equal respect for both genders as enjoined by scriptures. It is through a reorientation that groups such as Musawah seek to reinterpret social, legal, and scriptural norms. Such reorientations aim to contextualize Qur'anic verses such as 4:34 to read it contextually and conditionally (that only those men who actually earn can claim a degree of superiority over their wives. If a man does not provide for his wife, he will not have the stated privilege. Thus, such conditionality makes male superiority anything but a standard for all men over all women).

Contextuality and conditionality in reading and interpreting religious scripture to make current socioeconomic realities intelligible are hallmarks of a modernist, reformist approach within Islam. Reformist positions have been critiqued on a number of grounds. The backlash against reform from the "tradition" consists of the allegation that modernist impulses for change or the premise of sticking to "essentials" while seeing many other norms as historically contextual is owed to an uncritical overadherence to modern values to the extent that a need for an alignment with modernity may dispel other important essentials in the scripture.[18] Movements that are based on reformist positions have also received criticism for the links they engender between sociological and political implications. For example, Lila Abu-Lughod argues that movements such as Musawah and the Global Muslim Women's Shura Council resort to a human rights model that separates Muslim women from their own cultures and obscures the structural, political, and economic factors that contribute to women's suffering.[19] Saba Mahmood points out that an imperialist logic is at play when Islamic cultural practices such as veiling or "honor killings" are declared in need of remedy, consequently justifying Western military and other kinds of intervention in Muslim societies.[20] They argue that outside agents seeking progressive change need to pay closer attention to the everyday unfolding of women's lives to see that it is not Islam or tradition per se that need to be the starting points of change but other socioeconomic realities tied to imperial projects that need to be highlighted and targeted for the welfare of Muslim communities.

A conversation on gender is never easy, and, as the above paragraph demonstrates, especially when religion/Islam is involved, gender sits on so many busy cultural-political intersections that invoking gender reform can have the unintended consequence of making strange bedfellows—that is, reformists and imperialists on the one hand, conservative traditionalists and progressive anthropologists on the other. In order to reroute the journey of gender justice away from problematic intersections, Musawah embarked on an initiative called the Global Life Stories Project. The intention of this project is precisely to underscore the importance of (legal) reform away from abstract modernist notions and to situate the possibilities of change in the everyday lives of Muslim women. In mounting such an initiative, Musawah's goal is to add texture and dimension to the different ways in which change may be aimed and achieved, leading to different scenarios for men and women as well as for Muslim women from different parts of the world. While "religion" or "religious" tradition is not the same everywhere and women's lives are not solely about tradition, Musawah argues that tradition is neither inconsequential to women's everyday realities. It is toward a deeper understanding of the various layers of society—ranging from the geopolitical to the domestic—in which religious norms are imbricated that the Global Life Stories Project sought to underpin cultural and eventually legal reform.[21] The idea that addressing religious norms can be an effective measure of change (and not just a superficial imperial tactic that does nothing for women) is supported by studies that demonstrate an effectiveness of religious ideas to influence people's worldviews and change their actions accordingly.[22]

Musawah engages scholars and clergy who wish to locate change from within the tradition by bringing to bear on it new lenses of inquiry and analysis. A case in point is the work of Sadiya Shaikh, whose reformist stance engages certain tenets of Sufi traditions that "offer resources on the deepest human imperatives in Islam."[23] Shaikh argues that while Sufi traditions have not been free of politics either, its "deepest religious and existential priorities . . . and a rigorous spiritual interrogation of all human claims to power and supremacy . . . presents a fruitful opportunity to critique gender discrimination."[24] It is with these Sufi principles that Shaikh advocates a re-exploration of the underlying foundations of Muslim legal traditions and their implications for gender justice.

Internal movements for religious reform have generally focused on women and femininities, and less attention has been paid to men, masculinities, and gender relations in a broader sense. Even critical and reformist circles such as Musawah have been more focused on femininities than on masculinities. However, gender never means only women, and the relationship between religion and gender covers a wide spectrum. Questions around sexuality and sexual diversity anchor themselves within the intellectual and philosophical purview of liberal reform movements. However, more often than not, the critiques of and desire to re-engage tradition anew also usher alternative religious expressions. In the final section, I discuss Muslims' engaging alternative ideas and practices.

Seeking Alterity

The need to raise women's status in society has opened the window on several associated questions such as women's political and religious leadership, varied forms of masculinity, gender fluidity, and the acceptance of homosexuality. Questions surrounding these issues have not only shed critical light on dominant views on these matters; they have also opened up new spaces to engender a rethinking of belief and practice. A case in point is the Inclusive Mosque Initiative (IMI), which was founded by Muslim grassroots activists in 2012 as a network of women-led and women-run mosques that would be open to all, regardless of race, gender, creed, and sexual orientation. Since its inception, IMI has opened chapters in Zurich, Pakistan, Malaysia, and Kashmir. While "feminizing" the mosque space and culture was IMI's main intent, its deeply held commitment to tolerance and pluralism leads IMI to welcome other faiths to their mosques and even to hold interfaith prayers. In addition to prayers, *dhikr* (remembrance), and discussions of the Qur'an and Sunnah, IMI invites scholars, researchers, and specialists to give talks on a variety of issues ranging from hijab to masculinity to transsexuals. The participation of Muslims is open, thereby allowing Muslims of different creeds—Sufis, Salafis, progressives, unsure—to attend IMI mosques. While IMI is not a queer organization, it is acutely aware and willing to be responsive to the rights of members of the lesbian, gay, bisexual, transgender, and queer (LGBTQ) community.[25]

Sexual diversity is a vexed topic is most religions, and Islam in no exception. Having been significantly named, shamed, and therefore magnified by modernity, opposition to homosexuality is by no means confined to religion. However, such opposition is a feature of all fundamentalisms, rigidly scriptural forms of religion, and a great deal of mainstream religious opinions. But there are also dissenting voices who reread traditional religious sources to problematize "homophobic" interpretations. Among these is Scott Kugle, who, in his *Homosexuality in Islam*, makes the point that the canons of the tradition only speak of sexual acts; they contain nothing about sexual orientation.[26] Thus, for example, the story of the prophet Lot and the city of Sodom, which is present in the Qur'an as well as the Bible and has been held as the canonical negation of homosexuality—can and has been read differently. Among these alternative interpretations is one—backed up by scholarly analysis—that argues that the particular Qur'anic and biblical account is a story of oppressive power, miserliness, inhospitality, and arrogance; it is a story in which male sex acts are vilified for the abuse of power they represent in that particular context, not for sodomy—and certainly not for sexual orientation.

With such academic studies as a backdrop, LGBTQ movements are now also making their voices heard, calling for reform of official religion, and sometimes even setting up alternative religious communities and networks. A recent study by Andrew Yip and Sarah-Jane Page highlights how young people across many traditions are laying claims on the discourse of sexual diversity away from sexual deviance.[27] Consequently, even in conservative religious groups, young people took their faith as a support in helping to carve out their sexual identity. They find comfort in the belief that sexual orientation is God-given, claiming, "If God made me like this, this is who I am meant to be." Such a stance is not, however, well accepted by mainstream society and often leads to major points of conflict within religion as well as in secular societies. Some controversial groups in Islam include the UK-based Imaan and the Safra Project for women, along with the US-originating Al-Fatiha Foundation. The latter, which was founded in 1998 to offer a platform for believing and practicing LGBTQ Muslims transnationally, had several chapters in the United States and offices in Canada, the United Kingdom, Spain, and South Africa. However, an international Islamic group called Al-Muhajiroun, seeking an Islamic caliphate, declared in 2001 that members of Al-Fatiha were apostates. In spite of these pressures, a handful of mosques in the United States and South Africa have openly gay imams. However, these enterprises are not without resistance from many well-respected religious voices for allegedly defying Islam and its basic principles.[28]

Considered countercultural in the West in the first half of the twentieth century, the "alternative" spiritual milieu has expanded its influence to become increasingly mainstream in many countries, notably in the West. Its place in the mainstream arena has been facilitated by many aspects of globalization such as its easy relations with new media, revived and new healing and well-being practices, and the opportunities opened by entrepreneurial consumer capitalism.[29] In the West, as "spirituality" becomes prevalent in everyday matters ranging from education to health care to popular culture, Islamic spiritually in the form of Sufism has also made a comeback in the West and in Muslim-majority countries. Sufism appears in many shades—that is, as the fashionable "California Sufism," as a locus of prayer and contemplation, and as a way for many Muslim-majority nations to trace their own "authentic Islam" as it grew on their soil. The latter is especially relevant for much of South and Southeast Asia, which accompanies reforms along alternative lines—albeit not without tension. Returning to the example of Bangladesh, the local understanding of Sufism is an approach to Islamic belief and practice that emerged in Bengal through Mughal intervention—one that allowed for a certain hybridity and its de-emphasis on textuality.[30] A syncretic beginning subsequently tarred Bengali Islam as inadequately "Islamic." Attempts to reform it among more textual lines have often been entangled with other political and socioeconomic questions such as peasant rights, unequal land sharing arrangements, and political sovereignty. Textually oriented reform calls in the past twenty years, however, have come through Islamist ideas and the activities of various Middle Eastern charities and other welfare organizations. This has resulted in the growth and spread of political ideas and some cultural practices that critics consider too "Arab-centric" and therefore removed from how Islam arrived in and has been lived in Bengal. To resist such cultural "Arabization," Bengalis speak of attempts to carve out their own "authentic Islam" by reverting to the syncretism in religious practice and community sociability that constitutes Islam in its earliest era in Bengal. The anachronism in this notwithstanding, most people tend to think that such early syncretistic Islam and the spirituality underscoring it takes a more appreciative and affirming view of equal gender relations and is relaxed about the pluralization of family forms and intimate relations. However, these alternative expressions and accompanying mystical practices find it increasingly difficult to gain public and political acceptance. Recently local shrines and Sufi complexes have been the targets of Islamist onslaughts, and research shows that many shrine complexes have been adopting more rigid interpretations that are textually grounded in order to survive.[31] Recently, Baul mystics—a group of practitioners following the philosophy of eighteenth-century preacher Lalon Fakir, professing tolerance borne out of a mix between Islam and Hinduism by transcending religious dogma—have also come under serious attack.[32] While Lalon enjoys a huge commercial comeback through popular music, poetry, and clothing styles, real practitioners are under constant attack for practicing a "wrong religion." Weighed down by the rhetoric of religious authenticity, such philosophies and their address to gender equality remain at best fringe elements and irrelevant. Seeking alternate religious expressions and their implications for gender relation thus depends on many factors and varies in different parts of the world. These expressions are up against not only more orthodox Islamic narratives and expression but also state power that is often secular.

Conclusion

As the discussion above shows, gender and Islam are entangled in a variety of ways, and each of these entanglements lock Muslims into their tradition differently. Linda Woodhead argues that there are four main kinds of religious stances or orientations that people take concerning gender: consolidating (legitimating existing inequality), tactical (working within existing constraints to subvert them), questing (seeking alternatives for personal benefit rather than structural change), and countercultural (working for progressive structural change).[33] In the way that men and women live Islam conservatively or seek reformation and alterity, we see that some measure of one or more of these approaches are framed by norms and desires, going on to dictate expectations and outcomes.

Such negotiations shed light on not only the complexity of people's everyday lives but also the definition of and desire to rethink tradition.

As discussed earlier in this essay, the necessity for rethinking tradition in Islam can be motivated by a variety of intentions and agendas. New forms of colonization, imperialism, war, and all else that seek to undermine non-Western cultures by privileging assumptions inherent to Western ideas and interests often work as a filter through which Muslims' reflections on tradition must pass. Muslim communities are divided on how to set the right parameters of change so that certain values, norms, and lifeways are not lost to the whims of modernity. There is a genuine desire to disallow temporality to be informed by the short span of time that constitutes post-Enlightenment modernity. Many Muslims who seek to preserve tradition rightly argue that there is an arrogance in the assumption that everything good that has happened in the history of the world must have happened in the past two hundred years, and that there is no value to lifeways of the pre-Enlightenment era. That being said, as the discussion in this essay argues, there are realities that abound in the everyday lives of Muslims whose contestations are not as concerned with abstract notions of modernity and Enlightenment ideals as they are about the limits of pains, pleasures, and flourishing of mind, body, and spirit as they go through life. As Tanika Sarkar writes regarding changes in Hindu religion and culture in eighteenth-century India, there is an "argumentative universalism" that transcends the binary of acquiescing or rejecting modernity, especially since modern conditions are what largely inform the habitus of men and women today.[34] As a social scientist, I would like to see such an argumentative universalism be in conversation with tradition toward a re-envisioning of the welfare of Muslims and their communities. How would priorities around gender roles, expectations, and hierarchies be recalibrated, and how could tradition write the story of Muslim possibilities differently? Perhaps a good place to start, free of preconceived notions of gendered ideals, is not the verses on men's superiority over women (such as Q. 4:34) but rather Q. 4:1, which reads, "People, be mindful of your Lord, who created you from a single soul, and from it creates its mate, and from the pair of them spread countless men and women far and wide; be mindful of God, in whose name you make requests of one another."[35] The gender-unspecified pronoun here perhaps opens up productive possibilities for animosities and tensions in the everyday and allows the truth of the brute power that gender hierarchies wield to be legible by tradition in a way that Muslims feel the imperative to act upon injustices toward greater solutions.

Notes

1. "Bangladesh: Don't Lower Marriage Age," *Human Rights Watch*, October 12, 2014, https://www.hrw.org/news/2014/10/12/bangladesh-dont-lower-marriage-age.

2. "Islamists like Hifazat-e Islam Will Feel Encouraged if Bangladesh Lowers Marriage Age for Girls, Warns NHRC Chief," *Bdnews24.com*, June 30, 2015, https://bdnews24.com/bangladesh/2015/06/30/islamists-like-hifazat-e-islam-will-feel-encouraged-if-bangladesh-lowers-marriage-age-for-girls-warns-nhrc-chief.

3. For a discussion of the role of Christianity in sacralizing that patriarchal family unit, see Lyndal Roper, *The Holy Household: Women and Morals in Reformation Augsburg* (Oxford: Oxford University Press, 1992).

4. Grace Davie, Nancy Ammerman, Samia Huq, Lucian N. Leustean, Tarek Masoud, Suzanne Moon, Jacob K. Olupona, et al., "Religions and Social Progress: Critical Assessments and Creative Partnerships," in *Rethinking Society for the 21st Century: Report of the International Panel on Social Progress*, vol. 3, *Transformations in Values, Norms, Cultures*, ed. International Panel on Social Progress (Cambridge: Cambridge University Press, 2018), 641–76.

5. M. B. McGuire, *Lived Religion: Faith and Practice in Everyday Life* (New York: Oxford University Press, 2008).

6. Courtney Bender, *The New Metaphysicals: Spirituality and the American Religious Imagination* (Chicago: University of Chicago Press, 2010).

7. For a longer discussion of how religion may be defined in relation to social progress, see Davie et al., "Religions and Social Progress."

8. For a longer discussion of the meaning of social progress, see International Panel on Social Progress, ed., *Rethinking Society for the 21st Century*, vol. 1, *Socio-Economic Transformations* (Cambridge: Cambridge University Press, 2018).

9. Translation according to Yusuf Ali, *The Meaning of the Holy Qur'ān* (Lahore: Shaikh Muhammad Ashraf, 1934), modified slightly.

10. Omaima Abu Bakr, "The Interpretive Legacy of Qiwamah as an Exegetical Construct," in *Men in Charge? Rethinking Authority in Muslim Legal Tradition*, ed. Ziba Mir-Hosseini, Mulki Al-Sharmani, Jana Rumminger (Oxford: Oneworld, 2015), 44–64.

11. Lynn Welchman argues that based on certain Qur'anic verses, *qiwamah*, or male guardianship, acquires an ontological status—or a value system that exists on its own right. See Lynn Welchman, "A Husband's Authority: Emerging Formulations in Muslim Family Laws," *International Journal of Law, Policy and the Family* 25, no. 1 (2011): 1–23.

12. Saba Mahmood, *Politics of Piety: Islamic Revival and the Feminist Subject* (Princeton, NJ: Princeton University Press, 2005).

13. Lara Deeb, *An Enchanted Modern: Gender and Public Piety in Shi'i Lebanon* (Princeton, NJ: Princeton University Press, 2006).

14. Samia Huq, "Piety, Music and Gender Transformation: Reconfiguring Women as Culture-Bearing Markers of Modernity and Nationalism in Urban Bangladesh," *Inter-Asia Cultural Studies* 12, no. 2 (2011): 225–39.

15. See, for example, Jessica Stern and J. M. Berger, *ISIS: The State of Terror* (New York: Ecco, 2016).

16. Leila Ahmed, *Women and Gender in Islam: Historical Roots of a Modern Debate* (New Haven, CT: Yale University Press, 1992); Fatima Mernissi, *The Veil and the Male Elite: A Feminist Interpretation of Women's Rights in Islam* (New York: Basic Books, 1992); and Asma Barlas, *"Believing Women" in Islam: Unreading Patriarchal Interpretations of the Qur'an* (Austin: University of Texas Press, 2002).

17. Ziba Mir-Hosseini, Mulki Al-Sharmani, and Jana Rumminger, eds., introduction to *Men in Charge? Rethinking Authority in Muslim Legal Tradition* (Oxford: Oneworld, 2015), 4.

18. W. B. Hallaq, *Sharia: Theory, Practice, Transformations* (Cambridge: Cambridge University Press, 2009), 529.

19. Lila Abu-Lughod, *Do Muslim Women Need Saving?* (Cambridge, MA: Harvard University Press, 2015).

20. Saba Mahmood, "Secularism, Hermeneutics and Empire: The Politics of Islamic Reformation," *Public Culture* 18, no. 2 (2006): 323–47.

21. For further information, see Musawah, *Women's Stories, Women's Lives: Male Authority in Muslim Contexts* (Kuala Lampur: Musawah, 2016), https://www.musawah.org/resources/womens-stories-womens-lives-male-authority-in-muslim-contexts-arabic/.

22. For a discussion of how religious ideas and invocation of religious texts may influence changes, see Tarek Masoud, Amaney Jamal, and Elizabeth Nugent, "Using the Qur'ān to Empower Arab Women? Theory and Experimental Evidence from Egypt," *Comparative Political Studies* 49, no. 12 (2016): 1555–98.

23. Sadia Shaikh, "Islamic Law, Sufism and Gender," in Mir-Hosseini et al., *Men in Charge?*, 108.

24. Shaikh, 107.

25. For a more elaborate discussion on the IMI, see http://inclusivemosqueinitiative.org/.

26. Scott Siraj al-Haqq Kugle, *Homosexuality in Islam: Critical Reflection on Gay, Lesbian and Transgender Muslims* (Oxford: Oneworld, 2010).

27. Andrew Kam-Tuck Yip and Sarah-Jane Page, *Religious and Sexual Identities: A Multi-Faith Exploration of Young Adults* (Farnham, Surrey: Ashgate, 2013).

28. See, for example, Afdhere Jama, "5 Imams Who Are Openly Gay," *Islam and Homosexuality*, January 20, 2015, http://islamandhomosexuality.com/5-imams-openly-gay/. See also Susan Henking, "Coming Out Twice: Sexuality and Gender in Islam," *Religion Dispatches*, April 17, 2012, http://religiondispatches.org/coming-out-twice-sexuality-and-gender-in-islam/.

29. Kathryn Lofton, *Oprah: The Gospel of an Icon* (Berkeley: University of California Press, 2010).

30. For a discussion of how Islam arrived in Bengal, see Richard Eaton, *The Rise of Islam in the Bengal Frontier, 1204–1760* (Berkeley: University of California Press, 1993).

31. For a detailed understanding of how Sufi shrines and complexes are under attack and changing, see Peter Bertocci, "A Sufi Movement in Bangladesh: The Maijbhandari Tariqa and Its Followers," *Contributions to Indian Sociology* 40, no. 1 (2006): 1–28.

32. "Bauls under Attack: The Intolerance of Tolerance," editorial, *Daily Star*, August 1, 2016, https://www.thedailystar.net/editorial/bauls-under-attack-1262311. For greater detail on the life and teaching of Fakir Lalon Shah, see "Fakir Lalon Shah," based on an interview by Professor Maria Mies with Farhad Mazhar in Dhaka on January 28, 2004, https://www.scribd.com/doc/20481865/Fakir-Lalon-Sha.

33. Linda Woodhead, "Gender Differences in Religious Practice and Significance," in *The Sage Handbook of the Sociology of Religion*, ed. James Beckford and N. Jay Demerath III (London: Sage, 2007), 566–86.

34. Tanika Sarkar, "How to Think Universalism from Colonial and Post Colonial Locations: Some Indian Efforts," in *Universalism in International Law and Philosophy*, ed. Petter Korkman and Virpi Makinen (Helsinki: Helsinki Collegium for Advanced Studies, 2008), 239–54.

35. Seyyed Hossein Nasr, Caner K. Dagli, Maria Massi Dakake, Joseph E. B. Lumbard, and Mohammed Rustom, eds. *The Study Quran: A New Translation and Commentary* (New York: HarperOne, 2015), emphasis added.

The Problem of Race in Christianity

ELIZABETH PHILLIPS

When approaching the topic of Christianity and race, one feels the need either to present a multivolume work or, in the absence of that possibility, to throw up one's hands and say, "Yes, this is a huge problem. Where do we even begin?" In the setting of the Building Bridges Seminar, the former is not possible, and the latter would not do. I have chosen, instead, to present the following eight assertions and to admit that within this chapter's limited scope they can only be assertions. However, behind each of these assertions are shelves of books and articles that chronicle and debate them (and I have at least been able to gesture toward some of these in this essay's endnotes). I take these eight assertions to be at least some of the central considerations that must be on the table and with which we must come to terms if we are to engage in further considerations—both critical and constructive—about Christianity and race.

1. Race is just a *social construct*.

The divisions between groups of humans that have been named as distinctions of "race" have no basis in either historical or biological reality. In the West, the emergence of the idea of race is inextricably intertwined with colonialism and the slave trade. The concept of race as we know it today was not a reality described neutrally then unfortunately applied oppressively; rather, it came into existence for the purpose of explaining, justifying, and advancing the superiority of European powers over peoples from other parts of the world.[1] Particularly important here is that there is no such thing as "white" people. The social construction of "whiteness" as a racial category has never served any purpose other than to assert the superiority of so-called white people over other people who are categorized as Black or anything other than white.

2. Racism is not *just* a social construct.

Although it is extraordinarily important to grasp that the idea of race has been socially constructed rather than having any empirical reality, we must not misunderstand "social construct" as something that is therefore easily overcome by abandoning the idea of it. Racism does not go away simply because individuals decide not to believe in race or subscribe to racist ideologies. The social construction of race includes all the ways in which the superiority of "whiteness" has been systemically and structurally embedded in social and political realities for centuries. The strength, stability, and wealth of the societies of Europe, North America,[2] Australia, and New Zealand are historically dependent on the enslavement and subjugation of "nonwhite" others and are ideologically dependent upon the pervasive assumption that "white" is both normal and good, and nonwhiteness—especially Blackness—is exceptional and deficient.

3. The collusion of Western Christianity with the construction of race is undeniable.

Not only is the emergence of "race" inextricably tied to colonialism and the slave trade, it is also inextricable from Western Christian theology and practice. There is no simple causation traceable here; we cannot say that the social construction of race caused Western Christianity to become racist, nor can we say that the racism of Western Christianity caused the social construction of race. We *can* say, emphatically, that the history of Christianity in the West has been marked far more dramatically by racism than by antiracism.[3]

4. One way to trace this is by exploring the emergence of global Christian missionary movements in relation to colonialism.

Again, we cannot be simplistic here; it is not the case that all white missionaries have been brutal racists, particularly in local practice.[4] However, it is impossible to deny that for centuries the concepts of racial superiority and the practices of European empire and Christian mission were working in tandem with one another and most often were mutually beneficial.

5. Another way to trace this is by exploring Christian defenses of slavery and segregation in America.

Genesis 9 and 10 describe how, after the flood, the lineages of Noah's three sons (Shem, Ham, and Japheth) repopulated the earth. These three hereditary lines were read as the three "races": Shem's children were the Mongoloid race, Ham's descendants were the Negroid race, and Japheth's descendants were the Caucasian race. Chapter 9 includes the narrative of Ham seeing Noah naked; Shem and Japheth covering their drunk, naked father; and Noah later waking to declare, "Cursed be Canaan [Ham's son]; lowest of slaves shall he be to his brothers" (9:25) and "Blessed by the LORD my God be Shem; and let Canaan be his slave. May God make space for Japheth, and let him live in the tents of Shem; and let Canaan be his slave" (9:26–27). Having imposed the modern construct of race on these verses to argue for white supremacy, white interpreters then also imposed the modern institution of the slave trade on these verses to argue for its normative status in both nature and history. Although the imposition of modern race categories on this narrative is an obvious stretching of scripture to defend racism, there is a sense in which no such acrobatics were required to defend slavery. Throughout both testaments, the Bible speaks of slavery in either positive or morally neutral terms:

- Ham's son, Canaan, is made the slave of his brothers, with God's blessing (Genesis 9).
- Abraham is described as being blessed by God with male and female slaves (Genesis 12, 24).
- Leaders of God's people, including Joshua, David, and Solomon, are often described as having been told by God to take slaves (Joshua 9; 2 Samuel 20; 1 Kings 9).
- In the book of Judges, the Israelites do not expel the Canaanites but make them their slaves (Judges 1:28).
- Slavery is explicitly assumed, not prohibited, in the Ten Commandments (Exodus 20; Deuteronomy 5).
- All law codes in Hebrew scripture assume the legitimacy of slavery.
- Israelites are explicitly instructed in the law to take non-Israelites as slaves and instructed that slaves may be kept as possessions that are handed down to their children (Leviticus 25).
- Throughout the law and the prophets, fair treatment of slaves is often taught, but slavery itself is never rejected.
- Jesus never explicitly questions slavery in the Gospels.
- The parables of Jesus often have slaves as characters, and the narratives do not lead to questions about slavery.
- The New Testament epistles teach slaves to remain in slavery and obey their masters (1 Corinthians 7; Colossians 3).
- Slave owners and slaves are told to be good slaves and good slave masters in order to not bring disrepute to God (1 Timothy 6).

6. Yet another way to trace the racism of Western Christianity has arisen recently through the influence of Afro-pessimism.

Afro-pessimism, a critical approach adopted by Black scholars across disciplines in the arts and humanities, argues that analyses of racism up to now have only been scratching the surface.[5] The problem is not only the construct of race, nor is the problem only the unjust and oppressive realities tied to the construct; the problem is that the ontologies of "whiteness" and "Blackness" are deeply woven into every fiber of the metaphysics of the modern West. Attempts to establish racial justice or racial reconciliation continue to be partial and insufficient because racism cannot be addressed by the reduction of suffering alone. Racism is metaphysical because it is ontological; it ascribes being to whiteness and non-being to Blackness. Recently some Christian theologians have argued that the emergence, beginning in early Christianity, of supersessionist understandings of the universality of Jesus and Christianity transcending the particularity and ethnicity of Judaism easily became wedded to the emergence of race in colonialism and modern metaphysics, including explicit formulations of modern narratives of human progress that culminate in the universality of whiteness overcoming the insufficiency and particularity of Blackness.[6]

7. It is also true that Christianity has been at the forefront of some antiracist movements.

Even if Afro-pessimism is right that such efforts continue to only scratch the surface of racism (albeit in truly significant ways), it is important to note that Christians drew upon their scripture and tradition in activism that helped end the Atlantic slave trade, the enslavement of Africans and their descendants in America, and American segregation. None of these instances can be accurately portrayed as secular humanist justice overcoming the racist injustice of Christianity. Evangelicals and Quakers were among the activists at the forefront of the abolition movements in both Britain and America, and Black Christians were among the activists at the forefront of the American Civil Rights movement. Although scripture had been used to defend racism, slavery, and segregation, it was also used to defeat it. Appeals were made to scriptural texts and themes including:

- The exodus narrative (throughout the Pentateuch), in which YHWH is revealed as God who frees the oppressed and enslaved
- New Testament depictions of Jesus as coming to set free those who are captive and oppressed (especially in Luke 4, where he reads from Isaiah in the synagogue and says, "The Spirit of the Lord is upon me, because he has anointed me to bring good news to the poor. He has sent me to proclaim release to the captives and recovery of sight to the blind, to let the oppressed go free, to proclaim the year of the Lord's favor")
- New Testament descriptions of the church as a unified body that overcomes the barriers dividing people from one another, including both ethnic enmity and slavery (especially in Gal. 3:27–28: "As many of you as were baptized into Christ have clothed yourselves with Christ. There

is no longer Jew or Greek, there is no longer slave or free, there is no longer male and female; for all of you are one in Christ Jesus"; and Eph. 2:14: "For he is our peace; in his flesh he has made both groups into one and has broken down the dividing wall, that is, the hostility between us")

8. Not only have Black and womanist Christian theologies critiqued the racism of "white" Christianity, they have also drawn upon the antiracist resources of Christian scripture and tradition.

Themes have included the Blackness of Jesus, liberation, solidarity, intersectionality, community, and moral agency.[7]

The first six assertions have been crucial for clearing the ground and setting the historical and theoretical contexts in which we might have a scholarly conversation about race in Christian texts and traditions. The final two assertions are crucial for understanding why, even in the light of the histories behind my third through sixth assertions, it is meaningful for a group of scholars to approach Christian texts and traditions in relation to in/equalities in both critical and constructive registers. The history of racism in Christianity is undeniable, and the employment of Christian texts in support of racist ideologies and actions has been vociferous. Yet the social, political, and theological movements of abolition, civil rights, Black theology, and womanism have not found their strength or their voice in the rejection of Christian texts and traditions but in the redeployment of the liberative and transformative heart of these texts and traditions in which every human person is equally a child of God.

Notes

1. The history of "race" and racism has been chronicled in many places and in many ways. See, for example, George M. Fredrickson, *Racism: A Short History* (Princeton, NJ: Princeton University Press, 2002); Francisco Bethencourt, *Racisms: From the Crusades to the Twentieth Century* (Princeton, NJ: Princeton University Press, 2015); and Theodore W. Allen, *The Invention of the White Race: Racial Oppression and Social Control*, 2 vols. (London: Verso, 2012).

2. For a particularly compelling account of racism in America, see Ibram X. Kendi, *Stamped from the Beginning: The Definitive History of Racist Ideas in America* (New York: Nation Books, 2016).

3. For theological accounts of Western Christianity and race, see Willie James Jennings, *The Christian Imagination: Theology and the Origins of Race* (New Haven, CT: Yale University Press, 2010); and J. Kameron Carter, *Race: A Theological Account* (Oxford: Oxford University Press, 2008).

4. An especially poignant counterexample is Bartolomé de las Casas, called by some a colonial-era precursor of liberation theology. See Bartolomé de las Casas, *A Short Account of the Destruction of the Indies* (London: Penguin, 1992).

5. For a founding text, see Frank D. Wilderson III, *Red, White, and Black: Cinema and the Structure of U.S. Antagonisms* (Durham, NC: Duke University Press, 2010).

6. See especially Carter, *Race: A Theological Account.*

7. For introductions to Black and womanist theologies, see James H. Cone and Gayraud S. Wilmore, eds., *Black Theology: A Documentary History*, 2 vols. (Maryknoll, NY: Orbis, 1993); and Stephanie Y. Mitchem, *Introducing Womanist Theology* (Maryknoll: Orbis, 2002).

Nationality and Ethnicity in West Africa

An Economic and Religious Perspective on Inequalities

FRANÇOIS PAZISNEWENDE KABORÉ, SJ

Recent research by the African Development Bank, the World Bank, and the International Monetary Fund confirm that Africa is one of the drivers of the world's economic growth. According to the 2018 edition of the African Development Bank's Economic Outlook on Africa, per capita income growth increased by more than 3.5 percent for eight years in a row for at least 67 percent of the fifty-four sovereign states of Africa. Unfortunately, during the same period job creation grew far less. For instance, between 2000 and 2008, jobs creation increased by 2.8 percent on average per year, which corresponds to around half of the income growth during the same period.[1] As a result, the absolute level of poverty increased as well as inequalities. The share of poor decreased from 56 percent in 1990 to 43 percent in 2012, but the absolute number of poor increased. Moreover, inequalities increased as the Gini coefficient, which measures the level of inequalities, rose from 0.52 percent in 1993 to 0.56 percent in 2008. This situation gave birth to the concept of *growth without jobs* to characterize economic growth in Africa.

In addition, the 2018 issue of the World Bank's Doing Business (https://www.doingbusiness.org/) suggests that five of the top ten fastest-growing economies are in Africa. Unfortunately, growth in African countries does not seem to benefit all citizens. As a matter of fact, despite the good news of economic growth, inequalities are rising in almost all African countries. Many sources of inequalities are often explored: capital intensive sectors that do not lead to job creation (such as the mining sector); knowledge or innovation sectors that benefit only a minority; the service sector, which is human capital intensive, and so on. The current research investigates the contribution of ethnicity and nationality to inequalities in an African setting. Do ethnicity and nationality affect inequalities? If so, in which direction is the impact? If so, what could be the mechanism of impact? To that end, this research provides, first, key working definitions of the main concepts. The second part discusses ethnic challenges of nation building in Africa, and the third part highlights the possible links between ethnicity, nationality, and inequalities in the context of West Africa.

Working Definitions

This section provides clarification of the key concepts of the topic discussed: inequalities, ethnicity, and nationality.

Inequalities from an Economics Perspective

Inequalities, per se, could be perceived just as differences, in a value-neutral way. To that extent, inequalities are the basis for price discrimination and consumer segmentation at the micro level and are a source of competitive advantages and trade at the macro level. Differences (and thus inequalities) in human capital, at an individual level, have led to theories of signaling, pricing mechanism, and so on, to elicit high-potential workers or consumers. At the macro level, differences in natural endowments and raw materials have led to theories of opportunity cost, specialization, and international trade.

Whether inequalities are considered from the perspectives of consumers or producers, from the micro or macro level, they easily could be perceived as drivers of economic growth. Along these lines, the research by Simon Kuznets suggests an inverted, U-shaped relationship between inequalities and economic growth. According to Kuznets's curve, inequalities would positively drive economic growth at the beginning. However, at some point they would rather negatively impact economic growth.[2]

In a nutshell, an economics perspective of inequalities will take them as given and then look at whether the sources of inequalities are unfair or unacceptable. Indeed, inequalities (understood as differences in capabilities, preferences, endowment) do not seem to be able to be suppressed and may not be suppressed entirely. If inequalities do exist, what is their magnitude, and to what extent can their magnitude be unacceptable? Last, but not least, what is the marginal impact of inequalities on individuals' or society's well-being?[3] Are these impacts positive or negative? This is where a religious and ethical perspective might add some value to the analysis, even if it might be questionable to think that an economics approach is value neutral.

Inequalities from a Religious Perspective

At the individual level, and more so from a religious and ethical perspective, inequalities refer to differences in treatment, in situations, or in options that people could face or experience. From a socioeconomic point of view, inequalities would then characterize the human-made unfair situation of a person or a group of people in which some have more opportunities than others. To that extent, this research focuses on unfair situations that a person or some people could experience based on their religious background. How could we grasp or measure these unfair situations?

At a national level, religion-based inequalities could be experienced as discriminatory laws for access to various national resources that should normally be considered as public goods. For instance, are there members from a religious group who are intentionally less represented in public service? Is there discrimination for access to public service? How many religious holidays are recognized for each major religious group? Are there subtle or compulsory religious requirements for access to some public offices?[4]

Ways to measure religion-based inequalities could also include representation in top-level government, in public government service in general, in the private dynamic sector (the business leaders), in civil society movements, and in freedom-of-speech policies in particular. In other words, these inequalities could also be expressed in terms of political, economic, and social rights violations based on religious backgrounds. Sociopolitical instability could also express the fragility of the social and national fabric due to the lack of cohesion between religions or between ethnic groups within a nation. In that sense, nationality and ethnicity generate inequalities whose mechanism of impact would be the unfair public treatment and consideration based on religious background. Amartya Sen's capability approach is an important tool for assessing inequalities. It also relates to the lack of empowerment to be able to benefit from opportunities because of inequalities in ethnicity, nationality, or religion.[5] Except for isolated cases that could draw attention to existing phenomena, data on such inequalities are extremely difficult to find or to gather. As a result, this reflection is based on general trends observed nationwide in a dozen countries in West Africa.

Nationality versus Ethnicity

On the one hand, ethnicity or an ethnic group is often understood as a social and cultural group whose members share a common and distinctive culture, religion, language, tradition, or the like. On the other hand, nationality or a nation defines the status of belonging to a particular nation. Nationality is often equated with citizenship, although this is not in practice the case in a few countries in the world, such as the United States and the United Kingdom. A national or someone who holds the passport of a country differs from a citizen, who is often considered to enjoy all rights within a particular country or nation. In a particular country—where country means a geographic area of land that has its own government, army, and so on—many nations might coexist; a single nation could also exist across many other countries. For instance, in West Africa, many nations coexist in Burkina Faso: the Mosse, the Fulani, and the Bissa among them; conversely, the people of the Akan nation are spread across several West African countries—namely, Ghana and Côte d'Ivoire.

Although the concept of *race* is often considered as not politically correct, race also plays an important role within countries. Race gathers together people with particular, similar physical characteristics or who are considered as belonging to the same type.

Note that *ethnicity* and *nationality* could be expressed within the same sociological groups in various shades on a spectrum. In this regard, ethnicity and nationality could be perceived as social constructs. However, whether they are social constructs or not, this research takes them as economic sociopolitical realities that matter. These working definitions allow us to realize that, in the context of Africa, it is often the case that many ethnic groups live together within the boundaries of a single nation. In addition, many ethnic groups live across boundaries. Such a situation does not favor nation-building.

Challenges of Nation-Building in Africa

The previous working definitions might give the impression that all these realities (ethnicity, nationality, race, inequalities, etc.) are static. They are rather dynamic realities insofar as they pertain to human beings who are social beings who are alive. A nation gathers together a large group of people with a sense of shared identity, religion, and culture. It could be said that, ideally, a nation is an ethnic group on a large scale. What does the map of Africa look like in that regard in precolonial times and currently?

Precolonial Africa: A Multitude of Micronations

In precolonial Africa, political and social life was happening essentially at the level of ethnic groups or small nations, with the exception of a few larger political entities that developed here and there: kingdoms in current Nigeria, the Zulu empire in South Africa, the Kingdom of Kongo, the Mosse Empire in current Burkina Faso, Mali, and Ghana Empire.[6] Except for these political organizations that developed to the point of reaching the status of nations, most social groups in Africa consisted in small ethnic groups, which made colonization easier in most parts of the continent. Ethnolinguistic maps reflect the fragmentation of Africa on the eve of colonization in the nineteenth century. We can recognize many linguistic areas such as the Bantu, the Voltaic, the Sudanese, and the Nilotic groups.[7]

After colonization, Africa was divided into five zones of occupation by the Western countries. Table 1, however, shows that most nations or ethnic groups in West Africa have a medium size or minority within the frontiers of their respective states. To that extent, Burkina Faso and Senegal are exceptions as the Mosse

Table 1: Mapping of Major African Ethnic Groups in West Africa

Country	Akan	Ibo	Fulfulde	Mosse	Tuareg	Yoruba	Wolof
Benin		x				x	
Burkina Faso			x	xxx	x		
Côte d'Ivoire	x		x				
Ghana	xxx		x				
Mali			x		xx		
Niger			x		x		
Nigeria		xx				xx	
Senegal			x				xxx

Notes: x = minority, xx = medium size, xxx = dominant ethnic group

in Burkina Faso and the Wolof in Senegal represent dominant majority ethnic groups.

The Berlin Conference 1884–85 and the Balkanization of Africa

It is not easy to understand the current sociopolitical map of Africa unless one refers to the Berlin Conference that took place November 15, 1884–February 26, 1885. When it became clear to many European powers that Africa was the frontier of their opportunities, this led to the so-called scramble for Africa. Otto von Bismarck, the chancellor of Germany, convened a meeting of the major political and economic powers from fourteen countries for the purpose of signing the Berlin Act, which provided principles to settle any dispute over colonial territories. In particular, it promoted the "principle of effective occupation," according to which any territory that is effectively occupied by a Western force belongs, not only de facto but also de jure, to that Western country. The continent of Africa was thus parceled out among the major colonial powers at the time: Belgium, Germany, Spain, France, Britain, Italy, and Portugal. Modern-day boundaries are largely a legacy of the colonial era.[8]

How did the "scramble" on Africa impact the current state of affairs in Africa? Obviously, the official map of Africa, which shows the borders of fifty-four independent states, does not respect the boundaries of ethnic groups. Indeed, given that boundaries were drawn not to benefit African populations but rather the colonizers, nations were divided along the lines of Western influence zones. For instance, the Dioula people in West Africa are scattered in various countries such as Mali, Côte d'Ivoire, and Burkina Faso.

Only a few nations are located in a single independent country: the Mosse people, who developed an empire starting in the eleventh century, are located in

Burkina Faso; the Zulus are in South Africa; the Wolof people, in Senegal; and so on.

The original Mosse Empire was actually a federation of states. Still, in 1932 the Mosse Empire was dismantled and partitioned into three parts—which were then assigned to the republics of Mali, Niger, and Côte d'Ivoire. In addition to the economic arguments, political disputes might have—more than anything else— played a significant role. The Mosse people would not submit to the French colonial administrations unless their emperor agreed. So the best way to weaken the power of the Mosse emperor was to divide, that is, to dismantle the empire into three parts.

When modern-day African countries gather together many nations or ethnical groups, if there is no mechanism to ensure the proper, optimal, and fair allocation of national resources across ethnical groups, then issues of inequality might indeed rise.

Religious Map of Africa

Before the advent of foreign religion, most nations in Africa had their traditional religions, which still constitute the religious and cultural background of most countries. Although Christianity came to North Africa as early as the second century, it was mostly in the fourteenth century—and primarily through the efforts of the Portuguese—that Christianity was brought to sub-Saharan Africa. However, it was mostly during Western colonization that Christianity spread over the different parts of Africa and penetrated the continent beyond its coastal areas.

As for Islam, it also started with North Africa, then spread to Eastern and Western Africa. Two different types of Islam developed in Africa: the first came through political conquest, while the second came through trade. The first developed into political Islam with some claims to organize sociopolitical life, using violence if needed. The second type of Islam was very peaceful, as it mostly spread through traders in West Africa.

Senegal and Burkina Faso are well known in West Africa for their religious tolerance. Burkina Faso is an example of a country where Islam spread through trade. The Muslim traders, initially Arab traders, would come from northern Africa, exchange goods from the desert for good from the savanna, the forest, and the sea. Ouagadougou, the capital city of the empire, would then serve as a meeting point or a market to purchase goods from the desert, from the savanna, and from the forest. To ensure their own security and the security of their goods, the traders requested that the Moogo Naaba (the emperor of Mosse) give them some land not far from his palace. In return, the Muslim traders would ensure that there would be an imam at the court of Moogo Naaba to pray for the emperor's good governance and for the prosperity of his empire. Until today, there is still an imam at the court of the Moogo Naaba.

Ethnicity, Nationality, and Inequalities

Politics, Electoral Democracies, and Ethnic Fragmentation

While colonization did not intend to favor a particular religion, pragmatically colonial administrations collaborated with religious people, especially with Christians. In Burkina Faso, for instance, the Dioula people and many other small ethnical groups were mostly Muslim. However, the colonial administration—which favored Christianity over Islam—was in charge of the country's educational system. It invested more in the education of people from the Mosse nation than from the other small ethnic groups because they were not Muslim but rather believers of the traditional religion and Christians.

In Burkina Faso, people from the traditional religion, who are the holders of traditional political power, initially stood away from modern education. As for Muslims, competition arose between those educated in the traditional madrassas and those educated through the modern system. The result was that, by the time of independence (1960s), Christians and people from lower social classes were better educated than any other nationals.

Since the fall of the Berlin Wall in 1989, the wind of democracy has been blowing upon sub-Saharan Africa. After the period of dictatorship in most countries (from 1960 to 1980), democracy was expected to favor more peaceful and dedicated civil, political, and economic life. Unfortunately, given the generally low level of education, political competition has translated into ethnic and religious competition. When political leaders have not had good economic and social development blueprints, it has been easy to appeal to their ethnic and religious base. This has led to more fragmentation of the social and political fabric in West Africa.

Economic, Social, and Religious Nexus

Table 2 captures the complex relationship between inequality, nationality, and ethnicity. The number of transitions in power or brutal change of power expresses the instability with the nation. Countries that have a higher number of power transitions tend to be countries that are ethnically fragmented, or at least they do not have a dominant ethnic group. If we consider the declared religions of the presidents, it could show which religion would easily be on the state media and eventually take advantage of public exposure. The distribution of religions among the citizens suggests that having various religions equally practiced helps foster stability. Out of the three countries where the three religions are equally important, only Côte d'Ivoire has experienced major social and political postelection unrest. That crisis, however, had clearly more ethnic than religious underpinnings.

Table 2: Level of social fragmentation and economic inequalities across countries

Country	Number of changes in power (1960–2018)	Gini index of inequalities[a]	Religious distribution	Official religion[b]
Benin	19	38.6		Christianity
Burkina Faso	9	39.8	Islam, Christian, Traditional	Christianity
Côte d'Ivoire (2016)	6	41.5		Christianity
Ghana	15	42.8	Christian, Islam, Traditional	Christianity
Mali (2013)	8	33.0	Islam	Islam
Niger (2011)	9	45.5	Islam	Islam
Nigeria (2015)	15	48.8	Islam, Christian	Islam
Senegal (2012)	5	40.3	Islam	Islam

Source: Data on the income Gini coefficient are taken from the "Human Development Reports" of the United Nations Development Programme, http://hdr.undp.org/en/content/income-gini -coefficient, accessed February 1, 2019.

[a]Developed by Italian statistician Corrado Gini in 1912, the Gini index/coefficient measures and ranks income distribution within a population. The higher a population's Gini index, the greater its inequality of income distribution.

[b]Often the religion has been made official by declaration of the president.

Conclusions: Toward a Shared Ethics of Equality

This research addresses the issues of inequality as it pertains to ethnicity and nationality. Based on the working definitions of the main concepts, this research shows that nation building is a challenge because most independent African countries are composed of many ethnic groups, and citizens identify with their ethnic group rather than with their modern political nation or country. Moreover, the colonial experience of African countries adds another factor: new religions (Christianity and Islam) add to the fragmentation of African countries. Given that Christianity and Islam and traditional religion share the values of fairness and justice and equality, these religions could be part of the solution. The first step in nation-building will consist of acknowledging that religions made choices that led to more inequalities (slavery, colonization, and so on). The second step will consist of a more proactive attitude to promote equality as well as fairness, despite the challenges of countries fragmented along social, economic, political, and religious lines. Given the regional insecurity in West Africa, further research would complement the current literature by focusing on ethnic and national fragmentation and violent extremism.

Notes

I wish to acknowledge the helpful comments of the participants of the 2018 Building Bridges Seminar, organized by Georgetown University (USA), in Sarajevo (Bosnia Herzegovina, July 18–22).

1. In Côte d'Ivoire, for instance, the 2018 recruitment test for civil servants of the judiciary system took place from June 25 to June 29, 2018. The government planned to fill 25 seats, and there were 1,069 candidates.

2. Simon Kuznets, "Economic Growth and Income Inequality," *American Economic Review* 45, no. 1 (1955): 1–28.

3. John Rawls, in a *Theory of Justice* (Cambridge, MA: Harvard University Press, 1971), suggests a principle of difference that acknowledges economic differences (or inequalities) provided they benefit the least of the society.

4. Media reported that in Chad a woman who refused to use the word "Allah" in a public swearing ceremony was denied public office. The woman had requested in vain to use the word "Dieu," given that the swearing formula was written in French.

5. Amartya Sen, *Development as Freedom* (New York: Alfred A. Knopf, 1999).

6. In the literature the Mosse Empire is often referred to as the Mossi Empire or Mossi Kingdoms. The correct form is either "Moogo Empire" or "Mosse Empire." Mosse is pronounced "Moosse."

7. For an online example of such an ethnolinguistic map of Africa, see http://renau dossavi.mondoblog.org/files/2015/05/ethnies-5.jpg.

8. For a map illustrating areas of the African continent controlled by European colonial powers in 1913, along with current national boundaries, see https://en.wikipedia.org /wiki/Colonisation_of_Africa#/media/File:Colonial_Africa_1913_map.svg.

Islam and the Challenge of Sociopolitical Equality

The Contribution of Religious Creed

SHERMAN A. JACKSON

Especially where religious creed is concerned, equality—certainly the popular version of "formal equality"—is a particularly complicated challenge for Islam. To begin with, as with any monotheistic religion founded on a claim to absolute truth, Islam (and I would imagine Judaism and Christianity as well) can hardly dispense with categories of exclusion that mark the boundary between it and its antitheses. To the extent that these categories (i.e., "non-Muslim," "Unbeliever") do any work at all, they almost have to imply a relationship of inequality. Second, "equality," as a now nonnegotiable sociopolitical construct, is not only chronologically modern but the product of a very particular mode of modernity—namely, Enlightenment liberalism. It was devised in part to domesticate religion, and it was introduced to the Muslim world as part of a colonial package. Not only would this naturally breed resistance but the fact that it postdated the crystallization of Islam's authoritative religious tradition meant that it did not contribute to the latter's substantive constitution. As such, unlike Greek thought or other early "foreign elements," Muslims must now *vindicate* and cannot simply *assume* the normativeness of formal sociopolitical equality. Finally, there are a number of practical ambiguities connected to sociopolitical equality that call for additional consideration.

Other authors in this volume have treated us to an impressive array of Qur'anic verses and Prophetic statements that leave no doubt about Islam's recognition of the inherent sanctity and equality of all individual human souls. As I shall show, however, other scriptural indicants, alongside Muslim Tradition itself, introduce complications. One way of reconciling these two "faces of Islam" might be to note that it is one thing to understand these materials in a presumed state of "nature" but quite another to consider them in an actual state of society. For, in a state of society, we immediately confront issues of power, sovereignty, political authority, and the physical and ideological integrity of the religious community as a whole. This is in addition to basic matters of collective pride and the acquisition of enough civilizational prestige to insulate one's "way of life" from the cultural, intellectual, and related predations of "others." Such considerations move us decidedly in a direction away from sociopolitical equality, even assuming our continued recognition of each other's equal humanity. We may ignore this unlovely fact out of convenience or perhaps scholarly politeness, or the artificial environment of the classroom may obscure its presence. But this will not likely alter what is really at stake in the politics of groups and nations. Indeed, few could ignore the resonances of all of this in the present debates over immigration, the Black Lives Matter movement, or the meaning of such slogans as "Make America Great Again." In short, pluralism is a fact that simply does not manage itself. And the way to reconcile it with equality is neither always simple nor self-evident.

For their part, modern Western states tend to reflect a "homogenizing" approach to pluralism, where all citizens are theoretically equidistant from a single national identity to which they are assumed to belong naturally or into which they are expected to assimilate. This, however, was not the case in premodern Islam, still the interpretive point of departure for many, if not most, Muslims today. Non-Muslims were not expected (or even fully allowed) to assimilate fully into the Muslim state or the dominant culture that shadowed it. Rather, non-Muslims were simply called upon to pay obeisance—and taxes!—in exchange for the right to physical security in maintaining their own separate religious identity and basic institutions. The notion of sociopolitical equality simply remained part of the "un-thought." As Muslims generally saw it, their "survival," let alone their transgenerational "flourishing," was barely distinguishable from a commitment to "Muslim supremacy." As one medieval jurist-theologian summarized the matter, speaking of the relationship between Muslims and non-Muslims, "We must remain mindful that, were 'they' to gain the upper hand over 'us,' they would annihilate us, seize our money and waste our blood."[1]

This view of the world underwrote a battery of legal restrictions on non-Muslims that were clearly designed to domesticate them, such that they could never challenge, let alone threaten, the Muslim state or society. In various times and places, these included, for example, restrictions on building churches, preaching in public, ringing church bells, constructing homes taller than those of Muslims, dressing in certain ways, and using certain modes of transportation (e.g., the quality of horse or mule one could ride).[2] While it would be nice to be able to attribute all such discriminatory restrictions to historical contingency, there were also scriptural injunctions that underwrote unequal rights and obligations for non-Muslims, again, based solely on their religious identity or creed. For example, the Qur'an bars non-Muslims from entering Mecca or from marrying Muslim women, and it requires non-Muslims to pay a special tax known as the *jizya*. Meanwhile, the Prophet Muhammad reportedly restricted execution as a punishment for murder as a crime of passion to Muslims or non-Muslims who kill Muslims, with Muslims who kill non-Muslims being exempt.[3] In sum, based both on Muslim scripture and Muslim Tradition, sociopolitical inequality was widely accepted if not extolled as a hallmark of a normatively functioning Muslim state and society.

And yet these and related restrictions must be seen as exceptions to an expansive regime of rights and protections that were grounded in a fundamental recognition of the right of non-Muslims to exist as non-Muslims in Muslim society. These even included authorization to engage in activities from which Muslims themselves were legally barred (for example, charging interest, drinking wine, and so on). In fact, non-Muslims were even exempted from punitive sanctions that applied absolutely to Muslims—adultery, for example, being potentially a capital offense for Muslims but not, generally speaking, for non-Muslims unless their community designated it as such.[4] My point here is that while religion-based sociopolitical inequality was normalized in premodern Muslim society, this was a two-way street that both privileged and penalized Muslims and non-Muslims alike. All of this, I think, must be factored into any attempt to bring Islam into conversation with the modern concept of formal sociopolitical equality.

Before proceeding, however, two additional insights might prove useful. First, "religious freedom" or the "rights" of non-Muslims in Islam were not proportional to the degree of substantive truth represented by their religious beliefs. Even as infidels with patently wrong or offensive beliefs, non-Muslims remained wholly within the protective sanctum of Islamic law, which itself recognized their religion, mutatis mutandis, as the definer of their private rights, on the one hand, and as endowing with them fundamental public rights, on the other. For example, Zoroastrians were allowed to marry their mothers or daughters because their religion allowed this, despite the fact that Muslim jurists openly condemned this behavior as obscene. And even Muslims who murdered non-Muslims could be punished, just not by execution, except according to the majoritarian Ḥanafīs, who saw no difference between Muslims and non-Muslims in this regard.[5] In short, placing non-Muslims outside of Islam did not place them outside of Islam's regime of "fundamental rights" nor did it restrict their right to freedom of conscience or belief.

Second, regarding the practical implications of formal sociopolitical equality, I am reminded of a story related by Stephen Carter, author of *God's Name in Vain*.[6] A Christian minister remarked to a prison warden that the Muslim inmates had no cause to complain because they enjoyed all the rights that Christian inmates had. Carter responded, "No doubt they do. But, were I a Muslim, I would want the rights I need to practice Islam, regardless of how these compared to the rights of Christians." On the one hand, this takes us part of the way back to David Hollenbach's point about how an unqualified, theoretical sociopolitical equality might be qualified in actual application.[7] On the other hand, it raises profoundly important questions about the very definition or the kind of sociopolitical equality we actually want.

While it should be clear, having said all of this, that equality is not a panacean charm that can be invoked unproblematically, religion-based inequality is a challenge that Muslims simply must confront today, especially given the ubiquitous adoption of the modern state system and its attendant concept of citizenship. As I see it, there are two "dimensions" to this challenge. The first relates to whether Muslims have the interpretive tools to confront the disharmony between the norms and precedents reflected in Muslim scripture and Tradition, on the one hand, and the norms and aspirations of the modern world, on the other. The second relates to how far Muslims can go in this regard without Western modernity ultimately domesticating Islam and the exchange between Islam and modernity ending up as a one-way street.

Taking the latter of these challenges first, it is extremely important to recognize that modern Muslim reactions to calls to banish sociopolitical inequality based on religion are often informed by a reaction not to sociopolitical equality itself but to the liberalism on which this call is perceived to be predicated. After all, liberalism is a modern Western construct. And many Muslims will resist assenting to the concept of formal sociopolitical equality as a means of resisting the authority of Western thought as a whole, which they see as a tool and proxy for Western domination. This is why it is important, I think, to remain open to non-Western understandings and instantiations of sociopolitical equality. For even if these diverge at points from Western understandings, they provide a platform for sustained, meaningful, and hopefully productive communication and exchange. For example, the Muslim commitment to sociopolitical equality may not include the abandonment of Islam's categories of exclusion, that is, "kāfir" or "unbeliever." From a Western perspective, this may look like a complete contradiction of equality since the exclusion of persons from Christianity often implied their exclusion from the body politic, as we learn from Locke and others. But listen here to the eighteenth-century master jurist Aḥmad al-Dardīr advise Muslims on the treatment of their non-Muslim parents: "And he should physically guide the blind parent, even if the latter is a kāfir, to church, and he should deliver him or her to his or her place of worship and provide him or her with money to spend during their religious holidays."[8] To be sure, this still falls short of the formal equality we tend to recognize as the norm today. But there is clearly much to invest in here, including the ingratiation of Muslims with modern discourses on equality, on their own terms. In other words, what is reflected here is an "equality of respect" as opposed to a blind, formal equality. And especially given the substantive differences between Islam and Christianity (and other religions), the value of an equality of respect should not be simply dismissed out of hand. After all, all over the world, including in America, minorities can often only smile at the majority's obliviousness to the domination that lurks beneath the minority's "right" to be equal to the majority. Meanwhile, the liberal disdain for categories of exclusion, which are seen as unavoidably divisive, risks both forfeiting the possibilities inherent in this concept and alienating Muslims from discussions on equality by barring critical aspects of their own religious lexicon and worldview.[9]

Regarding the question of the tools for reconciling problematic features of Muslim scripture and Tradition with modern sociopolitical equality, Muslim jurists have always recognized that those aspects of Islamic law and doctrine that were historically contingent remain valid only as long as the historical circumstances that engendered them prevail. Thus, when asked about the legitimacy of adjustments to the law based on sociohistorical change, the celebrated Shihāb al-Dīn al-Qarāfī (d. 1285) responded as follows: "Holding onto rulings that were based on custom and prevailing circumstances even after these have changed is a violation of unanimous consensus and an open display of ignorance of the religion."[10] Recent times have seen this principle indulged more explicitly and boldly. For example, as part of their renunciation of political violence beginning in 1997, the leader of Egypt's notorious al-Gamāʻah al-Islāmīyah, who assassinated Anwar Sadat in 1981, stated openly that Islamic history is not a binding source of law or doctrine.[11] This is hugely important, given that Muslim history, especially among radical movements, is not only inspirational but often accorded the status of religious texts in determining the normative relationship between Muslims and non-Muslims. Increasingly, however, even illiberal Muslims are openly acknowledging that they no longer live in the world of their ancestors and that the fears, attitudes, and anticipations that animated the latter have dramatically if not completely lost relevance and propriety. So too have the highly discriminatory practices they spawned. Especially because the bulk of these practices were discretionary and not based on any explicit scriptural indicants, there are almost no impediments to abandoning these rules in favor of more egalitarian arrangements.

But there is another dimension to all of this that further advances the cause of sociopolitical equality, especially regarding non-Muslim participation in public life. This is tied to the recognition that so much of what modern states (and even premodern states), including Muslim states, do is not based directly on scripture; it is essentially "extra-scriptural," or "secular," if you will, being matters of prudence rather than morality. As there are no scriptural indicants telling us what an efficient national health care plan, immigration policy, speed limit, or gun-control policy would actually look like, these things are ultimately adjudicated according to a secular logic of which Muslims and non-Muslims may partake on an equal footing, their religious affiliation being essentially irrelevant. As such, there may be no basis for discrimination between Muslims and non-Muslims regarding vast areas of the public domain.[12] This is clearly the upshot of what the influential contemporary jurist Shaykh Yūsuf al-Qaraḍāwī has in mind when he writes of non-Muslims: "As for . . . matters concerning civil, commercial, administrative and other forms of legislation, their status here is as that regarding any other legislation that may be appropriated from the East or the West, based on the consent of the majority."[13] The "majority" in this context, in other words, includes non-Muslims as simply part of the voting citizenry. Incidentally, Shaykh Yūsuf also saw a historically contingent element in the Qur'anic requirement that non-Muslims pay the *jizya* tax. Thus, he suggests that, since it was imposed in exchange for exemption from military service, it can now be dropped in exchange for military service.[14]

To conclude, Islam's relationship with the modern, Western notion of socio-political equality is fraught with ambiguity. But there is also clear promise here. And this is further reinforced in Western countries like America by an undercurrent of shared egalitarian sentiments born of the fact that at least one-quarter of America's Muslims are native-born converts whose cultural sensibilities, "existential" backdrop, and interpretive point of departure is not the embattled predicament of Islam in the so-called Muslim world but the ongoing, transgenerational negotiations of a liberal democracy. Let us hope that we will be able to capitalize on the possibilities of enhanced dialogue between Islam and Christianity on this critical topic. And let us remember that what we need in this regard is not a sophomoric competition over who can put forth the most utopian, highfalutin vision of equality but who can make and inspire a clear-eyed, good-faith commitment to what is possible, given the complex realities of the world and our mutual attachment to our respective religious traditions. Let us be among those men and women who have neither lost sight of their ultimate debt to God nor despaired of God's infinite grace.

Notes

1. This statement is from Ibn Daqīq al-ʿĪd (d. 1302). Translation mine.

2. For more on this, see Anver M. Emon, *Religious Pluralism and Islamic Law: Dhimmīs and Others in the Empire of Law* (Oxford: Oxford University Press, 2014), 119–36. One should note that Emon includes a number of overinclusive summaries of Islamic law based on his tendency to over-rely on Shāfiʿī sources.

3. See, e.g., Muḥammad b. Ismāʿīl al-Bukhārī, *Ṣaḥīḥ al-Bukhārī*.

4. This was the going opinion in the Ḥanafī and Mālikī schools, numerically the first and second largest, respectively, over most of premodern history.

5. Indeed, the Ḥanafīs held that a Muslim *could* be executed for the private murder of a non-Muslim. I use "private murder" here to distinguish it from murder that resulted from an act of publicly directed violence (e.g., Columbine High School, where the public as opposed to an individual is the target). In this case—that is, where a Muslim kills a non-Muslim in an act of publicly directed violence—all of the legal schools agree that the Muslim is to be executed. For more on this detail, see Sherman A. Jackson, "Domestic Terrorism in the Islamic Legal Tradition," *Muslim World* 91, nos. 3–4 (September 2001): 293–310.

6. Stephen L. Carter, *God's Name in Vain: The Wrongs and Rights of Religion in Politics* (New York: Basic Books, 2000).

7. See David Hollenbach, "The Challenges of a World of Inequalities for Christians Today," in this volume.

8. Aḥmad b. Muḥammad b. Aḥmad al-Dardīr, al-Sharḥ al-ṣaghīr, on the margins of Aḥmad al-Ṣāwī, Bulghat al-sālik li aqrab al-masālik ilā madhhab al-imām mālik, 2 vols. (Cairo: Muṣṭafā al-Bābī al-Ḥalabī wa Awlāduh, 1372/1952) 2:523.

9. I recognize that nomenclature here is a problem. Thus, Rashīd Riḍā, for example, once issued a *fatwā* in which he stated that it was forbidden or *ḥarām* to call Coptic Christians "*kāfirs*," not because they were not *kāfirs* according to Islam but because modernity had disfigured the meaning of the word to the point that it implied "atheist" or "antireligious." Still, if the only way we can have equality is to banish categories of exclusion, how does religion, or shall we say Islam, survive the hegemonic impositions of egalitarian discourse?

10. See Ahmad ibn Idris al-Qarāfī, *Al-Ihkam fi Tamyiz al-Fatawa 'an al-Ahkam wa Tasarrufat al-Qadi wa al-Imam* 231, edited by Abd al-Fattah Abu Ghuddah (Aleppo, Syria: Matba'ah Islamiyyah, 1967), 231.

11. See al-Gama'ah al-Islamiyah, *Initiative to Stop the Violence: Sadat's Assassins and the Renunciation of Political Violence*, trans. Sherman Jackson (New Haven, CT: Yale University Press, 2015).

12. For more on this point, see Sherman A. Jackson, "The Islamic Secular," *American Journal of the Association of Muslim Social Scientists*, no. 34 (2016): 1–26.

13. Yūsuf al-Qaraḍāwī, *al-Aqalliyāt al-dīnīyah wa al-hall al-islāmī*, 2nd ed. (Cairo: Maktabat Wahbah, 1999), 15–16. Translation mine.

14. Qaraḍāwī, 31. For many Muslims, of course, this entails a logic that comes perilously close to the slippery slope.

Caste and Social Class in the Christian and Islamic Communities of South Asia

SUNIL CALEB

Both *caste* and *social class* are expressions of inequality in human relationships. Although both Christianity and Islam have, theoretically, strongly stressed the equality of all human beings, the reality is that caste and social class have been—and continue to be—practiced by the adherents of both traditions. However, it must be noted that among Christians and Muslims alike, those who practice caste and social class distinctions are condemned by those who hold equality of human beings to be central to their respective faiths.

Behind caste and class is the concept of power, with those who belong to the higher caste or higher social class having the power to force other people into a particular profession or economic status in order that the upper caste or class may benefit. This concept also involves higher groups having the power to deny some benefits to people belonging to a so-called lower caste or class so that they may not challenge the hegemony of the upper caste or upper class. Those in the upper levels of caste or social class gain from this forced inequality because they are able to get other people to do work that they find unpleasant—for example, making the cleaning of dry toilets or disposing of dead animals the work of the Dalits (a name that the "Untouchable" castes in India have chosen for themselves)—or tasks they consider demeaning because of their notion that physical labor is somehow less dignified than intellectual work. Those of the upper castes and social classes seek material comfort for themselves without having to earn money to pay for it; they seek to keep wages low so that they do not have to deplete their savings and income in order to fund their lifestyle. They achieve these goals through the caste system.

Thus, the basic inequality exemplified by caste and social class is that of unequal power to obtain capabilities (as the Noble Prize–winning Bengali Indian economist Amartya Sen, would say). Capabilities are sets of abilities to obtain whatever we would choose for ourselves or for those who depend upon us ("functionings," as Sen puts it). Those who are lower in the caste and social class scale are unable to

access all the "functionings" that they would like for themselves and their dependents because the social system of caste and social class prevents them from doing
so. They are, for all practical purposes, powerless to change their situation. Change
can happen only when there is a concerted organization and struggle.[1] As Dr.
Bhimrao Ambedkar, the Indian Dalit leader, used to urge, Dalits must "educate,
agitate, and organise."[2]

Social Class

From a Marxian perspective, *class* is defined by the ownership of property. In
Marx's assessments of capitalistic industry, those who own the means of production are called the bourgeoisie, and those who have only their labor to sell are the
proletariat. Owing to the fact that the interests of these classes differ, Marxian
analysis sees the potential for conflict that can be resolved only when the means
of production are owned by everyone—that is, when the means of production are
nationalized. In the agrarian sense, the differences between the classes are
between those who are landlords and those who are landless—and, to some
extent, between those who hire laborers to cultivate their land and those who hire
themselves out to work on other peoples' land.[3] Max Weber saw social class as
having more to do with "status"—where status can originate from birth, education (schooling), area of residence, or other factors. Of course, social class most
often does coincide with economic class. Social class also functions on the basis
of the concept of honor, where the honor of a social class is of great significance.
It is guarded zealously by the leaders of that class, who punish severely any perceived slight—such as disrespect toward that class's elders or the marriage of an
upper-class woman to a man of a so-called lower class.[4]

Caste

Caste, according to Weber, labels situations where status distinctions are established not merely by conventions and laws but also by rituals.[5] Caste is primarily
a South Asian phenomenon and, hence, is found mostly in the Indian subcontinent.[6] Its four *varnas* (orders) are the Brahmins (members of the priestly
order), the Kshatriyas (rulers, administrators, warriors), the Vaishya (artisans,
merchants, tradespersons, farmers), and Shudras (laborers). There are also large
numbers of people who are *avarna* (literally, without caste; lacking the status of
belonging to one of the four traditional societal orders). Members of this category
are often called Dalit ("broken")—a label that has come to be preferred over
"Untouchable." What was once descriptive became prescriptive. This hierarchical system is extremely rigid and hard to break because it has been legitimized in
India by traditional interpretations of certain Hindu scriptures, notably the Rig
Veda and Manusmriti.

The notion of caste has a purity and pollution aspect to it that is missing in the concept of class. Those of the so-called upper castes consider themselves to be purer in some way than the lower castes and go to the extent of believing that Dalits (the so-called Untouchables) can actually pollute them by their touch—or, in some cases, even by the sight of them. Sociologically, of course, castes are endogamous marriage circles. Convention and rules forbid intercaste marriages—and, sometimes, interdining.

Social Class and Caste within Christianity

Perhaps I am right in saying that class distinctions have always been present within Christianity. One has only to read 1 Corinthians 11 to see that there were wealthier Christians who had trouble seeing themselves as part of the same class situation (Paul calls it "the Body of Christ") as those Christians who were slaves. They behaved in a manner that looked down on those who were poorer than themselves, even though it had not been long ago that they had accepted the Christian faith with its deep egalitarianism. Once Christianity became a state religion after the conversion of the emperor Constantine around 311–313 CE, class differences between Christians asserted themselves in a very strong manner. The church hierarchy came to be monopolized by members of the upper classes or the aristocracy. Within churches in Europe, it was common for the front pews in churches to be reserved for the upper classes—with the poor expected to sit at the back or in the galleries upstairs. Class was thus accepted within the church as something that was almost part of God's plan.

Two examples of this are the following. The first comes from the era of the Protestant Reformation in the sixteenth century, during which there was in Germany an uprising by oppressed peasants who, encouraged by the initial writings of the reformer Martin Luther, asserted that the Christian was the slave of no one but God. However, Luther soon came out against the peasant uprising with his treatise "Against the Robbing and Murdering Hordes of Peasants," in which he urged the princes to retaliate ruthlessly against the violent acts of the peasants, suggesting that they be "sliced, choked, stabbed, secretly and publicly, by those who can, like one must kill a rabid dog."[7]

In my second example, a Christian assertion that the class system has been divinely ordained is very clearly made by the popular hymn "All Things Bright and Beautiful." Written in 1848, one of its original stanzas (now almost always omitted from hymnals) reads,

The rich man in his castle,
The poor man at his gate,
God made them high and lowly,
And ordered their estate.

Actually, the class system in Europe influenced the Christian missionaries who came to India and encountered the caste system. Although they could perhaps see that the caste system was extremely oppressive toward the poorest, most did not take a strong stance against it. There were notable exceptions, of course. However, most seemed to believe it to be very similar to the class system back home and, thus, unobjectionable. Roberto de Nobili—the early seventeenth-century Jesuit Roman Catholic missionary priest in Madurai, India—consciously stressed his aristocratic origins in Italy and was thus able to live among the Brahmins as one who belonged to the Kshatriya (ruling and warrior caste, the second level in the caste hierarchy).

Because Christian missionaries in India did not take a firm enough stance against the practice of caste by their converts, caste practices have always infected the Christian population in the Indian mainland, especially in areas where significant numbers of members of various different castes converted to Christianity.[8] For example, in Kerala, India, which was the first area of India to receive the Christian message, there arose a community now known as Syrian Christians (mostly Orthodox and Roman Catholic) who are caste-practicing Christians.[9] Later, when Catholic and Protestant missionaries converted Dalits and members of other lower castes, they found that it was almost impossible to incorporate them into previously existing upper-caste congregations. Separate and parallel administrations had to be set up by the Vatican—and also within the Church of South India—to deal with this situation. In parts of the state of Tamil Nadu, the caste system is so entrenched that many of its church congregations are organized on caste lines and will not accept a priest/presbyter who comes from a different caste. Since large numbers of Dalits have converted to Christianity, the potential for caste conflict within Indian Christianity is always present.

Class and Caste among Muslims in India and Pakistan

Generally, it would be true to say that the Muslim population in India and Pakistan is composed of two fairly distinct groups. The first group, the Ashrafs, comprises descendants of the Muslim conquerors who came from Central Asia and set up kingdoms in the northern and western part of the South Asian subcontinent. The second group, the Ajlafs, are converts to Islam—mainly as a result of the efforts of Sufi preachers—from among the various Hindu castes in India. I believe it is fair to say that a large proportion of these converts were from the Dalit and Shudra castes who were attracted to Islam because it provided them a religion that did not discriminate against them, as did the upper-caste Hindus.[10]

Interestingly, in spite of Islam's own egalitarian teachings, the Ashrafs maintain a class hierarchy. At the top are the Sayyads, supposedly descendants of the tribe of the Prophet Muhammad and the first four Caliphs. Then there are the Shaykhs, who are said to be descendants of Arab and Persian immigrants as well as high-caste Hindu converts (like Rajputs). The next group is the Pastuns, who descend from members of the Pashto-speaking tribes of Afghanistan. Lastly are the Mughals, persons of Turkic origin who came with the Mughal armies. A strong aspect of endogamy is practiced: marriages across these categories are rare. We also find the presence of hereditary occupations or occupational specializations. For example, qasai (butchers) are a separate group within South Asian Islam. Some degree of restriction of interdining (commensality) can also be found, although such restrictions are much weaker than among Hindu castes.[11]

Conclusion

Although the founders of both Islam and Christianity stressed the equality of all human beings, their followers in India have been unable in practice to live up to that ideal and have allowed hierarchical social systems to permeate their communities. Notions of caste and enforcement of class hierarchy permeate both the Christian and Islamic communities of South Asia.

Notes

1. See Amartya Sen, "Capabilities and Well-Being," in *The Quality of Life*, ed. Martha Nussbaum and Amartya Sen, 30–53 (Oxford: Oxford University Press, 1993), 30–53.

2. See Sonali Campion, "Educate, Agitate, Organise: A Short Biography of Dr. B. R. Ambedkar," written in 2016, now posted on the website of the London School of Economics and Political Science, accessed May 28, 2019, https://blogs.lse.ac.uk/southasia/2016/04/14/educate-agitate-organise-a-short-biography-of-dr-b-r-ambedkar/.

3. Bastiaan Wielenga, *Introduction to Marxism* (Bangalore: Centre for Social Action, 1984).

4. Max Weber, "Class, Status, Party," in *Social Stratification*, ed. Dipankar Gupta (Delhi: Oxford University Press, 1992), 464ff.

5. Weber, 464ff.

6. See, for example, Morton Klass, *Caste: The Emergence of the South Asian Social System*, 2nd ed. (New Delhi: Manohar, 1993).

7. For the full text (in English translation) of this document from May 1525, see "Against the Robbing and Murdering Hordes of Peasants," in *Martin Luther*, ed. E. G. Rupp and Benjamin Drewery (London: Edward Arnold, 1970), 121–26.

8. See, for example, Jose Kananaikil, *Christians of Scheduled Caste Origin* (New Delhi: Indian Social Institute, 1983).

9. Ninan Koshy, *Caste in the Kerala Churches* (Bangalore: Christian Institute for the Study of Religion and Society, 1968).

10. Azra Khanam, *Muslim Backward Classes: A Sociological Perspective* (New Delhi: Sage, 2013), 121ff.

11. Imtiaz Ahmed, "Endogamy and Status Mobility among the Siddique Sheikhs of Allahabad, Uttar Pradesh," in *Caste and Social Stratification among the Muslims*, ed. Imtiaz Ahmed (Delhi: Manohar, 1973), 167ff.

Slavery

Source of Theological Tension

JONATHAN BROWN

For several centuries the elite unit of the Ottoman army, the Janissaries, was made up of soldiers who were the personal slaves of the sultan. But when the sultan Mehmed IV (d. 1693) began referring to them too comfortably as "my slaves," the Janissaries reminded him that they were the slaves of God alone.[1] When the English Standard Version Translation Oversight Committee met in 2010, one issue of debate was how to translate the Hebrew word *'ebed* and the Greek word *doulos*. Were they slave, servant, bondservant? The discussion was wide ranging, with expected detours into what *slave* meant to American audiences. Lexically, one scholar pointed out, *slave* was clearly the most accurate translation for the Old Testament Hebrew *'ebed*. But if this translation were followed across all instances of this noun and the related verb, readers would be left incomprehensible renderings like "slaving for God" instead of "worshiping God."[2]

One of the most interesting commonalities—or perhaps continuities—between Christianity and Islam is the scriptural conflation of worship and servitude. Although the fact is lost or obscured in many English translations of the New Testament, those telling the tale of Christ regularly referred to the faithful as the "slaves" (*doulos*) of the Lord.[3] In the Qur'an, a common term for human beings is "the slaves of God" (*'abīd/'ibād Allāh*), which we still find in Islamic names like 'Abdallah (The Slave of God), 'Abd al-Raḥman (The Slave of the Most Merciful), and Amat Allah (The Female Slave of God). This is an ancient trope. Even in Mesopotamia of the third millennium BCE, key terms for slave and worshipper were conflated such that it is not clear which was the original meaning and which was the derivative.[4]

With the unique exception of Gregory of Nyssa (d. 394), whose extreme asceticism led him to judge slavery as wrong for both philosophical and theological reasons, and the passionate reiteration of his arguments by the early German jurist Eike von Repgow (d. circa 1235), voices from the Abrahamic tradition (or, indeed, any tradition) prior to the late 1500s did not note any qualms about slavery's wrongness.[5] There was anxiety around slavery; but it was theological, not moral. How can a human worshipper (slave) of God be the slave (worshipper) of another of God's worshippers/slaves? Especially in Christianity and Islam, if the ideal believers are those humble and oppressed brothers and sisters who risk persecution to worship the True God, how do we explain one of them owning another as property? Slavery is the polar opposite of the egalitarian spirit of the community of the faithful. How is it explained and how is it justified in the light of humanity's common servitude before God?

Ethical Imperative of Equality and Empathy

The theological tension caused by slavery was clearly felt as far as we can reach historically back into the Islamic tradition. A report from a ninth-century text describing the Prophet's Companion Salman al-Farisi, which tells of how he came from Persia to Arabia as a slave and eventually became a follower of Muhammad, includes his account of how he "had been handed off from lord to lord almost ten times [*min rabb ilā rabb*]" before he was finally freed.[6] This language grated on the ears of later Muslim scholars, since the Prophet had made it clear subsequent to Salman's statement that slaves should not call their masters "my lord," nor should their masters call them "my slave [*'abdī*]." "For indeed," the Prophet explained, "you all are slaves, and the lord is God most high."[7] This is reminiscent of Paul's exhortation that masters not threaten their slaves since they both have the same Master (*kyrios*) in heaven (Eph. 6:9). The earliest known Arabic dictionary, from the mid eighth century, makes a point of beginning the entry on slave (*'abd*) by affirming, "Free or slave [*raqīq*], all are the slaves of God."[8]

One solution to the theological tension around slavery was to diminish the hierarchy between master and slave or at least to rhetorically collapse it, as with the Prophet's instruction that a master call his slaves "my boy" or "my girl" and that slaves call their master "my patron" (mawlāya). The Islamic Hadith corpus is full of exhortations replacing the master/slave dynamic with one of brotherhood. The best known is the hadith that serves as the foundation for sharia legal and ethical norms on the treatment of slaves. The Prophet states,

> Your slaves are your brothers, whom God has put under your control. Feed them from what you eat, clothe them from what you wear, and do not burden them with work that overwhelms them. If you give them more than they can do, then assist them.[9]

This collapsing of hierarchy is especially pronounced in the domain of ritual, in which Muslims are all equal before God. One hadith has the Prophet foretelling that the Muslim nation would one day be the greatest in terms of both the number of orphans and the number of its slaves, but that both should be treated as one's children. And "when your slave prays with you, he is your brother."[10] The theological dimension is more pronounced in another hadith in which the Prophet upbraids a Muslim for striking his slave by warning that "God has far more power over you than you have over him."[11]

That slavery was a mundane reality of the biblical and Late Antique Near East is well known. This meant that slavery was construed not as some moral crisis but as manifestation of God's distribution of wealth, happiness, trial, and tribulation among His creatures. Interestingly, in the Old Testament this aspect of divine fiat regarding the human condition is drawn on for ethical exhortation. On two occasions, the Torah reminds Jews to treat their own Jewish slaves well because the Jews were once slaves in Egypt (Deut. 15:15; 16:12).

This dimension is absent in the Qur'an, despite the exodus narrative featuring prominently in that holy book. The Qur'an notes that Pharaoh enslaved the Jews (Q. 26:22), but the book's recurring description of the Jews in Egypt is not the idiom of slavery but rather that of oppression (*yastaḍ'ifu*) (Q. 28:4). This serves as the model for how the Qur'an describes the predicament of the Muslims living under the oppression of the pagan Quraysh in Mecca before the establishment of the Muslim polity in Medina (Q. 8:26). And this change of fortune is not an ethical lesson but rather a theological one. As the Muslims in Medina faced ongoing conflict and wars, they should never despair of God's capacity to bring victory or shirk their responsibility to fight in God's path. For God had already once brought them out of oppression against fearful odds.[12]

It is interesting that the only Islamic scripture drawing on the divine fiat of worldly power for a lesson of empathetic ethics for slave owners is a forged hadith that first appears in the late eleventh century in the famous *Revival of the Religious Sciences of al-Ghazali* (d. 1111). This hadith only becomes well known in texts written after the fourteenth century CE. It adds a new clause onto already well-known statements by the Prophet:

> Fear God concerning those whom you rightfully possess, feed them from what you eat, clothe them from what you wear, and do not burden them with work they cannot bear. As long as you like them, keep them. And when you do not like them, sell them. And do not inflict pain on the creation of God (thus far all material found in well-known hadiths), *for indeed God made you their owners, but if He had willed, He could have made them own you.*[13]

It is also worth noting that, even when discussing this hadith, prominent Muslim scholars do not interpret it as we would expect. Ahmad Baba (d. 1627), often lauded for his proto-abolitionist thinking, notes that the hadith means that God has chosen to bless Muslims with Islam, but if He so chose, He could have made them unbelievers subject to enslavement.[14]

Theological Justification for Slavery

In the Abrahamic scriptures, the fact of slavery is unremarkable. It merits no more note than the existence of war or the power of husband over wife. In the Near East, slavery was first and foremost a product of warfare and the captives it produced. It was thus something that happened to those outside "the nation" and its communal and doctrinal boundaries. In the Near East and elsewhere, however, slavery was also the by-product of debt and the inability to pay it back. This is accepted in the Old Testament's acknowledgment of a degree of servitude for Hebrew debtors that was not as severe as the enslavement of non-Hebrews (Exod. 21:20–21; Lev. 25:43, 46). Debt slavery was part of the Roman world into which Christianity was born, although it seems to have diminished in late antiquity in the Near East. As it coalesced in the first century after the Prophet, the sharia prohibited enslavement due to debt.

For proselyting religions, however, in which "the nation" could conceivably encompass anyone and embracing the faith made one—until then a foreigner—a brother or sister of the believers, how was slavery to be explained? A pagan slave of a Christian or Muslim owner could convert to Christianity or Islam, yet they remained a slave. Augustine of Hippo (d. 430) and Isidore of Seville (d. 636) found the answer in the doctrine of original sin. If a Christian was a slave, then that slavery was God punishing them either for original sin or for some sin known to God. But this was no limitation on that Christian's capacity to worship or serve Christ. Nor was it a worldly injustice inflicted on that slave. Here church scholars drew on Stoic thought (and in the writings of the Hellenized Jew Philo of Alexandria), which saw slavery as an extreme instance of how a person's virtue and happiness depended on their ability to live within nature and react wisely to a world they could not control. The legal status of slavery was immaterial since it was just another material constraint. A person's moral standing and happiness was defined by how they dealt with such constraints.[15]

Slavery was equally a fact of life in the Qur'an, where it was merely another case of God giving some people more worldly wealth or power than others. God states, "We have apportioned among [people] their livelihood in the life of the world, and raised some of them above others in rank that some of them may take labor from others; and the mercy of your Lord is better than what they amass" (Q. 43:32). In another verse that uses lifespan, health, and freedom/slavery to stress God's omnipotence, the Qur'an explains that God has "favored some of you above others in worldly provision" (Q. 16:71). As the Prophet explained, slaves are merely fellow humans who happen to be put under the control of others.

Unlike previous Near Eastern traditions, Islamic law foreclosed all routes into slavery except capture in war. Following the Roman law tradition, Muslim scholars acknowledged that the default, natural status of a human being was freedom. Debt slavery, selling off one's children, relatives, or even oneself, was understood as prohibited by the time that Islamic legal manuals were being produced in the late eighth century, although these rules were sometimes not obeyed by Muslims in later centuries. Following the line that slaves came from outside the nation, it was also unanimously agreed by Muslim clerics that Muslims could not be enslaved (although there is no scriptural ruling for this). The only people who could be enslaved were non-Muslim captives of war; non-Muslims living under Muslim rule (*dhimmī*) and non-Muslims from states allied to the Muslim state were protected from enslavement.

Here Muslim scholars trying to firm up the theoretical underpinnings of Islamic law in its revealed sources were presented with another tension that, if not purely theological, protruded from how they had come to understand God's relation to man in law. The tight constriction that the *sharia* had introduced on the means of enslavement, combined with the unprecedented emphasis that Qur'an and Prophetic precedent placed on the immense virtue or emancipating one's slaves, led Muslim scholars to conclude even in the eighth century that "God wants freedom." As one scholar writing in the early 900s concluded, "God most high created Adam and fortified him against anyone owning him, and the same with Eve (Ḥawā')." Since all humankind came from these two, all were free.[16]

But this was clearly not true. It was not true in fact, and it was not true in the law that the Qur'an and the Prophet had brought, since the sharia allowed slavery and enslavement. How could this divergence be reconciled? Looking back on the accumulated body of Islamic law that had been derived from the Qur'an, Prophetic precedent, and communal practice over the previous three centuries, Muslim scholars in the tenth and eleventh centuries theorized slavery as a condition that was caused by a person's unbelief (*kufr*). This became the standard definition of slavery in Islamic law: a legal handicap resulting from unbelief. Enslavement was allowed as an earthly punishment for *kufr*.

Theological tension remained, however. First of all, this sharia etiology of slavery clashed with a major principle of Islamic theology regarding matters salvific. Muslim theologians agreed that non-Muslims who lived outside the Abode of Islam and had no access to any reliable information about intact revelation would not be held accountable by God for not following a prophet or the Prophet Muhammad. These people were known as the Ahl al-Fatra, roughly translatable as "People of Times of Vitiated Prophecy." This term was based in Q. 5:19 and the principle laid out in Q. 17:15 that "No bearer of burdens will bear the burden of another, and We would not punish [a people] until We had sent a messenger." Those who died in a time or place in which the message of the prophets had been lost would be judged independently on the Day of Judgment. Yet this qualification applied perfectly to precisely those pagan populations— Turks in Central Asia, Slavs on the steppes of Russia, and Africans from south of the Sahara—whom Muslims enslaved over the course of many centuries. If God did not hold their non-Muslim-ness against them on the Day of Judgment, how could Muslims hold it against them in this life? Ironically, the non-Muslim populations who did flout God's will by refusing to embrace Islam despite constant

daily and reliable contact with its teachings were that same group strictly protected against enslavement under the sharia: dhimmīs.

Finally, the Muslim legal-theological theorization of slavery in the sharia left
a second, unresolved theological tension. If enslavement was only justified by
understanding it as divine punishment for a non-Muslim captured in war against
Muslims, then why did the sharia hold without exception that slaves so taken
remained slaves even if they embraced Islam? Muslim scholars answered this by
proposing that the person remained a slave as an earthly punishment for their
erstwhile unbelief.[17] But even if we were to accept this, how could we account for
this slave's child? Following Roman law and not any Qur'anic or Hadith-based
ruling, the sharia traced slave status through the mother; if a child's father was
free but their mother was a slave, then that child was the property of the mother's
owner. (An exception occurred through another of Islam's unprecedented changes
to the slavery regime of the Near East: a child born of a man and his female slave
was free and of the same social standing as children born of a free wife). If a
pagan captured in war who embraced Islam remained a slave as a vestigial result
of his previous condition, surely this would not apply to a newborn child who, as
the Qur'an stated, did not bear the burdens of another. Here the efforts of Muslim
jurists and theologians gave out. As one famous fourteenth-century legal theorist
wrote, that person was a slave because this had been "established as a rule of the
Sacred Law (shar')," pure and simple.[18] In the end, the owner's property right
trumped two axioms of God's relation to man: the original, natural state of freedom into which humans are assumed to be born and the fact that the legal cause
of the person's enslavement—their unbelief—had been rendered moot by their
birth as a Muslim child to Muslim parents.

Notes

1. Feridun M. Emecen, "Osmanlı Hanedanına Alternatif Arayışlar Üzerine Bazı
Örnekler ve Mülahazalar," in Osmanlı klasik çağında hanedan, devlet ve toplum (Istan-
bul: Timaş Yayınları, 2011), 49.

2. David Instone-Brewer, "ESV Bible Translators Debate the Word 'Slave' at Tyndale House, Cambridge," Youtube, https://www.youtube.com/watch?time_continue=242
&v=Mx06mtApu8k.

3. Ceslaus Spicq, "Le vocabulaire de l'esclavage dans le nouveau testament," Revue
biblique 85 (1978): 201–26, at 204–6.

4. Lorenzo Verderame, "Slavery in Third-Millennium Mesopotamia: An Overview
of Sources and Studies," Journal of Global Slavery 3 (2018): 13–40, at 19–20; and Jonathan E. Brockopp, Early Mālikī Law: Ibn 'Abd Al-Hakam and His Major Compendium of
Jurisprudence (Leiden: Brill, 2000), 128.

5. See, for example, Gregory's commentary on Ecclesiastes 2:7 in Homily No. 4, in
his Homilies on Ecclesiastes; Stuart G. Hall, ed., Gregory of Nyssa, Homilies on Ecclesiastes: An English Version with Supporting Studies (Berlin: Walter de Gruyter, 1993), 73;

see also Eike von Repgow, *The Saxon Mirror*, trans. Maria Dobozy (Philadelphia: University of Pennsylvania Press, 1999), 125–26.

6. Ṣaḥīḥ al-Bukhārī: *kitāb manāqib al-anṣār, bāb islām Salmān al-Fārisī.*

7. Sunan of Abū Dāwūd: *kitāb al-adab, bāb lā yaqūlu al-mamlūk rabbī wa rabbatī*; and Ṣaḥīḥ Muslim: *kitāb al-alfāẓ min al-adab wa ghayrihā, bāb ḥukm iṭlāq lafẓat al-ʿabd wa'l-ama* . . . .

8. Khalīl b. Aḥmad, *Kitāb al-ʿAyn*, 3:83.

9. Ṣaḥīḥ al-Bukhārī: *kitāb al-aymān, bāb al-maʿāṣī min amr al-Jāhiliyya* . . . ; Ṣaḥīḥ Muslim: *kitāb al-aymān, bāb iṭʿām al-mamlūk mimmā yaʾkulu wa ilbāsihi mimmā yalbasu* . . . ; Sunan of Abū Dāwūd: *kitāb al-adab, bāb fī ḥaqq al-mamlūk*; Jāmiʿ al-Tirmidhī: *kitāb al-birr waʾl-ṣila, bāb mā jāʾa fī al-iḥsān ilā al-khadam*; and Sunan Ibn Mājah: *kitāb al-adab, bāb al-iḥsān ilā al-mamālīk.*

10. Sunan Ibn Mājah: *kitāb al-adab, bāb al-iḥsān ilā al-mamālīk.*

11. Ṣaḥīḥ Muslim: *kitāb al-īmān, bāb ṣuḥbat al-mamālīk wa kaffārat man laṭama ʿabdahu.*

12. The Qurʾan does use an ethics of reciprocity, however, in exhorting children to care for their parents, who had cared for them when they were young. See Q. 17:24.

13. al-Ghazālī, *Iḥyāʾ ʿulūm al-dīn*, 2:1249–50; translation mine, emphasis mine.

14. Aḥmad Bābā, *Miʾrāj al-Ṣuʿūd: Ahmad Baba's Replies on Slavery*, annotated and translated by John Hunwick and Fatima Harrack (Rabat, Morocco: Institute of African Studies, 1999), 35.

15. See Pierre Bonnassie, *From Slavery to Feudalism in South-Western Europe* (Cambridge: Cambridge University Press, 2009), 26; and William L. Westermann, *The Slave Systems of Greek and Roman Antiquity* (Philadelphia: American Philosophical Society, 1955), 156. See also Augustine of Hippo, *The City of God* [Dē cīvitāte Deī contrā pāgānōs | Concerning the City of God against the Pagans], Book 19:15, trans. Henry Bettenson (London: Penguin Classics, 1984), 874–75.

16. Ibn al-Mundhir, *Kitāb al-Awsaṭ min al-sunan waʾl-ijmāʿ waʾl-ikhtilāf*, ed. Khālid Ibrāhīm al-Sayyid, 11 vols. (Fayyoum: Dār al-Falāḥ, 2009), 11:428.

17. Mona Siddiqui, *The Good Muslim: Reflections on Classical Islamic Law and Theology* (Cambridge: Cambridge University Press, 2012), 48.

18. ʿAbd al-ʿAzīz al-Bukhārī, *Kashf al-asrār*, ed. ʿAbdallāh Maḥmūd ʿUmar, 4 vols. (Beirut: Dār al-Kutub al-ʿIlmiyya, 1997), 4:395, 399.

PART THREE

Inequality, the Bible, and the Christian Tradition

Inequality in the Old Testament

LESLIE J. HOPPE, OFM

My task is to provide context for considering various texts from the Hebrew Bible that relate to the inequalities of human existence. It is important to note that Christian churches have appropriated selected religious texts produced by adherents of the religion of ancient Israel and early Judaism as normative for their faith and life, calling this collection of texts the "Old Testament." The list of individual books that make up the Old Testament, however, is not the same among Christian churches. Protestant, Catholic, and Orthodox Christians differ as to which books are to be regarded as composing the Old Testament. For our purposes, only texts that *all* Christians include among the collection of books known as the Old Testament are considered here. These are the books of the Hebrew (rabbinic) Bible. Like all complex societies, ancient Israel struggled with issues that are related broadly to the topic of the seminar: inequality. These struggles are reflected in its religious literature. Because this literature was produced and edited over a long period of time, we should expect to find a diversity of perspectives and the development of sensitivities regarding issues of inequality/equality.

The Issue of Gender Equality/Inequality

The Old Testament begins with texts that deal with the issue of the equality of the male and female human creatures. The story of their creation in Genesis 2:18–22 subordinates the woman to the man. God created the man; the creation of the woman appears to have been an afterthought to deal with the man's loneliness. God created the woman from the man's rib to serve as his partner. Genesis 1:27, however, has male and female created at the same time. There is no hint of subordination. There is a single "humankind" made of male and female persons, all of whom are created in the image of God. The two Genesis narratives of the creation of human beings suggest that while the world of ancient Israel was definitely a man's world, there were those who were convinced of the fundamental equality of male and female according to God's intention and action in creation. Some legislation found in the books of Exodus and Deuteronomy also put men and women on an equal footing. That is, both men and women are to enjoy the Sabbath rest (Exod. 20:8–10; Deut. 5:14) and the celebrations during the feasts of Weeks (Shavuot) and Tabernacles (Sukkot) (Deut. 16:11–12, 14). Adult children were responsible for the care of both parents (Exod. 20:12; Deut. 5:16). Both male and female indentured slaves were to be treated the same way when gaining their freedom (Deut. 15:12, 15).

In the matter of community leadership, men occupy most positions—especially in official leadership. All cultic officials (priests and Levites) are men; women do not serve in the cultic sphere except by performing menial tasks (Exod. 38:8; 1 Sam. 2:22). This sets off ancient Israel from the more common pattern in the ancient Near East in which women did have a role in cultic activities. Similarly, communal leaders (elders) were males. In the domestic sphere, there was a division of labor that left husband and wife as interdependent; for example, both parents were responsible for the raising of their children (Deut. 21:18–21; Prov. 10:1).

In the period of the Israelite national states of Israel and Judah, political leadership was dominated by men. All monarchs of the Kingdom of Israel were men, as were the monarchs of the Kingdom of Judah except in one case. Athaliah (842–836 BCE) ruled the Kingdom of Judah as queen following the death of her son Ahaziah. She consolidated her position by assassinating all male members of the royal family (2 Kings 11:1–21). It is likely that she was able to gain support for her actions because she had a measure of influence and authority as the *gebîrāh*.[1] Athaliah, in turn, was assassinated after a seven-year reign (841–835 BCE), and no woman ever again ruled as queen over the Kingdom of Judah during the biblical period.[2]

Women, however, were recognized as charismatic leaders. Four women are called prophets in the Old Testament: Miriam (Exod. 15:20), Deborah (Judg. 4:4), Huldah (2 Kings 22:14; 2 Chron. 34:22), Noadiah (Neh. 6:14). There is also an unnamed woman prophet (Isa. 8:3). The biblical text calls these women "prophets" and offers no explanation for doing so. Apparently their service as prophets was not considered unusual. A case in point is Huldah. When a lawbook was found in the temple while repair work was in process during Josiah's reign, the king ordered his advisers to "inquire of the LORD" (2 Kings 22:13). Jeremiah was active at the time, but Josiah's courtiers did not seek his advice and instead turned to a female prophet named Huldah. She introduced her decision about the authenticity of the lawbook with the common prophetic formulary, "Thus says the LORD, the God of Israel" (2 Kings 22:15), thus asserting that she was speaking in the name of God. Again, the text offers no indication that consulting a woman or her giving a message from God was anything out of the ordinary.

It has become a commonplace to speak of ancient Israelite society as patriarchal in its ideology and social structure,[3] yet the word "patriarch" does not appear in the Hebrew Bible.[4] While familial relations provided a model for ancient Israel's social system, at least one tradition did not see that model in terms of "father/children." The word "brothers" (*achim*) occurs almost forty times in the book of Deuteronomy. Sometimes it refers to male siblings as in the law of Levirate marriage (Deut. 25:5–10), and other times it refers to one's fellow Israelites as in the law of the king (Deut. 17:20). This suggests that the Deuteronomic tradition sees the people of Israel as a community of siblings, that is, a community of equals. Biblical Hebrew is a gendered language in which masculine forms are used though the idea expressed may be inclusive. I believe that when Deuteronomy uses *achim* to speak of one's fellow Israelites, women are included as they are explicitly in Deuteronomy 15:12, 17b. This is not to suggest that men and women enjoyed complete equality in ancient Israelite society; rather, I suggest that the Israelite social system was not completely dominated by men as implied by the word "patriarchal." Property was passed down from father to son. Fathers and husbands controlled the sexuality of their daughters and wives. Still, male domination was not total. Women had significant roles in the domestic, religious, and political spheres. They could and did act independently. Although men and women were not totally equal in Israelite society, both men and women played interdependent and overlapping roles in Israelite society. For example, in the family husband and wife were genuine partners.[5]

Ethnic/Religious Inequality

The Old Testament reflects the Janus-like attitude that the people of ancient Israel had toward other peoples and nations. The Israelites believed that they were related, through Abraham's family, with the other nations in the eastern Mediterranean region. The Moabites and the Ammonites were thought to be descendants of Lot, Abraham's nephew (Gen. 19:17, 38). The Bedouin Arabs were considered descendants of Ishmael, Abraham's firstborn, on the basis of the tribal lists of Genesis 25:12–15, 19–20. The Midianites were descended from Abraham through his wife Keturah (Gen. 25:1–4). The Edomites were believed to be descended from Abraham's great-grandson Esau (Gen. 25:25; 36:8; Deut. 2:4–5). Ancient Israel's neighbors, however, were also competitors for the limited resources of the region. The Israelite tribes and the two Israelite kingdoms frequently found themselves in armed conflict with their immediate neighbors. It is not surprising, then, that Deuteronomy forbids the inclusion of Moabites and Ammonites into the Israelite community "to the tenth generation" (Deut. 23:3) although the book admonishes Israel not to hate the Edomites since they are kin (Deut. 23:7).[6]

Two important theological themes in the Old Testament also have had their effects on Israel's relationship with the nations. The call of Abraham asserts that "all the families of the earth" shall be blessed in Abraham (Gen. 12:3), reflecting a universalist thrust in the biblical tradition—a motif that finds expression in the Isaianic tradition as a vision of peace among all peoples:

> In days to come
>   the mountain of the LORD's house
> shall be established as the highest of the mountains,
>   and shall be raised above the hills;
> all the nations shall stream to it.
>   Many peoples shall come and say,
> "Come, let us go up to the mountain of the LORD,
>   to the house of the God of Jacob;
> that he may teach us his ways
>   and that we may walk in his paths."
> For out of Zion shall go forth instruction,
>   and the word of the LORD from Jerusalem.
> He shall judge between the nations,
>   and shall arbitrate for many peoples;
> they shall beat their swords into plowshares,
>   and their spears into pruning hooks;
> nation shall not lift up sword against nation,
>   neither shall they learn war any more.
>
> (Isa. 2:2–4)

At the same time, the notion of Israel's *election* carries with it a particularist emphasis:

> You are a people holy to the LORD
> your God; it is you *the LORD has chosen out of*
> *all the peoples on earth to be his people.*
>
> (Deut. 14:2)

From this theological assertion of Israel's election as the people of God flows the command to take possession of the land of Canaan by displacing those who lived in it. The violence that accompanied this displacement is the subject of Joshua 5:13–12:24. The slaughter of the people of Canaan is justified because they were seen as threats to the loyalty it owes to the Lord and as threats to ancient Israel's existence.[7] During the brief existence of the two Israelite kingdoms, both felt pressure from their neighbors. When the Mesopotamian empires began their militaristic and expansionist policy, both Israel and Judah survived only as vassal states. Eventually both Israelite kingdoms fell: Israel to Assyria and Judah to Babylon. The territory of the Kingdom of Israel was absorbed into the Assyrian provincial system in 721 BCE and a portion of its population was forced to migrate to various places in Mesopotamia. In 587 BCE, Judah suffered a similar fate as it fell to the Babylonians, with many of its people forced to migrate to other territories controlled by the Babylonians. It is not surprising, then, that "oracles against the nations" become standard fare in the Latter Prophets: Isaiah 13–23; Jeremiah 46–51; Ezekiel 25–32; Amos 1:2–2:16; Zephaniah 2:4–15; Nahum and Obadiah.

A negative attitude toward the nations in the prophetic tradition changes dramatically in the poetry of that unnamed prophet whose words are found in Isaiah 40–55. This prophet presents YHWH not simply as the patron deity of Israel but the Creator and Lord of all nations. The prophet affirms the election of Israel, God's servant, but also affirms the mission of Israel on behalf of the nations:

> But you, Israel, my servant,
>   Jacob, whom I have chosen,
>   the offspring of Abraham, my friend;
> you whom I took from the ends of the earth,
>   and called from its farthest corners,
> saying to you, "You are my servant,
>   I have chosen you and not cast you off."
>
> (Isa. 41:8–9)

> Here is my servant, whom I uphold,
>   my chosen, in whom my soul delights;
> I have put my spirit upon him;
>   he will bring forth justice to the nations.
>
> (Isa. 42:1)

To begin achieving this goal, the Lord chooses Cyrus, the Persian king, calling Cyrus his "anointed" (Isa. 45:1), asserting that God raised up a gentile king to bring about the restoration of Judah.[8]

The readiness to include the nations among those who worship the Lord continues in the collection of prophetic texts known as Third Isaiah (Isa. 56–66):

> And the foreigners who join themselves to the LORD,
>   to minister to him, to love the name of the LORD,
> these I will bring to my holy mountain,
>   and make them joyful in my house of prayer;
> for my house shall be called a house of prayer
>   for all peoples.
>
> (Isa. 56:6–7)

The book of Isaiah concludes with a vision of some gentiles serving as personnel in the Jerusalem temple (Isa. 66:20). The vision of Isaiah 40–66 is not universalism in the strict sense since the nations will not maintain their own religious identity but are to become worshippers of the God of Israel. It does call the Jews to see the gentiles in a new and positive light.

At the same time that these Isaianic texts were being composed, there were those who continued to view the nations as potential threats to the loyalty that Israel owes to its God. In particular, non-Israelite wives were thought to lead their husbands into idolatry, as the story of Solomon suggests (1 Kings 11). The belief that marrying non-Jewish women will inevitably lead to abandoning the service of the Lord alone led Nehemiah to warn Jewish men against marriage with gentile women (Neh. 13:22–27) and Ezra to call Jewish men to divorce their non-Jewish wives (Ezra 10:1-44). But Moses's wife Zipporah was the daughter of a Midianite priest (Exod. 2:16–22). When Aaron and Miriam criticized Moses for marrying a Cushite (Ethiopian or Nubian) woman, Miriam was struck with leprosy (Num. 12:1, 10).[9] In addition, the Bible contains the charming story of Ruth, a Moabite woman, who marries an Israelite man named Boaz. Ruth's great-grandson was David, king of Israel and Judah. The books of Esther and Daniel reflect that the nations threaten Israel's existence.

On the other hand, ancient Israel's literature shows an openness to the cultures of the ancient Near East. For example, the narratives of Genesis 1–11 demonstrate that Israel's theologians were ready to take elements from Egyptian, Mesopotamian, and Canaanite sources. For example, Psalm 29 is probably a Canaanite hymn in praise of the Baal that was appropriated by Israel as a prayer for rain that would bring with it agricultural fertility. Israel's laws in Exodus and Deuteronomy show that Israel drew on legal traditions and practices common to the ancient Near East. It is ancient Israel's wisdom traditions that show Israel's connections with the wider ancient Near Eastern culture. For example, Proverbs 22:17–24:34 is closely related to the "Instruction of Amen-em-ope" from Egypt. The protagonist of the book of Job is not an Israelite but a gentile. The book of Qoheleth (Ecclesiastes) likewise shows affinities with Mesopotamian texts.

Even in matters of cult and piety, there were some in Israel who were ready to adopt non-Israelite forms of worship. For example, King Ahaz of Judah (735–715 BCE) had an altar built like one he saw in Damascus and replaced the bronze altar of the Jerusalem temple with it (2 Kings 16:10–16). Some women participated in a ritual dedicated to the god Tammuz in the Jerusalem temple itself (Ezek. 8:14). Of course, the Bible considers such activities idolatrous. A unique aspect of the biblical tradition is its refusal to use images, rejecting idolatry with parodies such as the one found in Psalm 115:3–8:

Our God is in the heavens;
    he does whatever he pleases.

Their idols are silver and gold,
  the work of human hands.
They have mouths, but do not speak;
  eyes, but do not see.
They have ears, but do not hear;
  noses, but do not smell.
They have hands, but do not feel;
  feet, but do not walk;
  they make no sound in their throats.
Those who make them are like them;
  so are all who trust in them.

The people of ancient Israel believed that they and most of their immediate neighbors were related through Abraham, but they experienced these nations as threats to the absolute loyalty they owed to YHWH, their national deity, and as threats to their very existence in the land promised to their ancestors. At the same time, however, the biblical tradition reflects the cultural heritage of the ancient Near East that Israel shared with the other peoples of the region. The biblical tradition rejects the inclusion of the nations into the community of Israel but paradoxically envisions a future in which Israel and the nations will join in the worship of YHWH, the patron deity of ancient Israel.

Inequality on the Socioeconomic Level

Archaeology has uncovered material evidence of economic and social inequality in ancient Israelite society. For example, excavations of the Iron Age strata from both Tel el Far'ah (the biblical Tirzah) and Shechem revealed differences between the more elaborate housing of the wealthy and the more simple dwellings of the poor.[10] Inequalities did exist in the socioeconomic spheres of ancient Israelite society. This following presentation, however, will confine itself to discussion of these as they are found in selected texts from the Old Testament.

Ancient Israel had an agrarian economy. Although its economic system included merchants, artisans, soldiers, and government bureaucrats, most Israelites were subsistence farmers who worked small family farms. Ideally all Israelite families except those from the tribe of Levi were to have equal access to the means of production—that is, land.[11] The book of Joshua describes the apportioning of the land of Canaan among the Israelite tribes (see Josh. 13:1–21:45).

There were circumstances that made it difficult if not impossible for some Israelite farmers and their families to survive. Some of these circumstances were beyond the control of the individual farmer, such as drought, war, sickness, and pestilence, but there were some reasons for the farmer to become poor that were his responsibility. For example, the book of Proverbs asserts that laziness and dissipation are causes of that poverty:

> I passed by the field of one who was lazy,
>   by the vineyard of a stupid person;
> and see, it was all overgrown with thorns;
>   the ground was covered with nettles,
>   and its stone wall was broken down.
> A little sleep, a little slumber,
>   a little folding of the hands to rest,
> and poverty will come upon you like a robber,
>   and want, like an armed warrior.
>
> (Prov. 24:30–34)

It is important to remember that Proverbs is not engaging in a sociological or even a theological reflection on poverty. The book's intended audience was the sons of the wealthy. These young men, who were born into wealth, needed to realize that poverty will be the inevitable status of those who are lazy (Prov. 10:4) and who waste their resources foolishly (Prov. 21:17). Although they may have been born into wealth, that wealth could all flitter away if they were not diligent.

There were, however, developments in ancient Israelite society over which ordinary Israelite farmers had no control. Some of these have profound effects on their economic status. One such development was the establishment of the two Israelite national states with their respective bureaucracies. The institution of the monarchy made it more difficult to maintain an equitable agrarian economy in which ownership of land was based on a family-based inheritance system. The prophet Samuel warns those who wished to have a king:

> These will be the ways of the king who will reign over you . . . He will take the best of your fields and vineyard and olive orchards and give them to his courtiers.
>
> (1 Sam. 8:11, 14)

With a prebendal system replacing the family-based system of inheritance, ordinary farmers found themselves gradually pushed to the margins of the country's economic life.[12] The king distributed land to his supporters and courtiers.[13] Some farmers lost their land and became simply agricultural workers on the estates of those favored by the king. The number of the poor grew since in an agrarian economy those without land were poor. Productive and self-sufficient farmers became objects of charity. They were reduced to working for wages and to gleaning crops from fields that have been harvested by workers who were to leave some grain, grapes, and olives unharvested and therefore available to the poor (Lev. 19:9; Deut. 24:19–20).

Land that once supported individual Israelite families became added to the estates of the wealthy. Ancient Israel's prophets vehemently criticized the socioeconomic system that concentrated wealth (= land ownership) in the hands of a few, for example, Isaiah 5:8:

> Ah, you who join house to house,
>   who add field to field,
> until there is room for no one but you,
>   and you are left to live alone
>   in the midst of the land!

This concentration of land ownership in the hands of a few helped create a permanent debtor class. Various grains (wheat, barley, spelt) were the principal crops of the Israelite farmer, with bread made from these grains as the staple of the Israelite diet. The wealthy landowner who owned large estates devoted much of their land to the production of olives and grapes. Exporting the olive oil and wine made from these crops was very profitable. With less land devoted to grain production, the price of grain rose, and the landless farmers went into debt just to provide their families with bread. The rich became richer and the poor became poorer.

When the poor tried to redress the wrongs that were the result of an unjust economic system, often they had to deal with a judiciary that was corrupted by bribes that served to skew judicial decisions in favor of the people of means (Amos 5:7; Isa. 5:23; Mic. 3:9–11; Jer. 22:13–17). The prophets then were convinced that poverty was not the result of chance or fate—nor was it simply the result of personal failings on the part of poor people. On the contrary, poverty was the creation of the wealthy who disregarded the norms of traditional Israelite morality because of their greed (Amos 3:9; Hab. 2:9; Jer. 5:27; Ezek. 45:9; Mal. 3:5). The people of means used their economic and political power to become wealthier and more powerful. The response of the prophets to an unjust political and economic system was to announce divine judgment on those who benefited from such a system at the expense of the poor. For example, the prophet Amos informs the wealthy women of Samaria of the fate that awaits them:

> Hear this word, you cows of Bashan
>   who are on Mount Samaria,
> who oppress the poor, who crush the needy,
>   who say to their husbands, "Bring something to drink!"
> The Lord God has sworn by his holiness:
>   The time is surely coming upon you,
> when they shall take you away with hooks,
>   even the last of you with fishhooks.

(Amos 4:1–2)

Ancient Israel's prophets were convinced that poverty was an evil created by Israel's elite class. The people of means engaged in unjust and immoral practices to further enrich themselves at the expense of those without power or influence.[14] The prophets then announce divine judgment on an unjust social, economic, and political system.

The book of Deuteronomy held that poverty should not have existed in ancient Israel. The Lord provided for all Israel, and if people lived according to the values of traditional Israelite morality, poverty indeed would not exist:

> There will, however, be no one in need among you, because the LORD is sure to bless you in the land that the LORD your God is giving you as a possession to occupy, if only you will obey the LORD your God by diligently observing this entire commandment that I command you today.
>
> (Deut. 15:4–5)

An important duty of the king was to ensure that poor people would receive justice:

> Give the king your justice, O God,
>   and your righteousness to a king's son.
> May he judge your people with righteousness,
>   and your poor with justice.
> May the mountains yield prosperity for the people,
>   and the hills, in righteousness.
> May he defend the cause of the poor of the people,
>   give deliverance to the needy,
>   and crush the oppressor.
>
> (Ps. 72:1–4)

The reality, however, was far from the ideal. The kings of ancient Israel failed to maintain a society in which all persons had access to the means of agricultural production—that is, land. Too many Israelite peasant farmers had to sell their land and were reduced to agricultural laborers who worked on the estates of the wealthy or they became objects of charity.

The Old Testament depicts God as one who takes the side of poor people who live in a society that has relegated them to the margins of that society's economic life: "I know that the LORD maintains the cause of the needy, and executes justice for the poor" (Ps. 140:12). This suggests that poverty among the people of Israel is an anomaly that is contrary to the divine will. The biblical witness, in addition, recognizes that poverty exists because of decisions that people make. In some cases, difficult economic circumstances that individuals face are due to their own lack of diligence and care. In most cases, however, poverty exists among the Israelite people because of injustices committed by people of means—decisions that call for divine judgment.

Although Deuteronomy expresses the ideal that poverty should not exist among the people of Israel, it does recognize that there were poor people in the community of Israel. There were Israelite customs to help one's relatives who have serious economic problems. One such attempt was the institution of the *gō'ēl* (next-of-kin), which served to keep a family's land from being sold to someone outside the clan. The book of Ruth tells of how Boaz, a relative of the widow Naomi, purchased land that Naomi thought it necessary to sell. By purchasing that land, Boaz kept the land under the control of his extended family, which included Naomi (Ruth 4:1–4).

Circumstances made it all but impossible for some farmers to hold on to their land, but they still had to feed their children. Sometimes Israelite farmers enduring difficult times had no choice but to sell themselves or even their children as indentured slaves to settle debts.[15] The relatives of the person who became an indentured slave were to buy him back (Lev. 25:47–49). Deuteronomy regulates the practice of indentured slavery, limiting the time a person could serve as an indentured slave to no more than six years. The slave's service ends when the sabbatical year began (Deut. 15:1).[16] In addition, all indentured slaves, male or female, upon regaining their freedom were not to leave service empty-handed. Deuteronomy requires their former masters to provide what is needed for the newly freed slave to make a fresh start:

> Provide liberally out of your flock, your threshing floor, and your wine press, thus giving to him some of the bounty with which the LORD your God has blessed you. . . . You shall do the same with regard to your female slave.
>
> (Deut. 15:14, 17b)

King Zedekiah of Judah (597–586 BCE) sought to end the practice of debt slavery (Jer. 34:8–22) but was unsuccessful, and the practice apparently continued throughout the biblical period (2 Kings 4:1; Amos 2:6; 8:6; Mic. 2:9; Neh. 5:3–5). It is likely that the king's desire to free all indentured slaves was to make available the newly freed slaves for the defense of the kingdom in view of the threat posed to Judah by the expansionist policies of Babylon.

Another attempt at preventing the development of a permanent underclass appears in Leviticus 25. The fiftieth year after a series of seven sabbatical years was a "jubilee year," during which the land was restored to the family that originally owned it, and Israelite indentured slaves were to be returned to their ancestral land (Lev. 25:13–17). Although there is no evidence that this law was ever observed as required by the Torah, this does show that there was resistance to the establishment of a permanent debtor class.

Excursus: Chattel Slavery

The Old Testament accepts chattel slavery as a fact of life. Chattel slavery was common in the biblical period (1 Sam. 8:10–18; 1 Kings 10:2–5). Indeed, Solomon's temple was built by slave labor (1 Kings 9:20–22). Slaves were acquired in war (Deut. 20:11–14) or purchased from other countries (Lev. 25:44–46); thus, most chattel slaves were non-Israelites. Slavery was also a punishment for some crimes (Gen. 43:18). Slaves were the property of their owners. They could be sold to other people or bequeathed to one's heirs. They could even be branded like livestock. Proverbs mentions slaves several times without questioning the morality of an institution that held that one human being could own another like owning donkeys or oxen (Prov. 12:9; 22:7; 29:19, 21). Joseph was sold into slavery by his brothers (Gen. 37:27–28) but managed to rise to a most prominent position in Egypt (Gen. 41:37–45). The other descendants of Jacob were not so fortunate and became slaves in Egypt for four hundred years (Exod. 1:11–14; 12:40) until they were freed under the leadership of Moses (Exod. 13:3). Beyond these two examples, slaves play little role in biblical narratives.

The existence and acceptance of chattel slavery in ancient Israel is an example of Israel's setting firmly within the wider culture of the ancient Near East where slavery was common. The way such slavery is presented in the Old Testament shows that, in this case, the people of ancient Israel and their religious literature were at odds with their most fundamental self-definition:

> A wandering Aramean was my ancestor; he went down into Egypt and lived there as an alien, few in number, and there he became a great nation, mighty and populous. When the Egyptians treated us harshly and afflicted us, by imposing hard labor on us, we cried to the LORD, the God of our ancestors; the LORD heard our voice and saw our affliction, our toil, and our oppression. The LORD brought us out of Egypt with a mighty hand and an outstretched arm, with a terrifying display of power, and with signs and wonders; and he brought us into this place and gave us this land, a land flowing with milk and honey.
>
> (Deut. 26:5a–9)

The core narrative of ancient Israel's story can be described as a celebration of a people set free by a God who takes the side of slaves against their masters. For such people to maintain the practice of slavery of any kind is contrary to that people's self-definition.

Conclusion

The sacred scriptures of ancient Israel reflect the inequalities that were endemic to the wider ancient Near Eastern culture: men/women; native/foreign; rich/poor;

slave/free. At the same time, there is evidence of not only respect for the human person but also a move toward recognizing the fundamental equality of all people. The subordination of women is countered by the affirmation that God created male and female together. Rather than seeing the nations only as enemies, the scriptures have a vision of an eventual merging of Israel and the gentiles in the worship of the Lord. The texts also affirm that efforts must be made to ensure that there is no permanent underclass in Israel but that all should have an equitable share of the land that God had given for Israel. Finally, the Old Testament is the product of a people set free, and the existence of slavery, either debt slavery or chattel slavery, is in conflict with the Bible's basic view of the human person and Israel's self-definition.

Notes

1. The mother of the reigning king of Judah bore the title *gebîrāh* and apparently enjoyed some measure of authority in the royal household although the precise contours of that authority are not known.

2. During the Hasmonean period (164–163 BCE), Salome Alexandra succeeded her husband, Alexander Yannai, and ruled as queen over Judah from 76 to 67 BCE. She was succeeded by her son Hyrcanus II. The story of her reign is not found in the Bible but is known from the work of Flavius Josephus, a first-century Jewish apologist. See his *Antiquities of the Jews* xiii. 11, § 12; 15, § 16.

3. See Roland de Vaux's classic *Ancient Israel: Its Life and Institutions*, trans. John McHugh (New York: McGraw-Hill, 1961), 20; Raphael Patai, *Family, Love and the Bible* (London: Macgibbon & Kee, 1961), 114–24; and Norman Gottwald, *The Tribes of Yahweh: A Sociology of the Religion of Liberated Israel, 1250–1050* (Maryknoll, NY: Orbis, 1979), 315.

4. Carol L. Meyers, "Was Ancient Israel a Patriarchal Society?" *Journal of Biblical Literature* 133, no. 1 (Spring 2014): 8.

5. Meyers, 21–23.

6. According to Flavius Josephus (*Antiquities* 13.9.1), the Hasmonean king John Hyrcanus I forcibly converted the Edomites (Idumeans) to Judaism in 125 BCE.

7. While the book of Joshua describes the defeat of the Canaanites and the taking of their land as total and complete, the book of Judges 1:21–30 asserts that it was not. Judges tells stories of the continuing conflicts that Israel had with the Canaanites over possession of the land.

8. The title "my anointed" was proper to the kings of Judah. Applying it to a foreign king reflects the high regard the author of Isaiah had for Cyrus. The reason for the prophet's admiration was the decree of Cyrus allowing the Jews to return to Judah and his call for the rebuilding of the temple in Jerusalem. See 2 Chronicles 36:22–23; Ezra 1:2–4.

9. There is some question whether the "Cushite woman" was Zipporah. The text itself does not make this identification and it cannot be assumed. The "Cushite woman" is probably not Zipporah.

10. Alain Chambon, "Far'ah, Tell el- (North)," in *The New Encyclopedia of Archaeological Excavations in the Holy Land*, ed. Ephraim Stern (New York: Simon & Schuster, 1991), 2:439–40; and Edward C. Campbell, "Shechem," in *The New Encyclopedia of*

Archaeological Excavations, ed. Ephraim Stern (New York: Simon & Schuster, 1991), 4:1352–53.

11. Members of the tribe of Levi were to gain their livelihood from the cultic service (Num. 20–21; Deut. 10:9; 18:1).

12. In a prebendal system, the political leader rewards supporters by giving them a share in government revenues. In the case of the Israelite kingdom, the king gives land grants to his most loyal supporters, reducing the land available for the independent Israelite farmer.

13. The story of Naboth's vineyard (1 Kings 21:1–29, esp. 8–16) is an example of how a corrupt political system made possible the confiscation of land from its lawful owner.

14. Some scholars suggest that the prophetic tradition came to spiritualize the poor as those having a special relationship with God. See Albert Gelin, *The Poor of Yahweh* (Collegeville, MN: Liturgical Press, 1964); and A. George, "Poverty in the Old Testament," in *Gospel Poverty*, ed. Michael D. Guinan (Chicago: Franciscan Herald Press, 1977), 17. While such "spiritualization" may be a legitimate appropriation of some prophetic texts such as Zephaniah 2:3, it should not lead to neglecting the prophetic critique of unjust social and economic systems that have created and maintained poverty.

15. The indentured slave was not considered as chattel but a debtor who was repaying his debts by working as an unpaid agricultural worker for the person to whom he was indebted.

16. In Leviticus, the sabbatical year is a time of "rest for the land" (Lev. 25:4–5), when the land was not to be cultivated and no crops grown. Deuteronomy 15 transforms this time of "rest for the land" into a time in which indentured slaves are to be set free.

Old Testament Texts
for Dialogue on Inequalities

The Bible excerpts provided here are arranged not always in canonical order but in the order in which the planners of the 2018 Building Bridges Seminar felt it best to engage them. Some passages include subheadings that are not part of the original Hebrew text. Rather, they are provided by the NRSV editors and have been retained here, as some readers may find them useful.

Genesis 1:27

So God created humankind in his image, in the image of God he created them; male and female he created them.

Genesis 2:18, 21–22

18Then the LORD God said, "It is not good that the man should be alone; I will make him a helper as his partner." . . . 21So the LORD God caused a deep sleep to fall upon the man, and he slept; then he took one of his ribs and closed up its place with flesh. 22And the rib that the LORD God had taken from the man he made into a woman and brought her to the man.

Genesis 9:8–11

8Then God said to Noah and to his sons with him, 9"As for me, I am establishing my covenant with you and your descendants after you, 10and with every living creature that is with you, the birds, the domestic animals, and every animal of the earth with you, as many as came out of the ark. ¹¹I establish my covenant with you, that never again shall all flesh be cut off by the waters of a flood, and never again shall there be a flood to destroy the earth."

Genesis 12:1–4

¹Now the LORD said to Abram, "Go from your country and your kindred and your father's house to the land that I will show you. ²I will make of you a great nation, and I will bless you, and make your name great, so that you will be a blessing. ³I will bless those who bless you, and the one who curses you I will curse; and in you all the families of the earth shall be blessed."

⁴So Abram went, as the LORD had told him; and Lot went with him. Abram was seventy-five years old when he departed from Haran.

Leviticus 19:9–10, 13

⁹When you reap the harvest of your land, you shall not reap to the very edges of your field, or gather the gleanings of your harvest. ¹⁰You shall not strip your vineyard bare, or gather the fallen grapes of your vineyard; you shall leave them for the poor and the alien: I am the LORD your God . . . .¹³You shall not defraud your neighbor; you shall not steal; and you shall not keep for yourself the wages of a laborer until morning.

Leviticus 25:8–17, 35–46

The Year of Jubilee

⁸You shall count off seven weeks of years, seven times seven years, so that the period of seven weeks of years gives forty-nine years. ⁹Then you shall have the trumpet sounded loud; on the tenth day of the seventh month—on the day of atonement—you shall have the trumpet sounded throughout all your land. ¹⁰And you shall hallow the fiftieth year and you shall proclaim liberty throughout the land to all its inhabitants. It shall be a jubilee for you: you shall return, every one of you, to your property and every one of you to your family. ¹¹That fiftieth year shall be a jubilee for you: you shall not sow, or reap the aftergrowth, or harvest the unpruned vines. ¹²For it is a jubilee; it shall be holy to you: you shall eat only what the field itself produces.

¹³In this year of jubilee you shall return, every one of you, to your property. ¹⁴When you make a sale to your neighbor or buy from your neighbor, you shall not cheat one another. ¹⁵When you buy from your neighbor, you shall pay only for the number of years since the jubilee; the seller shall charge you only for the

remaining crop years. [16]If the years are more, you shall increase the price, and if the years are fewer, you shall diminish the price; for it is a certain number of harvests that are being sold to you. [17]You shall not cheat one another, but you shall fear your God; for I am the LORD your God . . . .

[35]If any of your kin fall into difficulty and become dependent on you, you shall support them; they shall live with you as though resident aliens.[36]Do not take interest in advance or otherwise make a profit from them, but fear your God; let them live with you. [37]You shall not lend them your money at interest taken in advance, or provide them food at a profit. [38]I am the LORD your God, who brought you out of the land of Egypt, to give you the land of Canaan, to be your God.

[39]If any who are dependent on you become so impoverished that they sell themselves to you, you shall not make them serve as slaves. [40]They shall remain with you as hired or bound laborers. They shall serve with you until the year of the jubilee. [41]Then they and their children with them shall be free from your authority; they shall go back to their own family and return to their ancestral property. [42]For they are my servants, whom I brought out of the land of Egypt; they shall not be sold as slaves are sold. [43]You shall not rule over them with harshness, but shall fear your God. [44]As for the male and female slaves whom you may have, it is from the nations around you that you may acquire male and female slaves. [45]You may also acquire them from among the aliens residing with you, and from their families that are with you, who have been born in your land; and they may be your property. [46]You may keep them as a possession for your children after you, for them to inherit as property. These you may treat as slaves, but as for your fellow Israelites, no one shall rule over the other with harshness.

Deuteronomy 15:1–18

Laws concerning the Sabbatical Year

[1]Every seventh year you shall grant a remission of debts. [2]And this is the manner of the remission: every creditor shall remit the claim that is held against a neighbor, not exacting it from a neighbor who is a member of the community, because the LORD's remission has been proclaimed. [3]Of a foreigner you may exact it, but you must remit your claim on whatever any member of your community owes you. [4]There will, however, be no one in need among you, because the LORD is sure to bless you in the land that the LORD your God is giving you as a possession to occupy, [5]if only you will obey the LORD your God by diligently observing this entire commandment that I command you today. [6]When the LORD your God has blessed you, as he promised you, you will lend to many nations, but you will not borrow; you will rule over many nations, but they will not rule over you.

[7]If there is among you anyone in need, a member of your community in any of your towns within the land that the LORD your God is giving you, do not be

hard-hearted or tight-fisted toward your needy neighbor. [8]You should rather open your hand, willingly lending enough to meet the need, whatever it may be. [9]Be careful that you do not entertain a mean thought, thinking, "The seventh year, the year of remission, is near," and therefore view your needy neighbor with hostility and give nothing; your neighbor might cry to the Lord against you, and you would incur guilt. [10]Give liberally and be ungrudging when you do so, for on this account the Lord your God will bless you in all your work and in all that you undertake. [11]Since there will never cease to be some in need on the earth, I therefore command you, "Open your hand to the poor and needy neighbor in your land."

[12]If a member of your community, whether a Hebrew man or a Hebrew woman, is sold to you and works for you six years, in the seventh year you shall set that person free. [13]And when you send a male slave out from you a free person, you shall not send him out empty-handed. [14]Provide liberally out of your flock, your threshing floor, and your wine press, thus giving to him some of the bounty with which the Lord your God has blessed you. [15]Remember that you were a slave in the land of Egypt, and the Lord your God redeemed you; for this reason I lay this command upon you today. [16]But if he says to you, "I will not go out from you," because he loves you and your household, since he is well off with you, [17]then you shall take an awl and thrust it through his earlobe into the door, and he shall be your slave forever. You shall do the same with regard to your female slave.

[18]Do not consider it a hardship when you send them out from you free persons, because for six years they have given you services worth the wages of hired laborers; and the Lord your God will bless you in all that you do.

Deuteronomy 16:11–12

[11]Rejoice before the Lord your God—you and your sons and your daughters, your male and female slaves, the Levites resident in your towns, as well as the strangers, the orphans, and the widows who are among you—at the place that the Lord your God will choose as a dwelling for his name. [12]Remember that you were a slave in Egypt, and diligently observe these statutes.

Deuteronomy 23:1–8[1]

Those Excluded from the Assembly

[1]No one whose testicles are crushed or whose penis is cut off shall be admitted to the assembly of the Lord.

[2]Those born of an illicit union shall not be admitted to the assembly of the Lord. Even to the tenth generation, none of their descendants shall be admitted to the assembly of the Lord.

[3]No Ammonite or Moabite shall be admitted to the assembly of the LORD. Even to the tenth generation, none of their descendants shall be admitted to the assembly of the LORD, [4]because they did not meet you with food and water on your journey out of Egypt, and because they hired against you Balaam son of Beor, from Pethor of Mesopotamia, to curse you. [5](Yet the LORD your God refused to heed Balaam; the LORD your God turned the curse into a blessing for you, because the LORD your God loved you.) [6]You shall never promote their welfare or their prosperity as long as you live.

[7]You shall not abhor any of the Edomites, for they are your kin. You shall not abhor any of the Egyptians, because you were an alien residing in their land. [8]The children of the third generation that are born to them may be admitted to the assembly of the LORD.

Deuteronomy 23:19–20[2]

[19]You shall not charge interest on loans to another Israelite, interest on money, interest on provisions, interest on anything that is lent. [20]On loans to a foreigner you may charge interest, but on loans to another Israelite you may not charge interest, so that the LORD your God may bless you in all your undertakings in the land that you are about to enter and possess.

Ruth 1:16–17

[16]But Ruth said,
"Do not press me to leave you
    or to turn back from following you!
Where you go, I will go;
    where you lodge, I will lodge;
your people shall be my people,
    and your God my God.
[17]Where you die, I will die—
    there will I be buried.
May the LORD do thus and so to me,
    and more as well,
if even death parts me from you!"

Ruth 4:13–22

The Genealogy of David

[13]So Boaz took Ruth and she became his wife. When they came together, the LORD made her conceive, and she bore a son. [14]Then the women said to Naomi,

"Blessed be the LORD, who has not left you this day without next-of-kin; and may his name be renowned in Israel! [15]He shall be to you a restorer of life and a nourisher of your old age; for your daughter-in-law who loves you, who is more to you than seven sons, has borne him." [16]Then Naomi took the child and laid him in her bosom, and became his nurse. [17]The women of the neighborhood gave him a name, saying, "A son has been born to Naomi." They named him Obed; he became the father of Jesse, the father of David.

[18]Now these are the descendants of Perez: Perez became the father of Hezron, [19]Hezron of Ram, Ram of Amminadab, [20]Amminadab of Nahshon, Nahshon of Salmon, [21]Salmon of Boaz, Boaz of Obed, [22]Obed of Jesse, and Jesse of David.

Nehemiah 13:23–27

Mixed Marriages Condemned

[23]In those days also I saw Jews who had married women of Ashdod, Ammon, and Moab; [24]and half of their children spoke the language of Ashdod, and they could not speak the language of Judah, but spoke the language of various peoples. [25]And I contended with them and cursed them and beat some of them and pulled out their hair; and I made them take an oath in the name of God, saying, "You shall not give your daughters to their sons, or take their daughters for your sons or for yourselves. [26]Did not King Solomon of Israel sin on account of such women? Among the many nations there was no king like him, and he was beloved by his God, and God made him king over all Israel; nevertheless, foreign women made even him to sin. [27]Shall we then listen to you and do all this great evil and act treacherously against our God by marrying foreign women?"

Isaiah 2:2–4

[2]In days to come
   the mountain of the LORD's house
shall be established as the highest of the mountains,
   and shall be raised above the hills;
all the nations shall stream to it.
   [3]Many peoples shall come and say,
"Come, let us go up to the mountain of the LORD,
   to the house of the God of Jacob;
that he may teach us his ways
   and that we may walk in his paths."
For out of Zion shall go forth instruction,
   and the word of the LORD from Jerusalem.

[4]He shall judge between the nations,
    and shall arbitrate for many peoples;
they shall beat their swords into ploughshares,
    and their spears into pruning hooks;
nation shall not lift up sword against nation,
    neither shall they learn war any more.

Isaiah 56:1–8

The Covenant Extended to All Who Obey

[1]Thus says the LORD:
    Maintain justice, and do what is right,
for soon my salvation will come,
    and my deliverance be revealed.
[2]Happy is the mortal who does this,
    the one who holds it fast,
who keeps the sabbath, not profaning it,
    and refrains from doing any evil.
[3]Do not let the foreigner joined to the LORD say,
    "The LORD will surely separate me from his people";
and do not let the eunuch say,
    "I am just a dry tree."
[4]For thus says the LORD:
To the eunuchs who keep my sabbaths,
    who choose the things that please me
    and hold fast my covenant,
[5]I will give, in my house and within my walls,
    a monument and a name
    better than sons and daughters;
I will give them an everlasting name
    that shall not be cut off.
[6]And the foreigners who join themselves to the LORD,
    to minister to him, to love the name of the LORD,
    and to be his servants,
all who keep the sabbath, and do not profane it,
    and hold fast my covenant—
[7]these I will bring to my holy mountain,
    and make them joyful in my house of prayer;
their burnt offerings and their sacrifices
    will be accepted on my altar;
for my house shall be called a house of prayer
    for all peoples.

⁸Thus says the Lord God,
    who gathers the outcasts of Israel,
I will gather others to them
    besides those already gathered.

Joel 2:28–29

God's Spirit Poured Out

²⁸Then afterward
    I will pour out my spirit on all flesh;
your sons and your daughters shall prophesy,
    your old men shall dream dreams,
    and your young men shall see visions.
²⁹Even on the male and female slaves,
    in those days, I will pour out my spirit.

Jeremiah 22:13–17

¹³Woe to him who builds his house by unrighteousness,
    and his upper rooms by injustice;
who makes his neighbors work for nothing,
    and does not give them their wages;
¹⁴who says, "I will build myself a spacious house
    with large upper rooms,"
and who cuts out windows for it,
    paneling it with cedar,
    and painting it with vermilion.
¹⁵Are you a king
    because you compete in cedar?
Did not your father eat and drink
    and do justice and righteousness?
    Then it was well with him.
¹⁶He judged the cause of the poor and needy;
    then it was well.
Is not this to know me?
    says the Lord.
¹⁷But your eyes and heart
    are only on your dishonest gain,
for shedding innocent blood,
    and for practicing oppression and violence.

Amos 2:6–7a

Judgment on Israel

[6]Thus says the LORD:
For three transgressions of Israel,
    and for four, I will not revoke the punishment;
because they sell the righteous for silver,
    and the needy for a pair of sandals—
[7]they who trample the head of the poor into the dust of the earth,
    and push the afflicted out of the way;

Psalm 72:1–4

Prayer for Guidance and Support for the King

Of Solomon.

[1]Give the king your justice, O God,
    and your righteousness to a king's son.
[2]May he judge your people with righteousness,
    and your poor with justice.
[3]May the mountains yield prosperity for the people,
    and the hills, in righteousness.
[4]May he defend the cause of the poor of the people,
    give deliverance to the needy,
    and crush the oppressor.

Exodus 15:20–21

The Song of Miriam

[20]Then the prophet Miriam, Aaron's sister, took a tambourine in her hand; and all the women went out after her with tambourines and with dancing. [21]And Miriam sang to them:

"Sing to the LORD, for he has triumphed gloriously;
horse and rider he has thrown into the sea."

2 Kings 22:14

So the priest Hilkiah, Ahikam, Achbor, Shaphan, and Asaiah went to the prophetess Huldah the wife of Shallum son of Tikvah, son of Harhas, keeper of the wardrobe; she resided in Jerusalem in the Second Quarter, where they consulted her.

Notes

1. Readers who may consult the original Hebrew text should note that the verse-numbering system in the Tanakh (Hebrew Bible) and the New Revised Standard Version of the Bible are one verse out of step with each other in the twenty-third chapter of Deuteronomy. Thus, Deuteronomy 23:1 in the English corresponds with 23:2 in the Hebrew, and so on.

2. See previous note.

For All of You Are
One in Christ Jesus?

The New Testament Witnesses on Ethnic, Economic, Social, Religious, Racial, and Gender Inequality

CHRISTOPHER M. HAYS

There is no longer Jew or Greek, there is no longer slave or free, there is no longer male and female; for all of you are one in Christ Jesus. (Gal. 3:28)

Wives, be subject to your husbands as you are to the Lord. . . . Slaves, obey your earthly masters with fear and trembling, in singleness of heart, as you obey Christ. (Eph. 5:22; 6:5)

Jupiter Hammon was the first published Black poet in America. Born into slavery in the household of an aristocratic British family in the American colonies in 1711, he became a preacher, a writer, and a poet.[1] He died in the 1790s in a young country whose Declaration of Independence from Britain states, "We hold these truths to be self-evident, that all men are created equal, that they are endowed by their creator with certain unalienable rights, that among these are life, liberty, and the pursuit of happiness." He remained a slave until the day of his death.

Hammon's writings reveal some of the complexities and contradictions of doing theology as an enslaved Black preacher. Hammon could, on the one hand, affirm the equality of all races and gently call into question the legitimacy of the institution of slavery by, for example, appealing to the account of Cornelius's conversion: "Come my dear fellow servants and brothers, Africans by nations, we are all invited to come, Acts x, 34. Then Peter opened his mouth and said, of a truth I perceive that God is no respecter of persons, verse 35. But in every nation he that feareth him is accepted of him. My brethern [sic], many of us are seeking temporal freedom, and I wish you may obtain it."[2] Nonetheless, at times Hammon would also cite the New Testament to reinforce the submissiveness of African slaves to their white masters. Thus, in one pamphlet Hammon invoked Ephesians 6, writing, "Now whether it is right, and lawful, in the sight of God, for them to make slaves of us or not, I am certain that while we are slaves, it is our duty to obey our masters. . . . The apostle Paul says, 'Servants be obedient to them that are your masters according to the flesh.'"[3]

Modern readers may blanch to hear that Jupiter Hammon used the biblical text not only to console and encourage but also to quiet his fellow slaves. Hammon was, however, reflecting on the Word of God in a particular situation, and out of the same scriptures he spoke on behalf of the equality of slaves and the authority of masters. For these reasons, it would be wise to have Jupiter Hammon in our minds as we explore the New Testament. Composed in a world just as marked by inequality as is the modern one—often directly in response to occasions of division, exclusion, and marginalization—the writings of the New Testament sometimes cast striking visions of human equality and on other occasions make disconcerting concessions to inequality and injustice. These concessions—however prudent they may have been in their historical context—have been used to justify practices that fly in the face of the Christian Scriptures' most egalitarian projections.

This exploration of the New Testament witness on inequality will proceed in two stages. The first stage provides an overview of a fistful of texts that poignantly relate to ethnic, gender, religious, economic, and social inequality—in fashions ranging from inspiring to disquieting.[4] The second stage of this essay identifies several theological concepts that underpin the New Testament teachings on inequality, in hopes that ferreting out (some of) the underlying logic of these texts might help tee up constructive conversation.

The New Testament on Equality and Inequality

I begin the task of describing some of the New Testament texts most pertinent to the various forms of inequality under consideration. Because these passages are among the most disputed paragraphs of the Bible, presenting each of them in a few hundred words is slightly more foolhardy than roller-skating through a lumber mill since concision prohibits me from engaging the sort of circumspect bibliographic safety checks that ensure colleagues are not disgruntled by being omitted from discussion. Thus, I beg the readers' understanding of the selective nature of this survey.

John 4:4–27: The Samaritan Woman at the Well

It seems appropriate to start with a bit of Jesus. In the fourth chapter of the Gospel of John, Jesus's encounter with a Samaritan woman at the well of Jacob thrusts us into topics of ethnicity, religious convictions, and gender. In this exchange, Jesus runs roughshod over a number of the prejudices of his Jewish religious contemporaries, who would have viewed the woman with contempt for reasons of her Samaritan ethnicity, with its attendant religious commitments, as well as her gender (to say nothing of her dubious sexual virtue).[5]

Resentments between the Jews and the Samaritans hearkened back half a millennium, when the Assyrians invaded the Kingdom of Israel and settled colonists in the geographic region that would become Samaria. The unexiled Israelite population interbred with the colonizers (2 Kings 17:23–24), resulting in a race of what later Judeans considered "half breeds."[6] As the centuries passed, that population developed a distinctive set of theological commitments, most notably affirming only the first five books of the Jewish canon, identifying Mount Gerizim as the proper site of ritual sacrifice (rather than Jerusalem), and looking forward to the eschatological arrival of a prophet like Moses (Deut. 18:18–22) called the Taheb.[7]

The ethnic and religious tensions between the Samaritans and Jews are on full display in this passage when Jesus asks for a drink from the woman and she, in surprise, responds, "How is it that you, a Jew, ask a drink of me, a woman of Samaria?" (John 4:9). The Evangelist clarifies, "Jews do not share things in common with Samaritans" (*ou gar sugchraomai Ioudaios Samaritais*). This expression implies that Jesus had disregarded Jewish conventions of ritual purity by asking to share a vessel with a Samaritan woman, given that Samaritan women were considered perpetually impure (or at least perpetually suspect); as one early rabbinic tradition put it, "The daughters of the Samaritans are [deemed unclean as] menstruants from their cradle" (m. Nid. 4:1).[8]

Unflapped by the woman's surprise at his indifference toward typical Jewish ritual sensitivities, Jesus engages her in a theological conversation about true worship. He brushes aside both Samaritan and Jewish preoccupations with worshipping exclusively on their respective mountains and declares the imminent arrival of a time in which "the true worshipers will worship the Father in spirit and truth" (John 4:23). Jesus does not deny that Jews are the proper national conduit for salvation ("for salvation is from the Jews"; v. 22), but he refuses to circumscribe the benefits of that salvation to the Jews. The long and the short of this exchange is that Jesus ultimately identifies himself as the Messiah (vv. 25–26)—likely understood from the Samaritan perspective as the Taheb[9]—and offers eternal life to this unlikely Samaritan woman (v. 14).

As this conversation reaches its theological climax, the disciples show up (having been grocery shopping in town) and are "astonished that [Jesus] was speaking with a woman" (v. 27). This is not indication that Jesus tended to get tongue-tied around girls but rather a reflection of the strong rabbinic sense that it was unseemly for a religious teacher to fraternize with women. Traditions dating as early as the second century BCE say that a sage should "talk not much with womankind. . . . He that talks much with womankind brings evil upon himself and neglects the study of the law and at last will inherit Gehenna" (m. Ab. 1.5).[10] This is not to imply that Jewish men never talked with women but rather that

Jesus's extended private conversation with a Samaritan woman of dubious sexual virtue would have been highly impolitic for a Jewish religious leader like himself.[11]

In brief, this passage reveals that Jesus departed dramatically from the exclusivist Jewish and chauvinistic tendencies of many his contemporaries.[12] He extended the offer of eternal life to hated races and to women and in the process diminished some of the exclusivist features of Jewish theology (although by no means preaching a generic religion disconnected from the history and theological commitments of Israel).

Acts 2: Pentecost and the Birth of the Jerusalem Community

Although Jesus focused his ministry primarily on the Jewish people, the evangelists indicate that a mission to the Gentiles would follow his death (see John 12:20–32; Matt. 28:19; Mark 7:27).[13] This concern comes to the fore in the book of Acts, which narrates the spread of the apostolic message from Jerusalem to Judea and Samaria and on to the Gentiles (Acts 1:8). This expansion is already foreshadowed in Acts 2, when the Holy Spirit fell on the disciples and they spoke in a variety of foreign languages; Luke rehearses the litany of countries from which the witnesses of the event hailed (vv. 9–11), both to underscore the veracity of this conflagration of glossolalia and to indicate that it presaged the proclamation of the gospel among all the nations.

Peter interprets this event for the onlookers. He explains that this outpouring of tongues is the fulfillment of the prophecy of Joel 2:28–32, which looked forward to a time in which God would pour out his Spirit on "all flesh." That prophecy emphasized in particular that people from diverse social classes and both genders would be recipients of God's Spirit: "your sons and your daughters shall prophesy . . . Even upon my slaves, both men and women, in those days will I pour my Spirit" (vv. 17–18).

Acts goes on to narrate how this democratic distribution of the Spirit augured socioeconomic change: in the wake of the mass conversion which ensued that day in Jerusalem, economic sharing and egalitarian social sentiment came to characterize the early Christian community. Luke narrates, "All who believed were together and had all things in common [*hapanta koina*]; they would sell their possessions and goods and distribute the proceeds to all, as any had need" (v. 44–45).

New Testament scholars are agreed that this text, and in particular the phrase *hapanta koina* evokes the practiced of idealized ritual friendship, summarized in the maxim *koina ta filōn* (friends have all things in common).[14] Not to be confused with casual socialization, "ritual friendship" was confined to upper-class members of Hellenistic society. In such relationships, "friends"—while maintaining private property—would engage in forms of hospitality, commensality, and generosity that put their resources at the disposal of their friends, ideally giving expression to their deep personal and moral ties.[15] Of course, this was a recipro-cally beneficial relationship; "friends," being of high social status, were in a posi-tion to repay any favors in the future.[16]

What is remarkable is that Acts 2 narrates how the values of ritualized friend-ship were instantiated across social boundaries in Jerusalem. Although ritual friendship was effectively a horizontal and elite relationship, the Jerusalem Christians brought its ideals to fruition across social classes, between those who were well-off and those who were poor. Believers opened their homes and tables to one another, and the wealthy shared their goods with poor people who would never be able to reciprocate in kind. Thus, Acts unfurls an egalitarian vision of transformed social and economic relationships, as a result of unity in the Holy Spirit being poured out on "all flesh," both men and women and, imminently, on Samaritans and gentiles as well.

Acts 10–11: The Conversion of the First Gentile

Nonetheless, extending the Jewish people's religion to other peoples was no sim-ple matter, especially given that a major portion of Jewish religious practice aimed to underscore precisely that they were not like other nations, by means of strict dietary regulations, calendrical observances, and, in the case of men, the adoption of circumcision. Adjudicating the relevance of such boundary-marking practices was a defining debate of apostolic Christianity since Christianity spread so rapidly among non-Jews. The conversion of Cornelius in Acts 10–11 is therefore a pivotal narrative insofar as Cornelius is the first gentile whose conver-sion to Christianity is narrated in the book. Acts had mentioned proselytes, such as Nicolaus of Antioch (Acts 6:5),[17] who had previously converted to Judaism and thus adopted typical Jewish ritual behavior; but Cornelius is a "God-fearer"[18]—a gentile who was interested in Judaism and in many ways pious and yet was unwilling to adopt the food laws, Sabbath observance, and circumcision that showed Jews to be Jews. For this reason, his conversion is represented as a water-shed moment in the history of Christianity.

When Peter comes to visit Cornelius, he explains that merely crossing Corne-lius's threshold represented a violation of Jewish cultural and ritual piety: "It is unlawful for a Jew to associate with or to visit a Gentile"; but he goes on to say, "God has shown me that I should not call anyone profane or unclean" (Acts 10:28). Thus, Peter imitates Jesus's own willingness to defy religious taboos sep-arating Jews from other ethnicities. He then goes on to declare, quite remarkably, "I truly understand that God shows no partiality, but in every nation anyone who fears him and does what is right is acceptable to him." (vv. 34–35)

On the face of it, this is a ludicrous affirmation; the whole history of Israel is predicated upon the notion that God does have one elect nation. But with this sentence, Peter calls to mind Deuteronomy 10:17, which states, "the Lord your God is God of gods and Lord of lords, the great God, mighty and awesome, who is not partial and takes no bribe, who executes justice for the orphan and the widow, and who loves the strangers, providing them food and clothing."[19]

Deuteronomy 10 denies that God is partial specifically in relation to the perversion of justice on behalf of the rich or the poor. But Peter surmises that God's economic impartiality extends into the ethnic sphere; the same God who is not partial toward rich or poor is also impartial toward Jew or gentile. This exegetical maneuver is probably not unwarranted given that Deuteronomy 10:18 also describes God as one who "loves the strangers/sojourners"—which is to say, the foreigners living amid the Israelites.

On this basis, Peter proclaims the gospel to Cornelius. Peter's bold decision is ratified by God, who sends the Holy Spirit upon Cornelius, just as God had done upon the apostles in chapter 2, thereby confirming that there is indeed no partiality with God. Thus, in Acts 10 ethnic distinctions are overcome in ways that entail the relativization of certain Jewish religious commitments (purity laws and circumcision) without the complete evacuation of the unique historical and theological content of the Christian message (for Peter relates to Cornelius the apostolic kerygma in vv. 36–43).

Galatians 3: All of You Are One in Christ Jesus

Moving along from Jesus and Peter, it is perhaps Paul who makes the most far-reaching statements about equality in the people of God. Nonetheless, the letters ascribed to him also include the New Testament statements that most directly affirm conservative patriarchal hierarchies. In what follows, we will briefly look at both sides of that coin.

On the inclusive side, Galatians 3:26–29 declares emphatically that membership in the Christian community, which entails being "in Christ," effectively overcomes the divisions between Jew and Greek, slave and free, male and female.[20] It is likely that this threefold pairing reflects a subversion of some form of Jewish prayer formula in which the Jewish man thanks God that he was not born a heathen, a brutish man (or in other versions, a slave), or a woman.[21] The Jewish formula may itself be epiphenomenal on a much earlier Greek saying (which can be traced to Thales in the six century BC) that expresses gratitude for being born a human rather than a beast, a man rather than a woman, and a Greek rather than a barbarian (Diogenes Laertius, *Vit. Phil.* 1.33; cf. Plutarch, *Marius* 46.1).[22] Thus, Galatians 3:28 subverts old chauvinisms based on ethnicity, gender, and social class, affirming that even those of "despised" races, gender, and social classes are one in Christ with those whom a given society most privileges.

In the strictest sense, this passage denies any distinction between Jew and Greek, slave and free, male and female, insofar as all are equally children of God, equally Abraham's offspring, equally heirs according to the promise. This does not necessarily and explicitly entail, however, that these distinctions cease to hold any relevance within the community of faith. As we will see, other Pauline texts affirm that within the church and the household, distinct roles still apply. The great hermeneutical question is whether this unity in Christ should suggest progressively greater equality in the future operation of the household and the Christian community. In this vein, Richard Longenecker has argued, "These three couplets also cover in embryonic fashion all the essential relationships of humanity, and so need to be seen as having racial, cultural, and sexual implications as well . . . pointing the way toward a more Christian personal and social ethic."[23]

Romans 14: Dietary and Calendrical Disputes

However significant the conversion of Cornelius may have been, and however strongly Paul insisted that "there is neither Jew nor Greek," the first decades of Christianity continued to be marked by religious disputes over the ritual practices that identified the Jews as the people of God. Paul encounters this issue repeatedly throughout his career, including in Romans 14. In this epistle, Paul confronts a Christian congregation composed of both Jews and gentiles, in which a number of disputes relevant to their different ethnicities had emerged. Chapter 14 specifically responds to a dispute over whether members of the congregation (most likely, Jewish members) should continue to attend to kosher food laws (14:2) and calendrical observances such as the Sabbath and Jewish holidays (14:5).[24] Paul explains that, although he personally has no qualms about eating food traditionally considered unclean by the Jews (v. 14; cf. Mark 7:15), it is vital that this religious dispute be adjudicated in a way that respects the faith of all, ensuring that nobody be pressured to behave in a way that would violate their conscience or, as they understand it, dishonor God (Rom. 14:4–6, 20–23). Likewise, he encourages believers who are not sensitive to these traditional dietary and calendrical observances not to cause any offense to their brother, for "if your brother or sister is being injured by what you eat, you are no longer walking in love" (v. 15). Thus, Paul's counsel to set aside certain Jewish religious practices, for all gentiles and for many Jews, is not taken as a creedal absolute but is itself relativized in the service of fostering harmony between Jewish and gentile believers as well as between Jewish believers with different theological convictions.

Philemon: No Longer as a Slave but as More than a Slave—a Beloved Brother

If the dramatic-sounding elimination of distinctions between Jews and Greeks in Galatians 3 seems to have been somewhat qualified by Romans 14, the same could be said of Paul's teachings on slavery in his letter to Philemon. Paul wrote from prison to a fellow Christian, Philemon, regarding his runaway slave, Onesimus, who had fled his master and sought the intercession of Paul. Paul converted Onesimus during his imprisonment, making Paul his spiritual "father" (v. 10).

Paul explains that, while he was in prison, Onesimus cared for him (vv. 11, 13) and that he very much desires Onesimus to stay with him.[25] Still, Paul recognizes that keeping Onesimus, the slave of his spiritual brother Philemon, with him without the consent of Philemon would be "a breach of Christian fellowship."[26] Therefore, he sends Onesimus back with the request that Philemon not punish Onesimus for his flight but, indeed, voluntarily return Onesimus to Paul to continue to care for him, this time also on Philemon's behalf.

The tricky question of this epistle is whether or not Paul is instructing Philemon to grant Onesimus his freedom. After all, verse 16 indicates that Philemon should receive Onesimus "no longer as a slave but more than a slave, a beloved brother." This phraseology reflects the fact that, upon conversion, Onesimus had become part of the family of Abraham (*à la* the logic of Galatians 3) and therefore Philemon's brother. Nonetheless, his status as a brother does not necessarily entail that he be manumitted; in first-century Christianity one could be considered his master's spiritual brother and legal property. Accordingly, most commentators argue that Paul stops just shy of asking Philemon to free Onesimus, even though manumitting Onesimus would certainly be one way in which Philemon might allow him to return and continue to care for Paul.[27] It is probably most balanced to interpret this text as implying a preference for the freedom of Onesimus, without describing slavery as categorically incompatible with Christian brotherhood.[28] Nonetheless, if Church tradition is right in identifying this slave with the Onesimus who was bishop of Ephesus forty to fifty years later (Ignatius, *Eph.* 1:4), it may just be that this little epistle made it into the Pauline letter collection precisely because one early bishop treasured it as, effectively, the document that secured his own manumission.[29]

Ephesians 5–6: Reaffirming the Subordination of Wives and Slaves to Husbands and Masters

It might be too strong to say that in Romans 14 and in Philemon Paul is backpedaling in relation to the subjects of ethnicity and slavery. But in the disputed Pauline epistles, some have thought Paul's direction of argumentation to have been completely reversed.

In Ephesians 5 and 6, for example, one encounters one of the Pauline household codes or Haustafeln, in which the author lays out his vision of the relational dynamics of a properly functioning Christian household.[30] Here many have perceived a dramatic reversal of the social vision of Galatians 3 (which is just one reason why some have argued that Paul was not in fact the author of Ephesians). Although Ephesians 5:21 indicates that, speaking generally, interpersonal Christian relations should be characterized by mutual submission, the ensuing household code qualifies that sentiment, describing relationships of mutual obligation in which the submission is unidirectional.[31]

The first of these relationships is that between husband and wife, in which wives are told to be subject to their husband "as you are to the Lord" (v. 22), in everything (*en panti*), just as "Christ is the head of the church" (v. 23), for the husband is the head (*kephalé*) of the wife just as Christ is the head of the church (v. 22).[32] Traditional commentators emphasize that "Paul viewed the wives as equal to the husbands qualitatively, even though subordinate with regard to lines of authority."[33] According to this logic, Ephesians 5 is not seen as a contradiction of Galatians 3; rather, Galatians 3 is read as making a case for equal access to salvation without entailing functional or structural egalitarianism in the church or in families. Grasping the nettle more firmly, Elisabeth Schüssler Fiorenza has argued, "The instruction to the wives clearly reinforces the patriarchal marriage patterns and justifies it christologically."[34]

Ephesians goes on to instruct slaves to "obey your earthly masters with fear and trembling, in singleness of heart, as you obey Christ" (6:5). As in the case of marriage relationships, the subordination of slaves to masters is characterized in potent theological terms, as a reflection of the subordination the Christian has to the Lord Jesus. Ephesians emphasizes that slaves should obey "with fear and trembling[35] . . . as slaves of Christ, doing the will of God [*ek psuché*] from the heart" (6:5, 6). At least within the Pauline canon, therefore, the fact that in Christ there is no male or female, slave or free, does not mean that in the household such distinctions become irrelevant. In the household, one remains a slave to one's master just as one is a slave to Christ; the subject of one's husband just as one is a subject of Christ.

It is notoriously difficult to analyze this text in an evenhanded fashion. Certain commentators decry the patriarchalism of these texts as a betrayal of the principles on display in Galatians 3. Others who do not consider the ancient household codes normative for the Christian family or church in twenty-first-century Western society argue that the text does not endorse the subordination of the woman to the husband but contend that the husband should be mutually subordinated to the wife (*à la* 5:21).[36] This is, in my opinion, not the most candid reading of the text as a historical document since the epistle does reaffirm the other fundamental hierarchies of the ancient household: father over child and master over slave.

This is not to say that this epistle simply recapitulates typical Greco-Roman household structures or morality. Such a reading dramatically fails to appreciate the countercultural force of telling husbands to love their wives "just as Christ loved the church and gave himself up for her. . . . husbands should love their wives as they do their own bodies. . . . Each of you, however, should love his wife as himself" (Eph. 5:25, 28, 33). In a society in which women were viewed as intrinsically inferior to men, in which husbands often ignored, denigrated, abused, and cheated on their wives (lamentably, such practices were not limited to the first century) without considering such behavior to be morally deficient, the vision that a husband should imitate Christ by sacrificing himself for her is a dramatic advance on dominant Greco-Roman morality.[37]

Similarly, Ephesians 6 follows up the imperatives to slaves by saying "masters, do the same to them" (v. 9). This implies that masters should treat their slaves in such a manner that remembers that God is master of all, and that they will one day receive their recompense from that judge with whom "there is no partiality" (v. 9). While this may fall short of an egalitarianism that modern readers consider the logical outworking of Galatians 3, it is certainly an improvement upon popular Greco-Roman morality.

For this reason, Gerd Theissen (adopting language from Ernst Troeltsch) famously referred to the morality of the Deutero-Pauline and Pastoral Epistles as *Liebespatriarchalismus*, "love-patriarchalism." "This love-patriarchalism [*Liebespatriarchalismus*] takes social differences as a given, but it softens them through the requirement of concern for others and of love, a requirement which is applied specifically to the one who is socially stronger, while submission, loyalty and respect are asked of the one who is socially weaker."[38] Theissen avers that, even though this love-patriarchalism was nowhere near as radical as the sort of fraternal equality that marked the earlier and supposedly more socially homogenous Christian groups, within the more socially stratified Pauline communities, this love-patriarchalism offered a "realistic" and durable way to express Christian brotherhood.[39]

1 Timothy 2: I Permit No Woman to Have Authority over a Man

If one can at least identify in Ephesians 5–6 a significant advance on Greco-Roman popular morality as it relates to women and slaves (if not an ideal realization of Galatians 3:28), it is rather more difficult to make the same case for 1 Timothy 2:8–15 (a letter putatively from Paul to Timothy, the leader of the church in Ephesus), which sharply adjures, "Let a woman learn in silence with full submission [*en pasé hupotagé*]. I permit no woman to teach or to have authority over a man; she is to keep silent" (vv. 11–12). This text seems to break significantly with, for example, Romans 16:7, which praises the woman Junia as prominent among the apostles and recognizes that the woman Prisca was the leader of a house church (we also know from Acts 18:26 that she was a teacher of Apollos, a subsequent leader of the church in Ephesus).

This passage is a hotbed of interpretive controversy. Interpreters have scrambled to identify a situation in the ancient Ephesian community that would explain why the author would utter prohibitions which seem out of step with Pauline teaching in other epistles. Without rehearsing the long litany of suggestions that have been proffered, various extenuating circumstances in Ephesus may have contributed to these instructions.[40] The author may be responding in part to Christian women being caught up with a controversial new social tendency in which upper-class women defied dominant social mores of modesty, encouraged abortion and/or infanticide, and disparaged traditional female roles as wives and mothers. If Christian women in Ephesus were adopting these values, they may well have brought disrepute upon the still fragile Christian movement, contributing to the already common perception that Christians disrupt the order and stability of society.[41]

Additionally, it appears that false doctrine was being propagated in Ephesus (see 1 Tim. 6:3–10) and that the women in the Christian community—who were considered more susceptible to being led astray, given the low levels of education for women that prevailed in that cultural context—were not only being convinced by these false teachers but were also disrupting the church gatherings to advocate for these perspectives.[42] The combination of these social and doctrinal factors may explain why the author, in that circumstance, forbade those women from speaking in the congregation and instructed them to abandon their scandalous behavior, to accept instruction in proper doctrine, and to affirm the goodness of traditional femininity and the value of the family.[43]

One of the goals of reconstructing the circumstances in Ephesus that precipitated this prohibition of women teaching and wielding authority is that such reconstructions allow modern interpreters to circumscribe the applicability of 1 Timothy 2 to situations similar to those allegedly in play in Ephesus instead of construing it as normative for all women everywhere. While I do emphatically reject the belief that women are somehow less fit to teach or exercise authority in the church or society, it is nonetheless worth clarifying that the argument being made in 1 Timothy 2 is not entirely susceptible to an "occasional" interpretation. The author grounds his prohibitions of women teaching and exercising authority in Genesis 1–3. A woman should not teach or have authority but remain silent, he explains, "for [gar] Adam was formed first, then Eve; and Adam was not deceived, but the woman was deceived and became a transgressor" (1 Tim. 2:13–14).

The argument here is twofold. In the first place, the author appeals to something akin to primogeniture, the notion that a child who is born first is worthy of special authority; accordingly, the fact that Adam is created first is taken to imply that God wills that men should exercise authority over women. In the second place, Eve's deception by the serpent is taken to be prototypical of a female susceptibility to being deceived, which in turn is adduced as another reason why women should not teach or have authority over men.[44] I hasten to add that I think this is a bad line of argumentation; primogeniture is frequently undermined within the Old Testament canon and, if Eve is prototypical of deception, Adam therefore is prototypical of willful rebellion (hardly a trait that commends men as capable leaders).[45] Still, I am convinced that this is the most plausible account of the argument in 1 Timothy 2, however much it flies in the face of my own perspective and, indeed, even of other Pauline texts.

With this I will draw to a close this entirely too long and entirely too short overview of New Testament texts on inequality. Certain passages cast a vision of dramatic ethnic, gender, and socioeconomic equality (John 4; Acts 2 and 10;

Gal. 3), while others (Rom. 14, Philem.) pull their punches a bit, and some even reinforce gender and social inequality (Eph. 5–6; 1 Tim. 2). On the topic of religious equality, the New Testament texts do relativize certain religious and ritual practices (circumcision, food laws, calendrical observances, approved locations of temple worship, etc.), but they do not abandon all notion of historical particularity or theological exclusivism in relation to other religions (John 4; Acts 10).

The next challenge is to ask *why* the New Testament authors came to these conclusions. To do so, I will briefly lay out some of the underlying logical convictions apparently at play in the egalitarian (or nonegalitarian) movements on display in the New Testament.

The Underlying Logic of Equality and Inequality in the New Testament

Without proposing a prescriptive scheme for how to promulgate a Christian vision of equality based on the New Testament, it may be helpful to lay out some of the motivations and deep theological concepts that animate the early Christian movement toward greater or lesser degrees of equality and which may prove relevant in thinking about inequality in the twenty-first century. The following five concepts are by no means exhaustive nor even necessarily are they all endorsed by the present author, but they are important in the passages under consideration and therefore merit some explicit comment.

Love of Neighbor

Arguably the most important ethical principle of Christianity is the notion that one ought to love one's neighbor as oneself. This idea occurs repeatedly in the Gospels, being Jesus's second answer to the question, "Which commandment in the law is the greatest?" (Matt. 22:34–40; cf. Mark 12:28–34); the first commandment is said to be love of God with all one's heart, soul, mind, and strength (Deut. 6:5). Luke's Gospel actually combines the commandment to love God with the commandment to love one's neighbor as oneself (Luke 10:27), using a single imperative verb (*agapéseis*) to govern two different objects (God and neighbor), ostensibly because Luke perceives love of God to be inconceivable without a corresponding love of neighbor. Luke's Jesus then goes on to elaborate precisely what it means to love one's neighbor by telling the parable of the Good Samaritan,[46] a parable relevant to the topic of inequality insofar as it rejects the supposition that Jews are morally superior to Samaritans.

The command to love one's neighbor as oneself, originally issued in Leviticus 19:18, reemerges repeatedly in the New Testament (James 2:8; Rom. 13:9–10; Gal. 5:14), and even Paul and James agree that "the whole law is summed up in [that] single commandment" (Gal. 5:14; cf. James 2:8). We saw this consideration invoked in Romans 14:15 in the context of adjudicating theological-practical dispute over dietary and calendrical observations. Given that the New Testament authors identified love of neighbor as central to Christianity, and given that it takes very little theological imagination to see how the principle would be applicable to other dynamics of inequality, it certainly merits careful attention.[47]

Imitation of Christ's Self-Sacrifice

A second, key lens for New Testament ethics is the notion of *imitatio Christi*, the imitation of Christ, specifically with regard to his self-sacrificial death. Jesus himself exhorts his disciples, "whoever does not carry the cross and follow me cannot be my disciple" (Luke 14:27; cf. 9:23). Paul likewise enjoins the Philippian church, "let the same mind be in you that was in Christ Jesus. . . . He humbled himself and became obedient to the point of death—even death on a cross" (Phil. 2:5, 8).

The New Testament authors apply the notion of *imitatio Christi* to both ethnic and gender inequality. John connects Jesus's self-sacrificial death with the integration of gentiles into the people of God (John 10:14–16; 12:20–23, 32). The connection is at very least chronological (indicating that the gentiles are not as a population incorporated into the people of God until after the death and resurrection of Jesus). But atonement theology also indicates that the sacrifice of Christ is sufficient to forgive the sins of Jews and gentiles alike, and by that token it renders superfluous the temple cult and various other purity regulations traditionally considered necessary to facilitate access to the house of God (Eph. 2:11–22; cf. Heb. 9–10). In relation to gender, Ephesians 5:25–26 construes Christ's sacrifice for the church as exemplary of the ways husbands are to love their wives. This categorically rules out any sort of domineering or abusive male leadership in a marriage, even if the analogy does reinforce a matrimonial hierarchy.

Additionally, 2 Corinthians 8 applies the theme of imitation of Christ specifically to matters of economic inequality, as Paul asks the Christians in the city of Corinth to provide financial aid to impoverished believers in Jerusalem. In an argumentative one-two punch, Paul first tells the (relatively well-off) members of the Corinthian congregation about the generosity of the extremely indigent Christians in Macedonia, who gave according to and even beyond their own means, veritably begging Paul for the privilege to contribute to the needs of the saints in Jerusalem (2 Cor. 8:2–5). He follows this parenetic jab up with a rhetorical right-hook, contrasting the generosity of the poor Macedonians with the self-sacrifice of Jesus, who, "though he was rich [in his celestial, preexistent state], yet for your sakes he became poor, so that by his poverty you might become rich" (2 Cor. 8:9). Thus, the sacrifice of Christ in becoming a poor peasant and itinerant preacher (Luke 9:58; cf. 2:23–24, in light of Lev. 12:8) is used as an example to the Christians in Corinth. They should imitate Jesus's example and relieve the penury of their brothers in Jerusalem by means of their own abundance. This is, interestingly, the only place in the New Testament where we find a noun that could be translated "equality" (2 Cor. 8:13–14). Using the word *isotés* (translated "fair balance" in the NRSV), Paul exhorts the Corinthians, through their generosity, to bring about financial equality "between your present abundance and their need" (2 Cor. 8:13–14).[48]

Paul applies Christ's self-sacrifice to the topic of economic inequality, but Jesus's example could readily be made paradigmatic for any number of other moral issues. As Ralph Martin puts it, "Paul's time-bound insight has far-reaching ramifications for our world so tragically divided into privileged—at economic, social, cultural, and educational levels—and disadvantaged."[49]

Family

A third concept with far-reaching ramifications for the topic of inequality is the affirmation that all believers are part of the family of God or the family of Abraham. These terms are used somewhat interchangeably in Galatians 3:26–29, as Paul explains that those who are "in Christ Jesus" are also "children of God" (Gal. 3:26), since Jesus is the Son of God par excellence. Furthermore, insofar as Christ is the seed of Abraham (cf. Gal. 3:16), those who are in Christ Jesus are also part of the family of Abraham (Gal. 3:29). It is on this basis that Paul makes his claim that in Christ there is no longer Jew or Greek, slave or free, male or female, precisely because all are equally members of the family of God (Gal. 3:28).

The same logic is worked out further when Paul makes his appeal to Philemon on behalf of the slave Onesimus. Paul explains that, because of Onesimus's conversion, the slave has become Philemon's "beloved brother" (*adelphos agapeton*) (Philem. 16); Paul indicates that this theological truth ought to change the way in which the master sees his slave. So also, when warning against divisions within the Roman church over matters of religious convictions, Paul instructs the Romans not to "do anything that makes your brother or sister [*adelphos*] stumble" (Rom. 14:21).

In a similar vein, Jesus describes his followers as his true family; in contradistinction to his biological family, Jesus avers, "whoever does the will of my Father in heaven is my brother and sister and mother" (Matt. 12:50). He clarifies that the pursuit of the Kingdom of God entails that one must "hate father and mother, wife and children, brothers and sisters, yes, and even life itself" (Luke 14:26), precisely because of the thoroughgoing nature of one's commitment to the Kingdom and imitation of the suffering Messiah.[50] But if the concept of the family of God entails a relativization of one's obligations to one's biological family, that same logic benefits the gentiles, whose lack of consanguinity with the Jews ceases to be an obstacle to their equal incorporation in the family of God.

The Impartiality of God

The affirmation that all nations can be children of God is related to the belief in divine impartiality. As already seen in Acts 10:34, Peter appealed to the impartiality of God[51]—the notion derived from Deuteronomy 10:18 and other places—to help explain his decision to proclaim the gospel to Cornelius, a gentile. Paul makes a similar argument in regard to Jew-gentile relations in Romans 2:11 (similarly, see 1 Pet. 1:17) and applies the same sentiment to church hierarchies in Galatians 2:6. Additionally, Ephesians 6:9 warns masters to treat their slaves justly, invoking the fact that they and their slaves have a single master in heaven "and with him there is no partiality." Since the New Testament explores the concept of God's impartiality with relation to matters of ethnicity and slavery, and the Old Testament applies divine impartiality to economic matters, we may also find that the concept has traction in relation to topics such as gender or religion as well.

The Created Order

In the interest of being honest about some of the stickier bits of the New Testament, I present a final argument which underlies some of the teachings on inequality in the New Testament, even if this approach will strike many interpreters as, in varying degrees, problematic. The argument in question is the appeal to the created order, or the events described in the creation narrative of Genesis 1–3. As sketched above, 1 Timothy 2:11–15 appeals to the account of Genesis 2:7–24, invoking the sequence in which male and female were created as expressing something of the normative will of God for the subordination of women to men. The fall narrative of Genesis 3:1–19 is also cited as prototypical and representative of women's vulnerability to deception, which is itself adduced as evidence that they are unfit to lead or teach men.[52]

I have already indicated some of the reasons why the argumentation of this passage is problematic (without explicitly broaching my skepticism about the historical referentiality of the text), and it certainly bears discussing whether an unsatisfying application of this sort of argument should give us pause as to whether or not it continues to have contemporary, prescriptive potential for reflections on inequality. Nonetheless, it is also worth noting that a similar line of argumentation is invoked in Ephesians 5:28–31, in which the author instructs husbands to "love their wives as they do their own bodies," on the grounds that husband and wife are in fact one flesh, an argument he bases on a citation of Genesis 2:24. Here an argument for a more egalitarian treatment of women and men within a marriage relationship (and I say "more egalitarian" because Ephesians 5 does not endorse a fully egalitarian conception of marriage) is based on an argument from the created order in Genesis 2, working somewhat in the opposite direction as the appeal to the created order in 1 Timothy 2.

Conclusion

Having completed our survey, can we now conclude that the New Testament is a prophetic voice against inequality? On occasions such as these, it seems prudent to recur to the German word *Jein*—a mixture of *ja*, yes, and *nein*, no. With respect to subjects of ethnicity and nationality, the New Testament does indeed arrive at a full-throated endorsement of the equality of Jew, Samaritan, and gentile; however much God may have used the nation of Israel to bring the gospel and salvation to the nations, all nations are equally incorporated into the people of God through the Messiah, Jesus. National and ethnic distinctions are not erased, but all are embraced as part of the people of God.

Initially, one might feel similarly enthusiastic about the witness of the New Testament regarding economic and social equality, as the texts of Acts 2 and 4 and of 2 Corinthians 8 lay out a stirring vision of sacrificial Christian sharing in which the rich voluntarily donate their property in order to provide for the needs of the poor, sharing lives and tables together. But one is pulled up short when one reflects on the persistence of slavery in the early Christian community; how can we say that the church abandoned economic exploitation when rich Christians continued to benefit from the labor of their enslaved brethren? Similarly, with relation to gender, Paul may have declared enthusiastically that in Christ there was neither male nor female, and women such as Junia and Priscilla may have been teachers and apostles, but some epistles also endorse the subordination of women to men in the home and in the church.

When it comes to creedal matters, John 4, Acts 10–11, and Romans 14 bespeak the significant relativization of historically vital religious boundary markers between Jews and Samaritans, and Jews and gentiles (e.g., the proper place of worship, dietary laws, circumcision, holy days); these texts affirm that all people are equally acceptable to God, who is impartial. But this notion hardly entails the evacuation of all particularism since the New Testament texts emphatically insist on monotheism and on the kerygmatic particulars of Jesus's life, death, and resurrection as key criteria for religious orthodoxy and acceptance by God.

On the one hand, then, the New Testament has, within its own cultural context, a dramatic and far-ranging witness on matters of inequality. On the other hand, I would emphasize that the New Testament writings are occasional texts. I do not think they should be considered writings that pretend to crystallize the final and absolute expression of God's will for all times and place. In any scenario, they certainly do not advocate for an unalloyed sort of equality in the diverse facets of human life under examination in this book.[53] Perhaps, then, as we discuss these texts, we can do so with something of the same sensitivity with which we would read the poetry of Jupiter Hammon,[54] whose heart stretched longingly toward a future of greater equality, even as his vision, exegesis, and imagination were somewhat circumscribed by his own historical horizon.

Perhaps he would have applied to himself, and to us, the same counsel he gave to the young slave woman, Phillis Wheatley, who would later come to outstrip him as a poet:

Come you, Phillis, now aspire,
And seek the living God,
So step by step thous [*sic*] mayst go higher,
Till perfect in the word.[55]

Notes

1. Sondra O'Neale, "Jupiter Hammon and His Works: A Discussion of the First Black Preacher to Publish Poems, Sermons and Essays in America," *Journal of the Interdenominational Theological Center* 9 (1982): 100–103.

2. Jupiter Hammon, *America's First Negro Poet: The Complete Works of Jupiter Hammon*, Empire State Historical Publications Series 82 (Port Washington, NY: Kennikat, 1970), 73.

3. Jupiter Hammon, *An Address to the Negroes in the State of New-York* (New York: Carroll and Patterson, 1787), 7.

4. As will become abundantly apparent, the discrete topics of inequality under consideration in this Building Bridges conference are entangled in the New Testament texts, and I make no effort to comb the knots out of the intertwined scriptural teachings on these topics for fear that doing so in such a short space would ultimately distort the scriptural witness. Additionally, while I recognize the importance in contemporary conversation of distinguishing between racial, ethnic, and national forms of inequality, I do not consider these categories to be emic to the New Testament; so on the present piece I move with a certain naïveté between speaking of these distinct but interrelated forms of inequality. Likewise, I do appreciate that economic inequality and social class are distinct phenomena, but they are closely enough connected in the New Testament that the effort required to treat them separately in such a brief piece would not be proportional to the benefit yielded.

5. See the circumspect treatment of Craig S. Keener, *The Gospel of John: A Commentary* (Grand Rapids, MI: Baker, 2003), 605–8, 622.

6. This is the colorful phrase of D. A. Carson, *The Gospel according to John*, The Pillar New Testament Commentary (Leicester: Inter-Varsity Press, 1991), 216. See, further, Bruce J. Malina and Richard L. Rohrbaugh, *Social-Science Commentary on the Gospel of John* (Minneapolis: Fortress, 1998), 98.

7. For an overview of Samaritan history and theology, see H. G. M. Williamson and T. Kartveit, "Samaritans," in *Dictionary of Jesus and the Gospels*, ed. Joel B. Green, Jeannine K. Brown, and Nicholas Perrin, IVP Bible Dictionary Series (Downers Grove, IL: IVP Academic, 2013), 832–36.

8. See Malina and Rohrbaugh, *Social-Science Commentary on the Gospel of John*, 98–99; Keener, *Gospel of John*, 598, 600; and Carson, *Gospel according to John*, 218.

9. Francis J. Moloney, *El Evangelio de Juan*, trans. José Pérez Escobar (Estella, Spain: Verbo divino, 2005), 155; and Keener, *Gospel of John*, 619–20.

10. Wrapped up in this tradition are both the assumptions that religious teaching was a male affair in Judaism and a broader supposition that it was suspicious for men and women to be left alone together.

11. See further Malina and Rohrbaugh, *Social-Science Commentary on the Gospel of John*, 100–101; and Keener, *Gospel of John*, 594–97, 621–22.

12. In fact, the New Testament makes so many statements in favor of gentiles and criticizes so many errors of Christian Jews and non-Christian Jewish leaders (see, e.g., Matt. 23:31–33; John 8:37–39, 44–47; 1 Thess. 2:14–16; Rev. 2:9; 3:9) that some later readers have found justification for anti-Semitism in the New Testament. Obviously, using the New Testament for anti-Semitic purposes grossly abuses the text, given that most of the New Testament authors were themselves Jews, that Jesus was Jewish and was identified as the Jewish Messiah, and that the logic of the acceptance of the gentiles depends on them being incorporated in the family of Abraham. See discussion of Galatians 3:26–29, in the section headed "Galatians 3: All of You are One in Christ Jesus."

13. See, e.g., Mark 10:5–6; the gospels narrate only a small handful of interactions with gentiles.

14. Diogenes, *Laertius* 8.10; 10.11; Plato, *Resp.* 424A; 449C; *Leg.* 739C; and Aristotle, *Eth. nic.* 8.9.1, 1159b31–32.

15. Aristotle described the like-mindedness of friends by saying that friends were "one soul living in two bodies" (Diogenes, *Laertius* 5.20; and Aristotle, *Eth. nic.* 9.8.2, 1168b8). Luke alludes to that same proverb in Acts 4:32: "The whole group of those who believed were of one heart and soul [*kardia kai psuché mia*]."

16. For a detailed analysis, see Christopher M. Hays, *Luke's Wealth Ethics: A Study in Their Coherence and Character*, Wissenschaftliche Untersuchungen zum Neuen Testament II, vol. 275 (Tübingen: Mohr Siebeck, 2010), 201–9.

17. He was identified by Irenaeus (*Haer.* 1.26.3) as the founder of the Nicolaitan sect decried in Revelation 2:6, 15; Eckhard J. Schnabel, *Acts*, Zondervan Exegetical Commentary on the New Testament (Grand Rapids, MI: Zondervan, 2012), 334.

18. Irina A. Levinskaya, *The Book of Acts in Its Diaspora Setting*, vol. 5, *The Book of Acts in Its First Century Setting* (Grand Rapids, MI: Eerdmans, 1996), 121.

19. Psalm 82:1–14 invokes God's putative impartiality to ask when God will give justice to the needy and the vulnerable; Job 34:19 affirms that God has no partiality toward the rich as opposed to the poor; and 2 Chronicles 19:7 warns against the perversion of justice by judges, on the basis of God's impartiality. See Craig S. Keener, *Acts: An Exegetical Commentary*, 4 vols. (Grand Rapids, MI: Baker Academic, 2012–2015), 2:1796–97.

20. These same categories are evoked again in 1 Corinthians 7, in which context Paul encourages all to remain in the same status in which they existed upon conversion. A similar phraseology occurs in Colossians 3:11 as well.

21. This form of the prayer can certainly be traced as early as 150 CE (*t. Ber.* 7:18; *b. Men.* 43b), but may well go back further.

22. See *Theological Dictionary of the New Testament* [*TDNT*], edited by G. Kittel and G. Friedrich, translated by G. W. Bromiley, 10 vols (Grand Rapids, MI: Eerdmans,

1964–1976), 1:777; Richard N. Longenecker, *Galatians* Word Biblical Commentary 41 (Dallas: Word Books, 1998), 157; and F. F. Bruce, *The Epistle to the Galatians: A Commentary on the Greek Text*, New International Greek Testament Commentary (Grand Rapids, MI: Eerdmans, 1982), 187–88.

23. Longenecker, *Galatians*, 157.

24. Judaism obviously did not enjoin vegetarianism, but because of the strict regulations surrounding the Jewish diet, it was not uncommon for Jews living in the Diaspora simply to eschew meat altogether (Dan. 1:16; 2 Macc. 5:27; Josephus, *Vita* 14). These sensitivities, in the context of Romans 14, probably overlap with the preoccupation witnessed in 1 Corinthians 10 that the meat for sale in the market may have been sacrificed to a pagan deity, according to which some might fear that eating it would imply partaking unwittingly in a pagan cultic meal. Likewise, the concern about wine, mentioned in v. 21, may evince a related concern that the wine on sale may have been offered as a libation to a pagan deity; James D. G. Dunn, *Romans 9–16* Word Biblical Commentary 38B (Dallas: Word Books, 1998), 827. On Sabbath and Jewish holidays, see, e.g., Dunn, *Romans 9–16*, 799–802, 805, 810–11; and Douglas J. Moo, *The Epistle to the Romans*, New International Commentary on the New Testament (Grand Rapids, MI: Eerdmans, 1996).

25. Prisoners in this period were not cared for by the jailers but depended on friends from the outside to provide for their needs.

26. Peter T. O'Brien, *Colossians and Philemon* Word Biblical Commentary 44 (Waco, TX: Word Books, 1982), 294.

27. So, e.g., Markus Barth and Helmut Blanke, *The Letter to Philemon: A New Translation with Notes and Commentary*, Eerdmans Critical Commentary (Grand Rapids, MI: Eerdmans, 2000), 368–69, 411–22, 492; O'Brien, *Colossians and Philemon*, 302–3. *Pace*, e.g., Risto Saarinen, *The Pastoral Epistles with Philemon and Jude*, Brazos Theological Commentary on the Bible (Grand Rapids, MI: Brazos, 2008), 207–8.

28. Dennis Hamm, *Philippians, Colossians, Philemon*, Catholic Commentary on Sacred Scripture (Grand Rapids, MI: Baker Academic, 2013), 54–56.

29. O'Brien, *Colossians and Philemon*, 268; cf. Barth and Blanke, *Letter to Philemon*, 141; and Bruce, *Epistle to the Galatians*, 189.

30. Bear in mind that the first-century household included not only one's immediate or extended biological family members but also one's slaves, freedpersons, and even select clients.

31. Harold W. Hoehner, *Ephesians: An Exegetical Commentary* (Grand Rapids, MI: Baker Academic, 2002), 732.

32. While *kephalé* has been the subject of much lexical debate, in this context the term seems to denote a relationship of authority. For detailed discussion, see Wayne A. Grudem, "Does kephalē ('Head') Mean 'Source' or 'Authority over' in Greek Literature: A Survey of 2,336 Examples," *Trinity Journal* 6, no. 1 (1985): 38–59; and Wayne A. Grudem, "The Meaning of κεφαλη ('Head'): An Evaluation of New Evidence, Real and Alleged," *Journal of the Evangelical Theological Society* 44, no. 1 (2001): 25–65.

33. Hoehner, *Ephesians*, 735–36.

34. Elisabeth Schüssler Fiorenza, *In Memory of Her: A Feminist Theological Reconstruction of Christian Origins* (London: SCM Press, 1983), 269.

35. A phrase used to describe the relationship of animals to humans in Genesis 9:2, although Paul uses it more softly in 1 Corinthians 2:3; 2 Corinthians 7:15; Philippians 2:12.

36. See, e.g., Craig S. Keener, *Paul, Women and Wives: Marriage and Women's Ministry in the Letters of Paul* (Peabody, MA: Hendrickson, 1992), 168–72.

37. For more on women's roles in marriage, see Craig S. Keener, "Marriage," in *Dictionary of New Testament Background*, ed. Craig A. Evans and Stanley E. Porter (Downers Grove, IL: IVP Academic, 2000), 679–93.

38. My translation of Gerd Theissen, *Studien zur Soziologie des Urchristentums*, 3rd ed., Wissenschaftliche Untersuchungen zum Neuen Testament 19 (Tübingen: Mohr Siebeck, 1989), 268–69.

39. Theissen, *Soziologie des Urchristentums*, 269.

40. For reasonable surveys of interpretive opinions, see, e.g., I. Howard Marshall, *A Critical and Exegetical Commentary on the Pastoral Epistles*, International Critical Commentary (Edinburgh: T&T Clark, 1999), 452–67; and Philip H. Towner, *The Letters to Timothy and Titus*, New International Commentary on the New Testament (Grand Rapids, MI: Eerdmans, 2006).

41. Bruce W. Winter, *Roman Wives, Roman Widows: The Appearance of New Women and the Pauline Communities* (Grand Rapids, MI: Eerdmans, 2003), 97–122.

42. Keener, *Paul, Women and Wives*, 109–13.

43. See, e.g., George T. Montague, *First and Second Timothy, Titus*, Catholic Commentary on Sacred Scripture (Grand Rapids, MI: Baker Academic, 2008), 69; and Towner, *Letters to Timothy and Titus*, 234–35.

44. Cf. George W. Knight, *The Pastoral Epistles: A Commentary on the Greek Text*, New International Greek Testament Commentary (Grand Rapids, MI: Eerdmans, 1992), 143–44; Saarinen, *Pastoral Epistles with Philemon and Jude*, 57; and William D. Mounce, *Pastoral Epistles*, Word Biblical Commentary 46 (Dallas: Word Book, 2000), 131–42, 146, 148.

45. Genesis describes the selection of Isaac over Ishmael, Jacob over Esau, and Joseph over his ten older brothers; David and Solomon are selected as kings instead of numerous elder brothers.

46. For more complete discussion, see Hays, *Luke's Wealth Ethics*, 117–19.

47. Similar sentiments can be identified in non-Christian Jewish writings; see, e.g., *The Testament of Issachar*, 5.2; and Hays, *Luke's Wealth Ethics*, 117–18n52.

48. And in the present context, it most likely does imply some sort of general financial equality that goes beyond the rather vague term "fairness"; see further the discussion in *TDNT*, 3:343, 348; C. Spicq, *Theological Lexicon of the New Testament*, trans. and ed. J. D. Ernest (Peabody, MA: Hendrickson, 1994), 2:226, 230.

49. Ralph P. Martin, *2 Corinthians*, Word Biblical Commentary 40 (Waco, TX: Word Books, 1986), 268.

50. For further detail, see Christopher M. Hays, "Hating Wealth and Wives? An Examination of Discipleship Ethics in the Third Gospel," *Tyndale Bulletin* 60, no. 1 (2009): 47–68; and the extensive treatment of Stephen Barton, *Discipleship and Family Ties in Mark and Matthew*, Society for New Testament Studies Monograph Series 80 (Cambridge: Cambridge University Press, 1994).

51. Christ is also described as impartial in Colossians 3:25 and (in a manipulative fashion) in Matthew 22:16, Mark 12:14, and Luke 20:21.

52. In that same text the woman is also told "your desire shall be for your husband, and he shall rule over you" (Gen. 3:16).

53. This means, in turn, that we would do well to ask whether the equality is, in all topics, a litmus test for truth, holiness, and goodness. At present, this strikes me as a dubious supposition.

54. This is not to imply that the Christian canon is still open or that Hammon was divinely inspired, of course. The point is only that both Hammon's writings and the canonical writings are historically situated and that their ethical vision should be analyzed accordingly.

55. "An Address to Miss Phillis Wheatley," in Hammon, *America's First Negro Poet*, 50.

New Testament Texts for Dialogue on Inequalities

Some passages include a subheading. These are not part of the original Greek text. Rather, they are provided by the NRSV editors and have been retained here as some readers may find them useful.

Luke 10:25–37

The Parable of the Good Samaritan

[25]Just then a lawyer stood up to test Jesus. "Teacher," he said, "what must I do to inherit eternal life?" [26]He said to him, "What is written in the law? What do you read there?"[27]He answered, "You shall love the Lord your God with all your heart, and with all your soul, and with all your strength, and with all your mind; and your neighbor as yourself."[28]And he said to him, "You have given the right answer; do this, and you will live."

[29]But wanting to justify himself, he asked Jesus, "And who is my neighbor?" [30]Jesus replied, "A man was going down from Jerusalem to Jericho, and fell into the hands of robbers, who stripped him, beat him, and went away, leaving him half dead. [31]Now by chance a priest was going down that road; and when he saw him, he passed by on the other side. [32]So likewise a Levite, when he came to the place and saw him, passed by on the other side. [33]But a Samaritan while traveling came near him; and when he saw him, he was moved with pity. [34]He went to him and bandaged his wounds, having poured oil and wine on them. Then he put him on his own animal, brought him to an inn, and took care of him. [35]The next day he took out two denarii, gave them to the innkeeper, and said, 'Take care of him; and when I come back, I will repay you whatever more you spend.' [36]Which of these three, do you think, was a neighbor to the man who fell into the hands of

the robbers?" [37]He said, "The one who showed him mercy." Jesus said to him, "Go and do likewise."

Luke 14:25–27, 33

The Cost of Discipleship

[25]Now large crowds were traveling with him; and he turned and said to them, [26]"Whoever comes to me and does not hate father and mother, wife and children, brothers and sisters, yes, and even life itself, cannot be my disciple. [27]Whoever does not carry the cross and follow me cannot be my disciple. . . . [33]So therefore, none of you can become my disciple if you do not give up all your possessions."

John 4:4–27

[4]But [Jesus] had to go through Samaria. [5]So he came to a Samaritan city called Sychar, near the plot of ground that Jacob had given to his son Joseph. [6]Jacob's well was there, and Jesus, tired out by his journey, was sitting by the well. It was about noon.

[7]A Samaritan woman came to draw water, and Jesus said to her, "Give me a drink." [8](His disciples had gone to the city to buy food.) [9]The Samaritan woman said to him, "How is it that you, a Jew, ask a drink of me, a woman of Samaria?" (Jews do not share things in common with Samaritans.) [10]Jesus answered her, "If you knew the gift of God, and who it is that is saying to you, 'Give me a drink,' you would have asked him, and he would have given you living water." [11]The woman said to him, "Sir, you have no bucket, and the well is deep. Where do you get that living water? [12]Are you greater than our ancestor Jacob, who gave us the well, and with his sons and his flocks drank from it?" [13]Jesus said to her, "Everyone who drinks of this water will be thirsty again, [14]but those who drink of the water that I will give them will never be thirsty. The water that I will give will become in them a spring of water gushing up to eternal life." [15]The woman said to him, "Sir, give me this water, so that I may never be thirsty or have to keep coming here to draw water."

[16]Jesus said to her, "Go, call your husband, and come back." [17]The woman answered him, "I have no husband." Jesus said to her, "You are right in saying, 'I have no husband;' [18]for you have had five husbands, and the one you have now is not your husband. What you have said is true!" [19]The woman said to him, "Sir, I see that you are a prophet. [20]Our ancestors worshiped on this mountain, but you say that the place where people must worship is in Jerusalem." [21]Jesus said to her, "Woman, believe me, the hour is coming when you will worship the Father neither on this mountain nor in Jerusalem. [22]You worship what you do not know; we

worship what we know, for salvation is from the Jews. [23]But the hour is coming, and is now here, when the true worshipers will worship the Father in spirit and truth, for the Father seeks such as these to worship him. [24]God is spirit, and those who worship him must worship in spirit and truth." [25]The woman said to him, "I know that Messiah is coming" (who is called Christ). "When he comes, he will proclaim all things to us." [26]Jesus said to her, "I am he, the one who is speaking to you."

[27]Just then his disciples came. They were astonished that he was speaking with a woman, but no one said, "What do you want?" or, "Why are you speaking with her?"

Acts 2:1–18, 21 (citing Joel 2:28–32)

The Coming of the Holy Spirit

[1]When the day of Pentecost had come, they were all together in one place. [2]And suddenly from heaven there came a sound like the rush of a violent wind, and it filled the entire house where they were sitting. [3]Divided tongues, as of fire, appeared among them, and a tongue rested on each of them. [4]All of them were filled with the Holy Spirit and began to speak in other languages, as the Spirit gave them ability.

[5]Now there were devout Jews from every nation under heaven living in Jerusalem. [6]And at this sound the crowd gathered and was bewildered, because each one heard them speaking in the native language of each. [7]Amazed and astonished, they asked, "Are not all these who are speaking Galileans? [8]And how is it that we hear, each of us, in our own native language? [9]Parthians, Medes, Elamites, and residents of Mesopotamia, Judea and Cappadocia, Pontus and Asia, [10]Phrygia and Pamphylia, Egypt and the parts of Libya belonging to Cyrene, and visitors from Rome, both Jews and proselytes, [11]Cretans and Arabs—in our own languages we hear them speaking about God's deeds of power." [12]All were amazed and perplexed, saying to one another, "What does this mean?" [13]But others sneered and said, "They are filled with new wine."

[14]But Peter, standing with the eleven, raised his voice and addressed them, "Men of Judea and all who live in Jerusalem, let this be known to you, and listen to what I say. [15]Indeed, these are not drunk, as you suppose, for it is only nine o'clock in the morning. [16]No, this is what was spoken through the prophet Joel:

[17]'In the last days it will be, God declares,
   that I will pour out my Spirit upon all flesh,
     and your sons and your daughters shall prophesy,
   and your young men shall see visions,
     and your old men shall dream dreams.

¹⁸Even upon my slaves, both men and women,
> in those days I will pour out my Spirit;
> and they shall prophesy. . . .

²¹Then everyone who calls on the name of the Lord shall be saved.'"

Acts 2:42–47

⁴²They devoted themselves to the apostles' teaching and fellowship, to the breaking of bread and the prayers.
⁴³Awe came upon everyone, because many wonders and signs were being done by the apostles. ⁴⁴All who believed were together and had all things in common; ⁴⁵they would sell their possessions and goods and distribute the proceeds to all, as any had need. ⁴⁶Day by day, as they spent much time together in the temple, they broke bread at home and ate their food with glad and generous hearts, ⁴⁷praising God and having the goodwill of all the people. And day by day the Lord added to their number those who were being saved.

Acts 4:32–35

³²Now the whole group of those who believed were of one heart and soul, and no one claimed private ownership of any possessions, but everything they owned was held in common. ³³With great power the apostles gave their testimony to the resurrection of the Lord Jesus, and great grace was upon them all. ³⁴There was not a needy person among them, for as many as owned lands or houses sold them and brought the proceeds of what was sold. ³⁵They laid it at the apostles' feet, and it was distributed to each as any had need.

Acts 10:28–48

²⁸and he said to them, "You yourselves know that it is unlawful for a Jew to associate with or to visit a Gentile; but God has shown me that I should not call anyone profane or unclean. ²⁹So when I was sent for, I came without objection. Now may I ask why you sent for me?"
³⁰Cornelius replied, "Four days ago at this very hour, at three o'clock, I was praying in my house when suddenly a man in dazzling clothes stood before me. ³¹He said, 'Cornelius, your prayer has been heard and your alms have been remembered before God. ³²Send therefore to Joppa and ask for Simon, who is called Peter; he is staying in the home of Simon, a tanner, by the sea.' ³³Therefore

I sent for you immediately, and you have been kind enough to come. So now all of us are here in the presence of God to listen to all that the Lord has commanded you to say."

[34]Then Peter began to speak to them: "I truly understand that God shows no partiality, [35]but in every nation anyone who fears him and does what is right is acceptable to him. [36]You know the message he sent to the people of Israel, preaching peace by Jesus Christ—he is Lord of all. [37]That message spread throughout Judea, beginning in Galilee after the baptism that John announced: [38]how God anointed Jesus of Nazareth with the Holy Spirit and with power; how he went about doing good and healing all who were oppressed by the devil, for God was with him. [39]We are witnesses to all that he did both in Judea and in Jerusalem. They put him to death by hanging him on a tree; [40]but God raised him on the third day and allowed him to appear, [41]not to all the people but to us who were chosen by God as witnesses, and who ate and drank with him after he rose from the dead. [42]He commanded us to preach to the people and to testify that he is the one ordained by God as judge of the living and the dead. [43]All the prophets testify about him that everyone who believes in him receives forgiveness of sins through his name."

[44]While Peter was still speaking, the Holy Spirit fell upon all who heard the word. [45]The circumcised believers who had come with Peter were astounded that the gift of the Holy Spirit had been poured out even on the Gentiles, [46]for they heard them speaking in tongues and extolling God. Then Peter said, [47]"Can anyone withhold the water for baptizing these people who have received the Holy Spirit just as we have?" [48]So he ordered them to be baptized in the name of Jesus Christ. Then they invited him to stay for several days.

Romans 14:1–6, 13–23

[1]Welcome those who are weak in faith, but not for the purpose of quarrelling over opinions. [2]Some believe in eating anything, while the weak eat only vegetables. [3]Those who eat must not despise those who abstain, and those who abstain must not pass judgement on those who eat; for God has welcomed them. [4]Who are you to pass judgement on servants of another? It is before their own lord that they stand or fall. And they will be upheld, for the Lord is able to make them stand.

[5]Some judge one day to be better than another, while others judge all days to be alike. Let all be fully convinced in their own minds. [6]Those who observe the day, observe it in honor of the Lord. Also those who eat, eat in honor of the Lord, since they give thanks to God; while those who abstain, abstain in honor of the Lord and give thanks to God. . . .

[13]Let us therefore no longer pass judgement on one another, but resolve instead never to put a stumbling block or hindrance in the way of another. [14]I know and

am persuaded in the Lord Jesus that nothing is unclean in itself; but it is unclean for anyone who thinks it unclean. [15]If your brother or sister is being injured by what you eat, you are no longer walking in love. Do not let what you eat cause the ruin of one for whom Christ died. [16]So do not let your good be spoken of as evil. [17]For the kingdom of God is not food and drink but righteousness and peace and joy in the Holy Spirit. [18]The one who thus serves Christ is acceptable to God and has human approval. [19]Let us then pursue what makes for peace and for mutual edification. [20]Do not, for the sake of food, destroy the work of God. Everything is indeed clean, but it is wrong for you to make others fall by what you eat; [21]it is good not to eat meat or drink wine or do anything that makes your brother or sister stumble. [22]The faith that you have, have as your own conviction before God. Blessed are those who have no reason to condemn themselves because of what they approve. [23]But those who have doubts are condemned if they eat, because they do not act from faith; for whatever does not proceed from faith is sin.

Romans 16:1–7

[1]I commend to you our sister Phoebe, a deacon of the church at Cenchreae, [2]so that you may welcome her in the Lord as is fitting for the saints, and help her in whatever she may require from you, for she has been a benefactor of many and of myself as well.

[3]Greet Prisca and Aquila, who work with me in Christ Jesus, [4]and who risked their necks for my life, to whom not only I give thanks, but also all the churches of the Gentiles. [5]Greet also the church in their house. Greet my beloved Epaenetus, who was the first convert in Asia for Christ. [6]Greet Mary, who has worked very hard among you. [7]Greet Andronicus and Junia, my relatives who were in prison with me; they are prominent among the apostles, and they were in Christ before I was.

2 Corinthians 8:1–15

[1]We want you to know, brothers and sisters, about the grace of God that has been granted to the churches of Macedonia; [2]for during a severe ordeal of affliction, their abundant joy and their extreme poverty have overflowed in a wealth of generosity on their part. [3]For, as I can testify, they voluntarily gave according to their means, and even beyond their means, [4]begging us earnestly for the privilege of sharing in this ministry to the saints—[5]and this, not merely as we expected; they gave themselves first to the Lord and, by the will of God, to us, [6]so that we might urge Titus that, as he had already made a beginning, so he should also complete

this generous undertaking among you. [7]Now as you excel in everything—in faith, in speech, in knowledge, in utmost eagerness, and in our love for you—so we want you to excel also in this generous undertaking.

[8]I do not say this as a command, but I am testing the genuineness of your love against the earnestness of others. [9]For you know the generous act of our Lord Jesus Christ, that though he was rich, yet for your sakes he became poor, so that by his poverty you might become rich. [10]And in this matter I am giving my advice: it is appropriate for you who began last year not only to do something but even to desire to do something—[11]now finish doing it, so that your eagerness may be matched by completing it according to your means. [12]For if the eagerness is there, the gift is acceptable according to what one has—not according to what one does not have. [13]I do not mean that there should be relief for others and pressure on you, but it is a question of a fair balance between [14]your present abundance and their need, so that their abundance may be for your need, in order that there may be a fair balance. [15]As it is written,

"The one who had much did not have too much,
and the one who had little did not have too little."

Galatians 3:26–29

[26]for in Christ Jesus you are all children of God through faith. [27]As many of you as were baptized into Christ have clothed yourselves with Christ.[28]There is no longer Jew or Greek, there is no longer slave or free, there is no longer male and female; for all of you are one in Christ Jesus. [29]And if you belong to Christ, then you are Abraham's offspring, heirs according to the promise.

Ephesians 5:21–6:9

The Christian Household

[21]Be subject to one another out of reverence for Christ.

[22]Wives, be subject to your husbands as you are to the Lord. [23]For the husband is the head of the wife just as Christ is the head of the church, the body of which he is the Savior. [24]Just as the church is subject to Christ, so also wives ought to be, in everything, to their husbands.

[25]Husbands, love your wives, just as Christ loved the church and gave himself up for her, [26]in order to make her holy by cleansing her with the washing of water by the word, [27]so as to present the church to himself in splendor, without a spot or wrinkle or anything of the kind—yes, so that she may be holy and without

blemish. [28]In the same way, husbands should love their wives as they do their own bodies. He who loves his wife loves himself. [29]For no one ever hates his own body, but he nourishes and tenderly cares for it, just as Christ does for the church, [30]because we are members of his body. [31]"For this reason a man will leave his father and mother and be joined to his wife, and the two will become one flesh." [32]This is a great mystery, and I am applying it to Christ and the church. [33]Each of you, however, should love his wife as himself, and a wife should respect her husband.

6 Children, obey your parents in the Lord, for this is right. [2]"Honor your father and mother"—this is the first commandment with a promise: [3]"so that it may be well with you and you may live long on the earth."

[4]And, fathers, do not provoke your children to anger, but bring them up in the discipline and instruction of the Lord.

[5]Slaves, obey your earthly masters with fear and trembling, in singleness of heart, as you obey Christ; [6]not only while being watched, and in order to please them, but as slaves of Christ, doing the will of God from the heart. [7]Render service with enthusiasm, as to the Lord and not to men and women, [8]knowing that whatever good we do, we will receive the same again from the Lord, whether we are slaves or free.

[9]And, masters, do the same to them. Stop threatening them, for you know that both of you have the same Master in heaven, and with him there is no partiality.

1 Timothy 2:8–15

[8]I desire, then, that in every place the men should pray, lifting up holy hands without anger or argument; [9]also that the women should dress themselves modestly and decently in suitable clothing, not with their hair braided, or with gold, pearls, or expensive clothes, [10]but with good works, as is proper for women who profess reverence for God. [11]Let a woman learn in silence with full submission. [12]I permit no woman to teach or to have authority over a man; she is to keep silent. [13]For Adam was formed first, then Eve; [14]and Adam was not deceived, but the woman was deceived and became a transgressor. [15]Yet she will be saved through childbearing, provided they continue in faith and love and holiness, with modesty.

Philemon 10–16

[10]I am appealing to you for my child, Onesimus, whose father I have become during my imprisonment. [11]Formerly he was useless to you, but now he is indeed useful both to you and to me. [12]I am sending him, that is, my own heart, back to

you. [13]I wanted to keep him with me, so that he might be of service to me in your place during my imprisonment for the gospel; [14]but I preferred to do nothing without your consent, in order that your good deed might be voluntary and not something forced. [15]Perhaps this is the reason he was separated from you for a while, so that you might have him back for ever, [16]no longer as a slave but as more than a slave, a beloved brother—especially to me but how much more to you, both in the flesh and in the Lord.

PART FOUR

Inequality, the Qur'an, and the Hadith

Racial, Religious, and Gender Equality

Reflections on Qur'anic Texts

ABDULLAH SAEED

This chapter identifies some of the key issues associated with equality and inequality with reference to race, religion, and gender in the Qur'an. Rather than attempting to provide a comprehensive treatment of the topic, the focus in this essay is largely on what the Qur'an and to some extent the traditions of the Prophet Muhammad have to say on the topic, as an introduction to the texts selected for the Building Bridges seminar on equality. Given the complex nature of the debates associated with equality and inequality that is reflected even in the relevant Qur'anic texts, the treatment of each topic can only be brief.

Racial Equality

The starting point for equality is that from a Qur'anic point of view, human beings—all of them—originated from the same father and mother (Q. 4:1), understood to be Adam and Eve, and were created in the "best of molds" (Q. 64:3; Q. 95:4). Human beings are a creation of God—one of the wonders of God. The Qur'an says God gave dignity (*karama*) to human beings: "We [God] conferred dignity on the children of Adam and carried them by land and sea; We have provided good sustenance for them and favored them specially above many of those We have created" (Q. 17:70). This dignity is a fundamental characteristic of the human person. Essentially, human beings are among God's most favored creations (Q. 7:11). The Qur'an also says that God breathed from His Spirit into human beings, leaving an element of God's Spirit in the human person (Q. 15:29; Q. 38:72). At the level of creation, there is no fundamental difference between humans, and there is no inequality, based on the creation story.

After God created human beings—the first man and woman—God organized their offspring into tribes and communities (Q. 7:172) so that they might "recognize one another" (Q. 49:13). God did not create human beings identical to each other but differentiated between them in terms of their languages, colors, cultures, tribes, communities, religions, and laws (Q. 49:13). This difference is seen as an important aspect of God's plan for human beings and should not be considered negative. The equality of all human beings appears to be based on this idea of difference in the Qur'an.

On the equality between Arabs and non-Arabs and between people of different colors, which appears to have been an issue at the time of the Qur'an (610–632 CE), the Prophet Muhammad condemned discriminatory attitudes and affirmed the essential equality of all. The Prophet is reported to have said, "There is no superiority of Arabs over non-Arabs nor of non-Arabs over Arabs."[1] Similarly, in another hadith, the Prophet Muhammad said, addressing his companion Abu Dharr, "Look! You are no better than a white person or a black one; however, you may be preferred over him by God-consciousness."[2] In another example the Prophet Muhammad is reported to have advised Muslims, "If you were governed by a black slave with amputated ears and nose who leads you by the Book of Allah (The Qur'an), listen to him carefully and obey him."[3] The Qur'an also prohibits Muslims from using language that could offend others, including racist language: "O you who have believed, let not a people ridicule [another] people; perhaps they may be better than them; nor let women ridicule [other] women; perhaps they may be better than them. And do not insult one another and do not call each other by [offensive] nicknames" (Q. 49:11).

Despite this affirmation of the equality of all human beings in the Qur'an and the traditions of the Prophet, various forms of inequality still entered Muslim thought and practice. Following from what had been prevalent among pre-Islamic Arabs, in the post-prophetic period, many felt that those who belonged to certain Arab tribes had a higher social status than others. Regarding Arabs versus non-Arabs, in the ninth century CE, Persian Muslims were at the forefront of a movement that argued for equality with Arab Muslims, which is widely known as the Shu'ubiyya movement.[4] There is also an interesting body of literature about how Black people, many of whom were slave Muslims, were badly treated in Iraq in the ninth century CE and led the famous revolt known as the Zanj revolt.[5] Negative attitudes toward this or that race or ethnic group can be found in Arabic literary texts as well as views that counter such attitudes.

Related to this are the debates in Sunni tradition over whether the caliph should be from the tribe of Quraysh, the tribe of Prophet Muhammad, as well as debates in the Islamic legal tradition, for example, about whether there should be equality of social status in marriage between a husband and a wife. Social status could be determined by one's ethnic or racial identity, tribal identity, or social class.

Islamic tradition also accepted the idea that there could be free people and slaves. There is no common view among Muslims that slaves must be from a particular racial group, as slaves in Islamic history came from a vast array of racial groups. Slaves, despite the negative connotation, have also been at the forefront of leadership in many Muslim societies for much of Islamic history. Examples are the slave armies in the Abbasid period, the Mamluks of Egypt, and the Ottoman slave armies, from which well-known heads of state and generals emerged in various periods.[6]

In summary, although at a very foundational level all human beings belong to the same family and therefore should be considered "equal," there are areas where equality is not recognized. As Amr Osman has said,

> In practice, social stratification based on birth, lineage, wealth, profession, religion, gender, and knowledge always existed in medieval (and modern) Muslim societies. This stratification, at times influenced by Hellenistic and Persian cultures, was not necessarily associated with a denial of the essentially equal human nature of all individuals as God's creatures and servants, but it had implications, not necessarily sanctioned by Islam itself, with regard to the duties, rights, and social status of individuals as members in the community and citizens of the Muslim state.[7]

Religious Equality

Many Qur'anic references explain that God provided signs, evidence, and proof, along with the faculty of reason, for human beings to recognize the Creator and Sustainer God, yet only a few express gratitude to Him for creation and for everything He provides. Many people do not even acknowledge the existence of God. For the Qur'an, only a few people truly believe in God and submit to Him (Q. 49:14).

The Qur'an makes it clear that when it comes to how human beings respond to God's call, there are two categories of people: those who respond positively and submit to God—that is, the believers—and those who reject the call and refuse to submit, the nonbelievers. From a Qur'anic point of view, these two categories of people are not equal (as can be seen in Q. 14:35; Q. 24:51–54; Q. 24:55; Q. 39:32–35). The Qur'an states that believers will be the recipients of God's favor. God will make their works succeed and protect them (a point made in Q. 3:104; Q. 33:71; Q. 39:61; Q. 40:9). There is a hierarchy in the sense that those who believe and submit to God are above those who do not.

The issue of belief versus unbelief or faith versus lack of faith is a major concern of the Qur'an. The Qur'an says that human beings have been created for the purpose of entering into the servanthood of God (*ibada*) (Q. 51:56). In fact, this life is a testing ground for this very purpose (Q. 67:2). Some Qur'anic verses suggest that human beings can accept or reject God's call; they can submit to God or choose not to (Q. 18:29; Q. 17:15; Q. 2:256). The Qur'an recognizes the "superiority" of those who believe in God over those who do not.

With specific reference to the Muslim state and the relationship between Muslims and non-Muslims at a political level, the Qur'an also seems to differentiate between two categories of non-Muslims—non-Muslims who are at peace with the Muslim state and those who are hostile. Non-Muslims who are at peace can live, function, and interact with Muslims with relative ease and without facing any hostility from the Muslims or the Muslim state; their rights will be protected. From a Qur'anic point of view, Muslims should treat such non-Muslims kindly, justly, and fairly (Q. 29:46). However, those non-Muslims who were hostile and demonstrated their enmity toward the Muslim state were not given that flexibility. At the time, the Qur'an commanded the Prophet Muhammad to challenge the hostile forces and bring them under the control of the Muslim state (Q. 9:29).

These Qur'anic distinctions between the believer and nonbeliever, the Muslim and the non-Muslim, the non-Muslim at peace with the Muslim state and the hostile non-Muslim, paved the way for the Islamic tradition to create a hierarchical view of the members of a Muslim-governed polity. In the early development of Islam, in the post-prophetic period, Muslims developed a range of ideas that emphasized this hierarchical view. While all members of the Muslim polity had the same right to security of their persons and property as well as freedom of belief/religion, certain differences between Muslims and non-Muslims in that polity highlighted the inequalities between them. For example, non-Muslims were expected to pay a tax called *jizya* (Q. 9:29) to the Muslim state, largely in return for protection of their basic rights and exemption from participating in the military. A non-Muslim was not supposed to hold the office of the highest leader of the community—the caliph. Some Muslim scholars also extended this idea to sensitive or important positions in the state. In the Islamic legal context, non-Muslims also had certain disadvantages compared to Muslims. For example, traditionally a non-Muslim could not stand as a witness against a Muslim in certain legal cases in a Muslim court of law. According to some Islamic legal schools, a Muslim could not be killed in retaliation for the murder of a non-Muslim (although the opposite was allowed). In addition, non-Muslims, at certain times in different Muslim societies in the past, were expected to wear distinctive clothing, and restrictions were placed on some of their activities such as building houses that were taller than Muslims' houses or building places of worship.

In summary, the Qur'an makes it clear that believers in God are not on the same level as those who do not believe in God, nor do they share the same status. While the idea of the equality of all human beings is affirmed, when it comes to religious differences a degree of inequality is built into religious thought. Today, however, there is a lively debate among Muslims about the need to remove discriminatory ideas and legal positions that exist in traditional Islamic law and to move toward the equality of all people regardless of religious difference. In doing so, Muslims use the Qur'anic texts and the traditions of the Prophet that seem to emphasize equality and nondiscrimination and deemphasize those texts that are not in line with the notion of equality.

Gender Equality

It is not easy to give a simple overview of how the Qur'an treats the issue of equality between men and women. The Qur'an has much to say about women and the kinds of difficulties and challenges they faced in pre-Islamic Mecca and Medina and in the early part of the seventh century CE. The Qur'an looks at a wide range of these challenges and, based on its understanding of justice and fairness, addresses those situations where women were significantly disadvantaged, providing certain remedies or solutions to these problems.

There is nothing in the Qur'an's creation story to suggest that the woman had an inferior status or that she was subservient to the man. The man and woman were created from one soul (*nafs*) (Q. 4:1), a statement that was understood to indicate that man and woman are equal in dignity and humanity. There is no inequality at that level. There is also nothing in the Qur'an to suggest that women are somehow inferior to men in terms of their biological makeup or their physical, spiritual, emotional, or psychological characteristics. The Qur'an also appears to say that both women and men have rights over each other (Q. 2:228).

In fact, the Qur'an seems to suggest that women and men are equal on many fronts. When some women of the first Muslim community complained to the Prophet Muhammad about the lack of emphasis on women in the Qur'an, from their point of view, it was revealed to the Prophet that he should tell Muslims that men and women are essentially equal in the sight of God: "For men and women who are devoted to God—believing men and women, obedient men and women, truthful men and women, steadfast men and women, humble men and women, charitable men and women, fasting men and women, chaste men and women, men and women who remember God often—God has prepared forgiveness and a rich reward" (Q. 33:35). Men and women will have the same rewards from God. For instance, the Qur'an says, "Allah has promised to the believers, men and women, gardens under which rivers flow, to dwell therein, and beautiful mansions in gardens of everlasting bliss" (Q. 9:72). As long as they are believers, they will be treated similarly. Likewise, Muslim women are required to observe the same religious duties as men and are generally subject to the same punishments for crimes.

Socioeconomic Disadvantages

In the context of Meccan and Medinan societies and Arabian society in general, the Qur'an seems to recognize that socially, economically, and even politically, women had certain disadvantages compared to men. These disadvantages were largely related to societal values and practices of the time. In this environment, men held the most important roles in society. For example, men were tribal leaders and made decisions about war and peace. They also led economic and trade activities, including the caravan trade. This does not necessarily mean that women were not influential in society or that women were consistently dis-advantaged in the tribe or in Arabia more broadly. For instance, the Prophet Muhammad was employed by his wife Khadija, a very wealthy woman, in her business. There were certainly such cases, but most women were not in that fortunate position.

The Qur'an addresses a range of practices that were present in seventh-century Arabian society. Some tribes engaged in the practice of burying female infants alive. The reason given for this was usually fear of poverty or the parents' fear that the clan or tribe would be put in a situation where they would suffer shame. For example, the belief was that young girls or women could be sold into slavery if they were captured by opponents in war. This would put the tribe from which the women came in a difficult position, and ultimately the women could be a source of shame. The Qur'an found such practices contrary to its sense of justice and fairness. One very well-known Qur'anic verse (Q. 81:8–9) refers to those female infants who had been buried alive: when they are raised on the Day of Judgment, the infants would be asked, "For what sin [or crime] were they killed?" (Q. 81:9). This verse implies that burying an infant, in this case a female child, was a heinous crime that should not be tolerated.

The Qur'an also refers to other issues relevant to women, such as marriage and divorce, which is perhaps one of the most important topics in the Qur'an concerning women. Women were provided with extra protection and rights in marriage and divorce. For instance, women were given the right to consent to their own marriage. In a famous hadith, it is reported,

A girl came to her ['A'isha, the wife of the Prophet Muhammad] and said: "My father married me to his brother's son so that he might raise his own status thereby, and I was unwilling." She ['A'isha] said: "Sit here until the Prophet comes." Then the Messenger of Allah came, and I ['A'isha] told him (what the girl had said). He [the Prophet] sent word to her father, call-ing him, and he [the Prophet] left the matter up to her [the girl]. She said: "O Messenger of Allah, I accept what my father did, but I wanted to know whether women have any say in the matter."[8]

The bridal gift (mahr) or dowry was traditionally given to the father of the bride. The Qur'an did not see this as right and commanded Muslims to give it to the bride (Q. 4:4). The dowry was a gift given to the woman in return for giving her consent to the marriage. More importantly, in a culture where there was no social security, the dowry functioned as a type of insurance for the woman in case the marriage was dissolved or she was mistreated (Q. 4:20–21; see also Q. 4:24; Q. 2:237). The Qur'an commands Muslim men not to "take back the bride-gift" given to them (Q. 4:19).

Various other marriage-related rights are also mentioned in the Qur'an, such as maintenance (Q. 4:34) and the provision of other forms of financial support.

The Prophet is reported to have said, "Fear Allah concerning women! Verily you have taken them on the security of Allah."[9] From a Qur'anic point of view, the husband must not neglect the wife; he must maintain her and provide her with necessary support based on his available means (Q. 65:6–7). If, for some reason, the marriage does not work, the Qur'an suggests appointing an arbiter to whom both parties (the husband and the wife) can bring their concerns in order to help them resolve their differences (Q. 4:35). If that does not work, divorce would be the most practical option. Again, in the case of divorce, the Qur'an makes it clear that the wife should not be left without support (Q. 2:231). Other Qur'anic verses and traditions of the Prophet support the idea that the wife should be treated kindly and generously. The Prophet Muhammad advised his followers to treat women well: "I enjoin good treatment of women."[10] Some verses of the Qur'an emphasize kindness and love between husband and wife: "And among His signs is this: that He created for you wives amongst yourselves that you may dwell in tranquility with them; and He has put love and mercy between your hearts. Surely in this are signs for people who reflect" (Q. 30:21).

In the case of children, the Qur'an allocates significant responsibility to the father with regard to financial support and other forms of assistance (Q. 2:233). Even in the case of divorce, the father is expected to take responsibility for the welfare and expenses of the children.

Concerning inheritance, the Qur'an provides explicit and specific instructions on how an estate should be divided. This verse on inheritance is probably one of the clearest Qur'anic texts (Q. 4:11). The Qur'an makes it clear that it is not necessarily going to treat men and women equally; for example if the husband dies leaving a wife and children, the wife may receive one-eighth of the estate. If the wife dies leaving the husband and children, the husband gets a larger share. The inequality of shares can also be seen in the case of a son and daughter. Certainly, there is no equality in some instances when it comes to inheritance, but a number of Muslim scholars argue that inheritance was closely connected to structural issues in that society, and this is about fairness, not equality. From an early Islamic perspective, because at that time women were not often involved in generating wealth, and the responsibility for looking after the family was largely borne by men, a larger share was generally allocated to men. In pre-Islamic times many women did not receive a share of the inheritance at all, so the Qur'an took the position that women should receive at least some (Q. 4:7). Although the share was not equal to that of a man, at least in some cases, the fact that she received a share was important and was a major reform then.

Equality and the Debates on Qiwama

The Qur'an does not appear to support the view that the social and economic disadvantages women had in the early seventh century CE was normal or ideal; however, it recognized that, in certain cases, the advantages men possessed needed to be acknowledged so long as these social, political, and economic structures existed. The Qur'an makes reference to this by saying that men have a "degree" of advantage over women (Q. 2:228). This idea has historically been interpreted to mean that men are "superior" to women. The modern Shi'a scholar Muhammad Husayn Tabataba'i (d. 1981) argues—similar to Sunni scholars such as the Qur'an commentator al-Qurtubi (d. 1273)—that men have certain natural characteristics that apparently make men "superior" to women. These scholars believe that men have a "stronger rationality than women" or that men are stronger in terms of "bearing difficulties" and performing heavy tasks.[11]

This debate has been extended to what the Qur'an alludes to as *qiwama* (understood to mean "authority of men over women"), in the famous Qur'anic verse 4:34.[12] The verse has traditionally been seen to support the idea of men's "superiority" or "authority" over women. However, some Muslim scholars today suggest that the verse is about the requirement for husbands to take good care of their wives and to bear the necessary financial responsibility.[13] Verse 4:34 itself goes on to say that this responsibility is probably given to men for two reasons: the first is because God has given "certain advantages to some over others"; the second is because men—meaning husbands—"spend from their wealth." This responsibility therefore is linked to two issues. The first is cultural: politically and economically men had the advantage of having greater access to power and wealth in society. At the time when the verse was revealed, men generally fulfilled the responsibility of taking care of their families and wives. However, the Qur'an does not seem to say that this position should continue; it simply seems to acknowledge it. The second issue is economic and financial: from a Qur'anic point of view that is how society was then. Men, by and large, had more economic power and financial resources than women, hence the need to support women.

While Q. 4:34 is not necessarily a recommendation to maintain such advantages for men over women or even an endorsement of the status quo, many Muslim commentators have understood this text to mean that men are somehow "superior" to women. The famous Qur'an commentator al-Razi (d. 1210) expresses this view of men's "superiority" and explains why it should be the case. According to al-Razi, men are prophets and scholars, have major and minor *imama* (leadership), and carry out *jihad*. Men call for the prayer, deliver Friday sermons, perform spiritual retreats (*i'tikaf*) in mosques, bear witness in cases of *hudud* (prescribed punishment) and *qisas* (retaliation, in the case of murder), and have a greater share of inheritance.[14] These, in his view, make the issue of superiority clear.

Obviously, in earlier times, most Qur'anic commentators saw no reason not to adopt this view of the superiority of men. In their societies, the status of men and women was consistent with what the Qur'an appeared to say—their purpose was to find support for that position. Given that society operated along those lines, the

Qur'anic statement of what existed in the early seventh century CE was seen as normative to them.

In the area of traditional Islamic law, for example, jurists developed a whole series of rules for women that emphasized this inequality. For instance, jurists developed rules that restricted the degree of freedom available for the woman in the context of marriage, including freedom of movement, and the restrictions a husband could place on his wife in their marital home. Inequality also appeared in the rules developed for women to give evidence in court, where, in some cases, a woman's testimony often was equal to half that of a man, and where the blood money given in the case of murder or manslaughter of a woman was half that for a man.

Overall, the Qur'an reformed a range of cultural practices where women had significant disadvantage, providing remedies and support for women while also recognizing that men had advantages over women in that society. It therefore gave some extra responsibilities and perhaps even rights to men, without necessarily arguing that it should be normative throughout the centuries.

In the modern period, many Muslim women scholars have taken issue with the traditional interpretations of such texts. Hotly contested are issues such as qiwama and the view that a woman equals one-half of a man in a variety of legal matters. On the issue of qiwama, various scholars, including Amina Wadud and Asma Barlas, have argued that it is really a relationship based on the economic, cultural, and financial situation in which men and women functioned in the early seventh century CE and that has continued for much of Muslim history, until the modern period.[15] For them, men's role to protect and provide for the family was based on the economic and financial resources available to men at the time. Their view is that, if circumstances change and women are equally capable of having access to such economic and financial resources, then the responsibility or qiwama of men does not arise.[16]

Such scholars, including a number of male Muslim scholars, such as Fazlur Rahman (d. 1988) and Nasr Hamid Abu Zayd (d. 2010), have tried to argue that, from a Qur'anic point of view, gender equality should be assumed because it is supported by the reforms the Qur'an had introduced in relation to women.[17] Abu Zayd, for example, argues that the Qur'an explicitly endorses the spiritual equality of the sexes, equality in creation, and equality in religious duties and rights; it therefore could not sanction any inequality in society.[18]

In summary, the Qur'anic position on gender equality is not as clear-cut as it might be. The Qur'an introduced many reforms for women. It gave them many rights, but it also recognized that there were certain factors at work in society that gave men significant advantages over women. Recognizing this, the Qur'an seems to suggest that women may not necessarily be "equal" to men in certain circumstances. Yet, at the same time, it seems to point out that this inequality was because of structural issues in society then.

Conclusion

This chapter offers a brief overview of the Qur'anic treatment of equality, with particular reference to race, religion, and gender. As I indicated earlier, when attempting to provide a summary of the Qur'anic view of equality or inequality in these three areas, certain difficulties arise, in part because the Qur'an, revealed over a period of twenty-two years, had a variety of things to say on these matters. It seems to have looked at the political, social, economic, and cultural contexts of Mecca and Medina and the surrounding regions in the early part of the seventh century. It needed to support its fundamental view of human beings as essentially coming from the same family; it had to highlight that, among human beings, there are those who are comfortable with and live by God's call to them to recognize Him; and it had to minimize disadvantages for women, in the Meccan and Medinan societies in particular. For these reasons, the advice, instructions, and commandments the Qur'an provided were often related to the specific social and political contexts of the time.

Notes

1. Muhammad Nasir al-Din al-Albani, *Ghayat al-Maram: Takhrij Ahadith al-Halal wa al-Haram* (Beirut: al-Maktab al-Islami, 1980), 188n308. See also Ahmad b. Hanbal, *Musnad.* Hadith No. 22978.

2. Ahmad b. Hanbal, *Musnad,* Kitab Musnad al-Ansar, Bab Hadith Abi Dharr.

3. Muslim, *Sahih Muslim*, Kitab al-Imara. See also Bukhari, *Sahih al-Bukhari*, Kitab al-Ahkam.

4. See Roy R. Mottahdeh, "The Shu'ubiyah Controversy and the Social History of Early Islamic Iran," *International Journal of Middle East Studies* 7 (1976): 161–82.

5. "Zanj Revolution: Abbasid History," *Encyclopaedia Britannica* online edition, accessed March 16, 2020, https://www.britannica.com/event/Zanj-rebellion; and Ghada Hashem Talhami, "The Zanj Rebellion Reconsidered," *International Journal of African Historical Studies* 10, no. 3 (1977): 443–61.

6. David Nicolle and Angus McBride, *The Mamluks, 1250–1517 (Men-at-Arms)* (Oxford: Osprey, 1993); and Jem Duducu, *The Sultans: The Rise and Fall of the Ottoman* (Gloucestershire: Amberly, 2018).

7. Amr Osman, "Equality," in *The Oxford Encyclopedia of Islam and Politics*, Oxford Islamic Studies Online, April 3, 2018, http://www.oxfordislamicstudies.com.ezp .lib.unimelb.edu.au/article/opr/t342/e0157.

8. Al-Nasa'i, *Sunan al-Nasa'i*, Kitab al-Nikah.

9. Muslim, *Sahih Muslim*; https://sunnah.com/muslim/15/159.

10. Ibn Majah, *Sunan Ibn Majah*, Kitab al-Nikah.

11. Abdullah Saeed, *Reading the Qur'an in the Twenty-First Century: A Contextual Approach* (Oxon: Routledge, 2014), 118, citing Allama Muhammad Hussain Tabataba'i, *Tafsir Al Mizan*, www.shiasource.com/al-mizan/.

12. See Siel Devos, "The Feminist Challenge of Qur'an Verse 4:34: An Analysis of Progressive and Reformist Approaches and Their Impact in British Muslim Communities" (PhD thesis, SOAS, University of London, 2015), doi:10.13140/RG.2.1.1587.5920. On the issues related to *qiwama*, inequality, and hitting one's wife, see also the commentary on Qur'an 4:34 in Seyyed Hossein Nasr, Caner K Dagli, Maria Massi Dakake, Joseph E. B. Lumbard, and Mohammed Rustom, *The Study Quran: A New Translation and Commentary* (New York: HarperCollins, 2015).

13. Translation of Q. 4:34 according to M. A. S. Abdel Haleem, *The Qur'an* (Oxford: Oxford University Press, 2004).

14. Saeed, *Reading the Qur'an*, 114, citing Razi, *al-Tafsir al-Kabir*, tafsir of Q. 4:34.

15. Amina Wadud, *Qur'an and Woman: Rereading the Sacred Text from a Woman's Perspective* (New York: Oxford University Press, 1999), 62–63; and Asma Barlas, *"Believing Women" in Islam: Unreading Patriarchal Interpretations of the Quran* (Austin: University of Texas Press, 2002), 59–60.

16. Saeed, *Reading the Qur'an*, 121.

17. Fazlur Rahman, "The Status of Women in Islam: A Modernist Interpretation," in *Separate Worlds: Studies of Purdah in South Asia*, edited by Hanna Papanek & Gail Minault (Delhi: Chanakya, 1982), 299–301; and Fazlur Rahman, *The Major Themes of the Qur'ān* (Chicago: Bibliotheca Islamica, 1980), 49.

18. Saeed, *Reading the Qur'an*, 124; and Abu Zayd, *The Voice of an Exile*: *Reflections on Islam* (London: Prager, 2004), 176.

Qur'an and Hadith Texts for Dialogue on Human Nature, Gender, Ethnicity, Religion, and Inequality

In this chapter, we provide Qur'anic verses and hadiths selected for their usefulness to a deep discussion about Islamic notions of the nature of humanity and inequalities with regard to gender, ethnicity, and religion. Passages are according to the translation by M. A. S. Abdel Haleem. They are presented here not in canonical order but in the order preferred for the facilitation of dialogue by the 2018 Building Bridges Seminar planners.

Sūrat al-Tīn [95]:4–6

⁴We created man in the finest state ⁵then reduced him to the lowest of the low, ⁶except those who believe and do good deeds will have an unfailing reward.

Sūrat al-Isrā' [17]:70

We have honored the children of Adam and carried them by land and sea; We have provided good sustenance for them and favoured them specially above many of those We have created.

Sūrat al-Hijr [15]:26–30

²⁶We created man out of dried clay formed from dark mud—²⁷the jinn We created before, from the fire of scorching wind. ²⁸Your Lord said to the angels, "I will create a mortal out of dried clay, formed from dark mud. ²⁹When I have fashioned him and breathed My spirit into him, bow down before him," ³⁰and the angels all did so.

Sūrat al-Aʿrāf [7]:10–15

[10]We established you [people] on the earth and provided you with a means of livelihood there—small thanks you give! [11]We created you, We gave you shape, and then We said to the angels, "Bow down before Adam," and they did. But not Iblis: he was not one of those who bowed down. [12]God said, "What prevented you from bowing down as I commanded you?" and he said, "I am better than him: You created me from fire and him from clay." [13]God said, "Get down from here! This is no place for your arrogance. Get out! You are contemptible!" [14]but Iblis said, "Give me respite until the Day people are raised from the dead," [15]and God replied, "You have respite."

Sūrat al-Qasas [28]:4–6, 38–42

[4]Pharaoh made himself high and mighty in the land and divided the people into different groups: one group he oppressed, slaughtering their sons and sparing their women—he was one of those who spread corruption—[5]but We wished to favour those who were oppressed in that land, to make them leaders, the ones to survive, [6]to establish them in the land, and through them show Pharaoh, Haman, and their armies the very thing they feared. . . .

[38]Pharaoh said, "Counsellors, you have no other god that I know of except me. Haman, light me a fire to bake clay bricks, then build me a tall building so that I may climb up to Moses's God: I am convinced that he is lying."

[39]Pharaoh and his armies behaved arrogantly in the land with no right—they thought they would not be brought back to Us—[40]so We seized him and his armies and threw them into the sea. See what became of the wrongdoers! [41]We made them leaders calling [others] only to the Fire: on the Day of Resurrection they will not be helped. [42]We made Our rejection pursue them in this world, and on the Day of Resurrection they will be among the despised.

Sūrat al-Anʿām [6]:165

It is He who made you successors on the earth and raises some of you above others in rank, to test you through what He gives you. [Prophet], your Lord is swift in punishment, yet He is most forgiving and merciful.

Sūrat al-Hujurāt [49]:11–13

[11]Believers, no one group of men should jeer at another, who may after all be better than them; no one group of women should jeer at another, who may after all be better than them; do not speak ill of one another; do not use offensive

nicknames for one another. How bad it is to be called a mischief-maker after accepting faith! Those who do not repent of this behaviour are evildoers. [12]Believers, avoid making too many assumptions—some assumptions are sinful—and do not spy on one another or speak ill of people behind their backs: would any of you like to eat the flesh of your dead brother? No, you would hate it. So be mindful of God: God is ever relenting, most merciful. [13]People, We created you all from a single man and a single woman, and made you into races and tribes so that you should recognize one another. In God's eyes, the most honoured of you are the ones most mindful of Him: God is all knowing, all aware.

Sūrat al-Rūm [30]:22

Another of His signs is the creation of the heavens and earth, and the diversity of your languages and colours. There truly are signs in this for those who know.

Hadith: The Prophet's Farewell Sermon

O People, just as you regard this month, this day, this city as sacred, so regard the life and property of every Muslim as sacred. You will come to an encounter with your Lord and He will question you about your actions: Return the goods entrusted to you to their rightful owners. All usury is now suppressed; however, you are entitled to your capital, [with which] you are not to wrong anyone and you will not be wronged. O humankind, Your Lord is one; your ancestry is one. You are all of Adam, and Adam was made from dust. In God's eyes the most noble of you is the most pious. God is knowing and aware! An Arab has no superiority over a non-Arab except on the basis of piety.

Hadith: Sahih Muslim 2699

Abu Huraira reported God's Messenger as saying: ". . . whoever is slow to good deeds will not be hastened by his lineage [on the Day of Resurrection]."

Hadith: Sahih al-Bukhari 7142

Narrated Anas b. Malik: The Messenger of God said: "Listen and obey your ruler even if he be an Abyssinian slave whose head looks like a raisin."

Hadith: Jami' al-Tirmidhi 1430

From 'A'isha: "The Quraish were troubled by the case of a woman from the tribe of Makhzum who had committed a theft. So they said: 'Who will speak about her to the Messenger of God?' They said: 'Who would be so bold as to do it other than Usama b. Zaid, the one dear to the Messenger of God?' So Usama spoke with him, the Messenger of God said: 'Are you trying to persuade me in a case regarding one of the fixed penalties that God has laid down?' Then he stood up and addressed the people saying: 'Those before you were only destroyed because, if one of their nobility was a thief, they used to let him go free—whereas if a lowly person stole something they would impose the prescribed punishment on him. By God! Even of Fatima, daughter of Muhammad, were to steal, then I would cut off her hand.'"

Sūrat al-Rūm [30]:21

Another of His signs is that He created spouses from among yourselves for you to live with in tranquility: He ordained love and kindness between you. There truly are signs in this for those who reflect.

Sūrat al-Naḥl [16]:57–61

[57]They assign daughters to God—may He be exalted!—and the [sons] they desire to themselves. [58]When one of them is given news of the birth of a baby girl, his face darkens and he is filled with gloom. [59]In his shame he hides himself away from his people because of the bad news he has been given. Should he keep her and suffer contempt or bury her in the dust? How ill they judge! [60]Those who do not believe in the Hereafter should have the contemptible image, and God should have the highest one: He is the Mighty, the Wise. [61]If God took people to task for the evil they do, He would not leave one living creature on earth, but He reprieves them until an appointed time: when their time comes they cannot delay it for a moment nor can they bring it forward.

Sūrat al-Aḥzāb [33]:35

For men and women who are devoted to God—believing men and women, obedient men and women, truthful men and women, steadfast men and women, humble men and women, charitable men and women, fasting men and women, chaste men and women, men and women who remember God often—God has prepared forgiveness and a rich reward.

Sūrat al-Mujādila [58]:1

God has heard the words of the woman who disputed with you [Prophet] about her husband and complained to God: God has heard what you both had to say. He is all hearing, all seeing.

Sūrat al-Baqara [2]:282

Call in two men as witnesses. If two men are not there, then call one man and two women out of those you approve as witnesses, so that if one of the two women should forget the other can remind her.

Hadith: From Bukhari, Al-Adab al-Mufrad

Anas reported that the Prophet, may God bless him and grant him peace, said, "Someone who brings up two daughters until they come of age: that person and I will enter Paradise like these two," and he indicated his index finger and middle finger.

Sūrat al-Isrāʾ [17]:23–24

[23]Your Lord has commanded that you should worship none but Him, and that you be kind to your parents. If either or both of them reach old age with you, say no word that shows impatience with them, and do not be harsh with them, but speak to them respectfully [24]and lower your wing in humility towards them in kindness and say, "Lord, have mercy on them, just as they cared for me when I was little."

Sūrat al-Baqara [2]:47

Children of Israel, remember how I blessed you and favoured you over other people.

Sūrat al-Baqara [2]:62

The [Muslim] believers, the Jews, the Christians, and the Sabians—all those who believe in God and the Last Day and do good—will have their rewards with their Lord. No fear for them, nor will they grieve.

Sūrat al-Baqara [2]:256

There is no compulsion in religion: true guidance has become distinct from error, so whoever rejects false gods and believes in God has grasped the firmest handhold, one that will never break. God is all hearing and all knowing.

Sūrat al-Mā'ida [5]:5

Today all good things have been made lawful for you. The food of the People of the Book is lawful for you as your food is lawful for them. So are chaste, believing, women as well as chaste women of the people who were given the Scripture before you, as long as you have given them their bride-gifts and married them, not taking them as lovers or secret mistresses. The deeds of anyone who rejects faith will come to nothing, and in the Hereafter he will be one of the losers.

Sūrat al-Mā'ida [5]:55–58

[55]Your true allies are God, His Messenger, and the believers—those who keep up the prayer, pay the prescribed alms, and bow down in worship. [56]Those who turn for protection to God, His Messenger, and the believers [are God's party]: God's party is sure to triumph. [57]You who believe, do not take as allies those who ridicule your religion and make fun of it—whether people who were given the Scripture before you, or disbelievers—and be mindful of God if you are true believers. [58]When you make the call to prayer, they ridicule it and make fun of it: this is because they are people who do not reason.

Sūrat al-Tawba [9]:28–29

[28]Believers, those who ascribe partners to God are truly unclean: do not let them come near the Sacred Mosque after this year. If you are afraid you may become poor, [bear in mind that] God will enrich you out of His bounty if He pleases: God is all knowing and wise. [29]Fight those of the People of the Book who do not believe in God and the Last Day, who do not forbid what God and His Messenger have forbidden, who do not obey the rule of justice, until they pay the tax and agree to submit.

Hadith: Sahih al-Bukhari 1312–13

Sahl b. Hanif and Qays b. Sa'd b. 'Ubada were at Qadisiya and a funeral procession passed in front of them. They both stood up. When they were told, "This is one of the people of this country," they answered, "A funeral procession once passed in front of the Messenger of God and he stood up. He was told that it was a Jew, and he answered, 'Was he not a soul?'"

Sūrat al-Sajda [32]:18

So, is someone who believes equal to someone who defies God? No, they are not equal.

Sūrat al-Fāṭir [35]:19–22

[19]The blind and the seeing are not alike, [20]nor are darkness and light; [21]shade and heat are not alike, [22]nor are the living and the dead. God makes anyone He wills hear [His message]: you cannot make those in their graves hear.

Sūrat al-Hashr [59]:20

There is no comparison between the inhabitants of the Fire and the inhabitants of Paradise—and the inhabitants of Paradise are the successful ones.

Economic Equality and Inequality

An Introduction to Selected Qur'anic Texts

ABDULLAH SAEED

The Qur'an takes for granted the fundamental dignity of human beings in its discourse on the nature of the human person. This is probably most evident in the Qur'anic story of creation, in which the human being is described as God's vice-gerent (*khalifa*) on earth. The Qur'an makes it explicit that God created Adam and his soulmate, and there is no reference to any form of inequality between the man and the woman in this story; however, the essential dignity that men and women share does not necessarily mean complete equality between them in all respects. There are a multitude of differences among human beings in their skills, abilities, wealth, intelligence, power, prestige, and status, for instance. While these differences may be important in life, from a Qur'anic perspective, what matters is the extent to which a human being is prepared to recognize God, to be God-conscious, and to live an ethical and moral life in line with God's commandments, which were provided through a vast array of prophetic figures. Thus, while the Qur'an fundamentally recognizes the equality and dignity of all at some level, inequality is also a recognized part of life.

This essay focuses on one aspect of this equality: economic equality and the reality of economic inequality; however, there is no simple Islamic understanding of this. Even within the Qur'an itself, a multitude of texts provide a mixed picture of how the issue of equality should be understood. Within Islamic tradition, the topic of equality has also been explored differently by scholars in the past. Various forms of inequality—for example, concerning women and slaves—were institutionalized in traditional Islamic law, considered legitimate, and indeed appear to be endorsed to some extent by the Qur'an. The modern period is no different, and there are many different perspectives on these matters; however, given the contemporary emphasis on equality and nondiscrimination, many Muslim scholars and thinkers currently tend to emphasize the discourse on equality and attempt to show that the Qur'an emphasizes equality and deemphasizes inequality. In this sense, equality is viewed as an ideal to which Muslims should aspire. Naturally, modern discourses on equality outside of Islam have influenced the thinking of Muslim scholars, who are well aware of the modern context and its values and needs.

Given the difficulties associated with this topic and the diverse ways the issue of economic equality can be approached, some reflections on the issue of economic equality and inequality, as expressed in certain Qur'anic texts, are presented briefly in this chapter. By its very nature, this approach is selective; and, of course, there are many other valid approaches to the issue. This approach is also dictated by the fact that the task of this chapter is to introduce the Qur'anic texts that were studied by the 2018 Building Bridges Seminar and are provided in the chapter following this one for those who wish to study them further. Rather than attempting to weave these texts into a general discourse on equality/inequality, it is more useful simply to make some preliminary comments on economic equality/inequality in the Qur'an and to introduce each text on its own, briefly highlighting what the text is about, its context, and how a few select Qur'anic commentators see the key issues.

Economic Equality: Core Principles

The Qur'an establishes some general principles and specific commandments, laws, and institutions to govern how a Muslim's economic life is to be carried out; however, it does not establish a blueprint for economic transactions or relations. Rather, it emphasizes important principles and values, such as justice, moderation, honesty, and kindness (especially toward the disadvantaged).[1] Indeed, the Qur'an's concern in the economic sphere—as Maududi explained in a lecture in 1948—appears to be "that whatever the particular form of economic activity in operation, its underlying principles should always be the same." Economic activities should therefore "conform to the Islamic standard of justice and equity."[2]

Justice

The Qur'an does not seem to be too concerned with the issue of accumulating wealth. Rather, it demonstrates "fundamental concern for peace, justice, and well-being"—values that are to be reflected in the values and practice of every Muslim.[3] In the sphere of economics, as I have explained elsewhere, those involved in economic transactions are exhorted to "act fairly, truthfully, honestly and in a spirit of cooperation, to enter into transactions freely, without coercion, provide a fair description of the goods involved in a transaction and, when exchanging goods, ensure that proper standards of measure are used."[4] Moreover, those with wealth are to ensure that they do not exploit the vulnerable.

The Qur'an goes on to criticize transactions or practices that result in gross injustice. Indeed, it forbids injustice (*zulm*) and tyranny (*baghy*) in the strongest terms. The unjust are called to repentance. Those who conduct themselves in this way are called to repent. The community as a whole has a corresponding obligation to ensure that justice and acceptable standards of practice are maintained in the economic sphere and that injustice is avoided.

Fairness

The principle of fairness requires that economic transactions be fair. More specifically, Timur Kuran explains, it requires that the economic system "treat similar economic contributions similarly, and different contributions differently" and ensure that economic gains are "earned" while economic losses are "deserved."[5] Moreover, economic transactions should not be conducted in a discriminatory manner. There should be no distinction due to "race or colour or position" in how wealth is distributed or economic transactions are carried out.[6]

The Qur'an acknowledges that pursuing wealth is a legitimate goal as long as people do not resort to unfairness. For example, Kuran notes, employers should "pay 'fair' wages to . . . [their] employees and charge 'just' prices to . . . [their] customers."[7] Merchants should be honest with their customers, providing them with the information they need to make an informed purchase—including descriptions of "defects" in what customers are purchasing. The goal of this communication is to ensure that the purchaser is involved in a fair transaction and is in no way exploited.

Equal Access to Resources

Economic equality guarantees all people on earth have a fundamental right to "food and . . . means of livelihood."[8] Since God created the earth and all the natural resources it contains, Maududi asserts in his 1948 lecture, everyone has an equal right to such "wealth and sustenance." This includes the "water in the rivers and springs, timber in the forests, fruits of wild plants, wild grass and fodder, air, animals of the jungle, minerals under the surface of the earth and similar other resources." Such resources do not belong to only a few or to "a particular person, class, race or group of people."[9] All people are freely allowed to use these things to fulfill their basic needs. On the other hand, the principle of equality also means avoiding extravagance. According to Kuran, "extravagance violates the principle of equality because, by definition, it entails consumption well beyond the average level for society."[10]

Brotherhood/Sisterhood and Mutual Responsibility

The Qur'an's emphasis on equality comes from its acknowledgment that all human beings are related at a fundamental level. This brotherhood or sisterhood is based on the "God-consciousness" (*taqwa*) that people share.[11] Regardless of the amount of wealth a person has been given by God, the essential unity of all human beings remains. Stemming from human beings' fundamental kinship, the Qur'an emphasizes the principle of mutual responsibility. All people within a society are expected to benefit from the wealth it produces; to take steps to look after the vulnerable, poor, and needy; and to ensure wealth and resources are used to satisfy people's fundamental needs.

Wealth Distribution

The Qur'an also establishes specific principles for wealth distribution so that economic equality in society is maintained, at least to the extent possible.[12] Wealth should be distributed equitably and used to fulfill the "basic human needs" of everyone.[13] Indeed, "'selfish' wealth creation" is considered forbidden.[14] It also requires social balance. This means that while the Qur'an recognizes that people will acquire different levels of wealth, it "does not tolerate this divergence growing so wide that some people spend their life in luxury and comfort, whereas the great majority of people are left to lead a life of misery, hunger, and subsistence."[15] The Qur'an also establishes a number of mechanisms to ensure that wealth is distributed within society and not accumulated by only a few individuals.

However, the Qur'an's emphasis on economic equality does not mean that all people have exactly the same access to wealth. God granted people different levels of wealth, ability, aptitude, and so forth. This does not mean, by implication, that one person is superior to another because of their resources or attributes; nor do distinctions such as skin color, wealth, or social status change one's stature from God's perspective.

Keeping these broad principles in mind will enhance a close reading of the Qur'anic texts chosen for the 2018 Building Bridges Seminar. However, as the texts selected come from both the Meccan and Medinan periods of the Prophet Muhammad's mission, it is useful to say a few words about these contexts, emphasizing the different issues and themes that were relevant to each period.

Meccan Context (610–622 CE)

By the time of the birth of Prophet Muhammad around the mid-sixth century CE, Mecca was a "city-state." Its wealth and status in the region arose from two features: its religious prominence and trade.[16] Mecca was the home of the Ka'ba, an important religious shrine that housed various pagan deities and brought many travelers to the city for pilgrimage. Its role as a center of religious activity caused its settled population to grow and brought travelers to the "sacred enclave."[17] As the Ka'ba gained regional prominence as a religious site and more people traveled there to worship their gods, the economic status of Mecca also grew. The

Quraysh, Mecca's most predominant tribe, developed and fostered trade networks with visitors to the city that brought wealth and prosperity for some of its inhabitants. The city also hosted regular "markets and fairs," which were opportunities for establishing trading contracts as well as social occasions that brought people with common economic interests together, establishing "important social ties" as well.[18] The undeniable importance of trade and commerce as economic activities in Mecca is reflected in the language of the Qur'an, with "notions of reckoning and calculating, of earning and paying out wages, of selling and bargaining, of loans and pledges for debts, of loss and fraud, of weighing and balancing" permeating its commands, injunctions, and moral worldview.[19] This importance is also reflected in the prominent place that the "mercantile and aristocratic" classes had in Mecca as social elites.[20] However, the economic prosperity of Mecca was not evenly shared, and this divided the city economically and socially because the great wealth and prosperity of the city was only enjoyed by some, not by all. This was a matter that concerned Prophet Muhammad greatly even before he received the first Qur'anic revelations.[21]

In the Meccan period there were very few Qur'anic rules, regulations, or commandments regarding particular types of giving or how to provide financial support to those in need in a particular way. Instead, certain themes emerge from the verses dealing with economic matters. Generally speaking, the focus was on encouraging and exhorting the people of Mecca to be grateful to God, to be mindful of those who were not well off, and to share their wealth with those in need. More specifically, during the Meccan period there was a general exhortation to give, share, and care for the poor and the needy. In some cases, the Qur'an emphasizes a Muslim's duty to give to or provide for certain categories of people in society. These acts would be rewarded by God. Indeed, acts of charity such as freeing a slave, feeding orphans, and providing for the destitute ("a poor man lying in the dust") were evidence of having chosen God's path—the path of virtue (Q. 90:7–16).[22]

In the Meccan period there were also many reminders that God is the giver of wealth and prosperity. Just as God easily gives wealth, God can also take it away. God, in His wisdom, has also given to some more wealth than to others, which verses such as Q. 89:14–20 and 16:71 emphasize—a point Maududi makes in his aforementioned 1948 lecture. Both wealth and poverty can therefore be a test from God; however, in each circumstance God is concerned with the attitude of humankind and how a person acts in response.

While the unequal distribution of wealth might seem to be contrary to the principle of equality, this does not appear to be the case. Maududi, when lecturing on economic principles, asserted that what the Qur'an emphasizes appears to be equality of opportunity—that is, the importance of securing a livelihood and climbing the ladder of prosperity using a person's own specific capacity and talents. A person should not be prevented from doing so due to any social or other form of distinction that might take away their equal footing with others. A person must be able to engage with economic struggle equally at one's own level and in light of the conditions or state of affairs that have been given by God.

The Meccan period also established a requirement for those with wealth to give and share it. The Qur'an instructs those who are wealthy to share their means with those in need so that wealth is fairly distributed in society.[23] The Qur'an repeats the importance of people responding to poverty on several occasions. For example, terms from the Arabic root n-f-q (which has to do with spending or giving) occur more than seventy-five times in the Qur'an. The Prophet's early emphasis on giving underscores this importance. According to Fazlur Rahman, "The Meccan verses of the Qur'an are replete with the denunciation of the economic injustice of contemporary Meccan society, the profiteering and stinginess of the rich and their unethical commercial practices such as cheating in the weight and measurements etc."[24] The Qur'an is therefore unequivocal in criticizing those who are "affluent" (as in Q. 89:17–20) and do not make the effort to "support the destitute" (Q. 69:34). Indeed, the Qur'an declares that the poor are entitled to the wealth of the rich, and the wealthy must provide for those in their community who are economically disadvantaged.

Finally, the Meccan chapters of the Qur'an establish the close relationship between faith, giving, and sharing. The Qur'an stresses that the giving of wealth to those in need is not just an act of charity but a demonstration of "God-wariness" (*taqwa*) that will result in benefits in the afterlife.[25] Thus, giving not only has material benefits for those who are in need but also spiritual reward. The Qur'an says elsewhere, "You can never attain to piety unless you spend [in the cause of Allah] out of that which you like the most; and Allah surely knows well whatever you give away" (Q. 3:92). Those who fail to provide for the poor, needy, or destitute will be punished (as in Q. 74:43–44).

In sum, during the Meccan period the Qur'an did not establish many rules, regulations, or commandments for certain types of giving or for how to provide charitable support in a particular way. Generally speaking, the focus was on encouraging and exhorting the people of Mecca to be grateful to God and mindful of those who were not well off, thus to give and share. In contrast, during the Medinan period there was an emphasis on the establishment of a range of rules and institutions for the economic sphere.

Medinan Context (622–32 CE)

In the Medinan period the context changed significantly. In contrast to the situation in Mecca, the Prophet needed to manage the social and political community (*umma*) he had established there by instituting rules and regulations to govern the economic sphere. The principle of justice and the emphasis on helping the disadvantaged that were so important in the Meccan period continued to be so in the Medinan period. The most crucial difference between the two contexts is that in

Medina, the Prophet had established a community that he needed to manage where such principles would be applied. For instance, the general emphasis on justice that was apparent in Mecca was applied to the specific economic relations and transactions of Medina. The Qur'an now stressed the importance of keeping one's word; it strongly condemned the breaching of contracts and the breaking of a promise because, as I explained elsewhere, the fulfilling of a contract is a duty for which individuals will have to answer on the Day of Judgment. Indeed, the Qur'an commands believers to pay their debts, give full measure, return what is entrusted to them, and avoid fraud and cheating. Moreover, as Asad Zaman and Junaid Qadir have written, the Qur'an ensured that the accumulation of wealth could only occur in a way that was "just to all the parties concerned." It therefore disallowed "exploitation, arbitrary taxation, and any action that leads to social harm," and it established "restrictions on profit-based business practices that . . . [could] otherwise lead to social inequitable outcomes."[26]

Further observations can be made about the Medinan context that clearly distinguish it from the Meccan context. First, the Qur'an focused on several categories of people that should be assisted economically. The Qur'an was particularly concerned about the plight of the poor and needy in general as well as women, slaves, those who were indebted, orphans, and widows. Indeed, the changes the Qur'an introduced in the social and economic sphere that targeted the exploitation of the "poor, weak, widows, women . . . [and] orphans" are one of its "most striking features."[27]

Poor and Needy

The Qur'an establishes the believers' very clear social responsibility and obligation to provide for the poor and needy in their society. It explicitly condemns "stingy" behavior (as in Q. 4:36–37) and establishes institutionalized forms of giving—"religious tithes or taxes on wealth and agricultural lands"—to ensure their needs are met.[28]

Women

The Qur'an acknowledges the economic disadvantage many women experienced in Meccan and Medinan societies. In these societies at that time, women were generally not considered major creators of wealth. Wealth was usually generated by men through tribal warfare, trade, or other activities that women were generally not part of. Wealth also came from the distribution of inheritance that, again, was often received by male members of the family. Moreover, the marriage dowry that was traditionally given to women (wives) in Meccan and Medinan societies appears to have often been retained by the wife's father or her husband so that the wife had little access to this financial resource. Some women were also left without financial support or maintenance after divorce. The Qur'an therefore introduced major reforms in these areas. The new regulations also included limits on the number of women a man could marry. This also aimed to discourage men from marrying orphan girls for the sake of gaining access to the wealth left to them by their parents.

Slaves

The Qur'an established an entirely new ethic on the issue of slavery—a topic that Sayyid Qutb expounded while commenting on Q. 4:1–12 in his commentary, *Fi Zilal al-Qur'an* [*In the Shade of the Qur'an*]. Given that slavery existed in seventh-century Arabian society, the Qur'an could not ignore the important section of the community that slaves represented. Slavery was considered reprehensible, although the Qur'an did not ban the institution as such. Instead, it seems to have been concerned with the welfare of slaves, giving them new rights and emphasizing the importance of their emancipation. It strongly encouraged the community to free slaves, providing a whole range of opportunities to do so as a meritorious act. If a slave wanted freedom, the Qur'an also described ways of assisting in this process, allowing the slave to earn money by lawful means to go toward their freedom or by encouraging masters to provide money from their own resources for this purpose (Q. 24:32–33). Overall, the commands and exhortations of the Qur'an concerning slaves aimed to maintain fairness and to prevent injustice.[29]

The Indebted

The Qur'an strongly prohibited the common practice at the time of "doubling and redoubling . . . the principal if the date for repayment fell due and the debtor was unable to pay."[30] This practice commonly led to significant hardships for the debtor and, at times, the "enslavement of the debtor to the creditor."[31] Thus, the unfair, disproportionate, and "morally reprehensible" nature of increasing debt in this way led to its condemnation by the Qur'an.[32]

Orphans

On many occasions the Qur'an clearly condemns the exploitation of orphans, setting down legal provisions to protect their wealth and property (as in Q. 4:1–12). It also prohibits the practice of marrying orphans simply for the purpose of financial gain.

Widows

The Qur'an introduces rules for the protection of widows from neglect or exploitation and to ensure that their financial needs were met. For instance, it establishes a fixed share of inheritance for widows from their deceased husband's estate (as in Q. 4:12).

Some Institutions for Ensuring Economic Equality

Inheritance Laws

The Qur'an establishes various institutions in pursuit of some degree of economic equality in society. One of these was the laws of inheritance, which had an "important equalizing effect" by distributing wealth among the relatives of the deceased in a certain way.[33] Using specific formulas, these texts regulate the acquisition of wealth among eligible family members—a process that facilitates the distribution of societal wealth and corresponded to the Qur'anic idea of wealth as a trust.[34]

Zakat *and* Sadaqa

The Qur'an establishes two forms of giving for ensuring "distributive justice" in society: *zakat* and *sadaqa*. Zakat involves putting aside a specific portion of one's wealth for the poor and disadvantaged as well as for the welfare of society. It is a compulsory levy according to which all Muslims who fit certain criteria are expected to set aside (in many cases) 2.5 percent of their net savings each year. Islamic law dictates that Muslims who are above the age of majority, mentally sound, and have "unhindered possession of their wealth" above a certain amount must pay zakat.[35] Things such as gold, silver, animals, crops, currency, or any other items that could be exchanged for money all qualify as "wealth," but each particular item is "zakatable" only when it has reached its *nisab*, "the minimum amount owned by an individual for it to become subject to zakat."[36]

Zakat was used to reallocate some of society's wealth in large part to help the needy and disadvantaged in the community. Economically, it also encouraged Muslims who were wealthy to invest in items that were exempt from zakat because they did not count toward a person's net worth, including assets such as "equipment, factories and tools."[37] On the other hand, by ensuring that the needy and disadvantaged had some access to society's wealth, they were able to have some level of purchasing power, which also economically benefited society. Spiritually, zakat encouraged Muslims to avoid greed, materialism, or excess by ensuring that some of their wealth was given to others.[38]

Sadaqa is a voluntary levy, beyond that which is required by zakat. It can consist of any form of wealth, from currency to property to land, and it can be given as general charity or allocated for a particular purpose, such as a charitable endowment. Any Muslim is free to give sadaqa. However, if a person has children, they are encouraged not to give more than one-third of their total wealth as sadaqa at the time of the person's death. This is based on a hadith of the Prophet that limited sadaqa "to one-third the portion of an estate that can be bequeathed at the owner's discretion."[39] The giving of sadaqa is considered a virtuous act. It indicates a person's generosity and may be rewarded with God's favor or even Paradise.[40]

Prohibition of Riba

Riba literally means an "increase in" or "addition to" anything, but it technically referred, according to Maududi, to the "additional sum which the creditor charged from the debtor at a fixed rate on the principal he lent, that is, interest."[41] The practice of riba, says Abdullah Yusuf Ali, was "condemned and prohibited" by the Qur'an "in the strongest possible terms."[42] However, M. Raquibuz Zaman and Hormoz Movassaghi note that, except for the reference to "doubling and re-doubling," the Qur'an does not define riba.[43] This has historically made the prohibition somewhat difficult for scholars to apply.

In the pre-Islamic period the word "riba" was used to identify a class of business transactions. As Masood Mashkoor explains, the common feature of these transactions appears to be that a fixed amount was required over the principal due. There were several forms of transactions, including loans (*qard*), debts (*dayn*), and sales (*bay'*).[44]

The prohibition of riba in the Qur'an is preceded by the condemnation of several other modes of behavior that negatively affected the socially and economically disadvantaged in Mecca. The first Qur'anic verse containing the term "riba" (Q. 30:39) appears to have been revealed in the early period of the Prophet's mission in Mecca, and it commands the Muslims to provide financial support to those in need. Those who give based on charity (rather than riba) will receive a reward. The verse seems to be condemning the practice of riba and the resulting exploitation of the disadvantaged in the community.

The second verse, Q. 3:130, which was revealed in Medina, unequivocally prohibits riba. It also condemns the pre-Islamic practice of doubling and redoubling riba in cases where the debtor could not afford to pay his or her debt. Reports suggest that the pre-Islamic practice among the Arabs of the Hijaz region was to impose an increase on the debtor at maturity if the debtor was unable to pay the principal on time. The increase in the debt occurred after the contract was concluded and at the loan's maturity, due to the debtor's failure to meet the obligation. In sum, it appears that riba was prohibited primarily to protect the economically and socially disadvantaged in the community. The Qur'an commanded Muslims not to impose any charge on debtors if they were unable to pay their debts on time and to accept only the principal. Forcing further debt on an already poor and burdened debtor was considered unethical.

In the modern period riba has come to be discussed in Islamic finance scholarship predominantly in the context of interest-based financial transactions. However, among scholars there are certain disagreements as to whether the riba prohibited in the Qur'an applies to modern bank interest. Differences in opinion appear to stem from the issue of whether the emphasis should be on the rationale for the prohibition or on the legal form of riba that was conceptualized in traditional Islamic law. As a result, there tends to be two predominant views of riba. The first is that any increase charged in a loan transaction over and above the principal is riba and therefore prohibited. Because the modern banking system is based on interest, its practices are seen to be in conflict with this Islamic principle. The other is that riba relates to the exploitation of the economically disadvantaged by the affluent. This may or may not be an element in modern bank interest. The concern here for these scholars is the "moral intent" of the prohibition. Scholars such as Fazlur Rahman and Muhammad Asad tend to emphasize the moral aspect of the prohibition against riba. They argue that the reason for the prohibition is to prevent the exploitation of the needy and injustice, as formulated in the Qur'anic statement "Do not commit injustice and no injustice will be committed against you." However, in general, there is no consensus on which forms of interest practiced by the modern banking system may be considered acceptable.

In sum, a whole range of rules, regulations, laws, and institutions were introduced to establish economic justice for the weak and vulnerable in society that the expanding Muslim body politic was obliged to follow. The Qur'an introduced measures that aimed to bring about some type of balance and justice for those sections of the community that had been disadvantaged in one form or another. Categories of people who had previously been marginalized or excluded in society were specifically included in the economic reforms, guaranteeing them greater access to wealth.

Introduction to the Selected Qur'anic Texts

Given the large number of classical and contemporary scholars who have engaged with the issues covered by the Qur'anic verses selected for the present project, it is useful simply to focus on four Qur'anic commentators. For this purpose, I have chosen three scholars from the modern period: Abdullah Yusuf Ali, Abul Ala Maududi, and Sayyid Qutb. From the classical period, I have chosen Ibn Kathir (1300–1373), a scholar whose commentary is considered by many to be "textualist"—that is, based primarily on the texts of the Qur'an and traditions of the Prophet. His perspective remains very close to the *tafsir* tradition that emphasizes the approaches of the *salaf* (early Muslim ancestors). Ibn Kathir, Maududi, and Qutb each have a multiple-volume *tafsir* work (exegesis/commentary) to their credit: Ibn Kathir, *Tafsīr al-Qur'an al-ʿAẓīm*; Sayyid Abul Ala Maududi, *Tafhim al-Qur'an* [*The Meaning of the Qur'an*]; and Sayyid Qutb, *Fi Zilal al-Qur'an* [*In the Shade of the Qur'an*]. The *tafsir* of Abdullah Yusuf Ali is included in his widely used publication *The Holy Qur'an: English Translation of the Meanings and Commentary.* In what follows I rely on, and at times quote from, English translations of these sources, which are readily available online.[45]

Sūrat al-Fajr [89]:14–20

The Attitude of Human Beings toward God and Fellow Human Beings and the Need to Give

According to Maududi, Sūrat al-Fajr was revealed when the new Muslims were being persecuted in Mecca. Its major theme, he notes, is to "affirm the meting out of rewards and punishments in the Hereafter, which the people of Makkah were not prepared to acknowledge." Beyond this, the verses consider the moral state of society, criticizing the attitude of people who regard "worldly wealth, rank and position" as the criteria for "honor or disgrace." Such people, he observes, forget that God provides both wealth and poverty as a test/trial to determine a person's attitude and to see how a person will behave. Qutb points out that this chapter also criticizes people for failing to care for orphans. God will call people to account for their deeds (and failures).

The verses Q. 89:14–20 assure the believers that God will hold those who practice "corruption and tyranny" to account, Qutb asserts. As Ibn Kathir puts it, God "will bring all of the creation before Him and He will judge them with justice," and people will be rewarded according to what they have strived for. The verses go on to criticize those who assume they have been honored by God because they have "abundant provisions" and those who view poverty as an indication of God's disgrace or injustice. Qutb notes that both "wealth and poverty are two forms of a test which God sets for His servants." The point is that God should be obeyed in either circumstance. If a person is wealthy, they should thank God for that, and if they are poor, they should exercise patience.

The verses Q. 89:14–20 go on to rebuke those who fail to look after the orphans and poor in society, who love wealth, and who take advantage of the vulnerable in society. Believers will avoid such behavior. In commenting on this passage, Qutb says that the real issue is that when people are given wealth, they do not fulfill the duties demanded of the wealthy. They do not look after the young orphan who has lost his father and become, therefore, in need of protection and support. They do not urge one another to contribute to general welfare. Such mutual encouragement is indeed an important feature of the Islamic way of life.

Sūrat al-Balad [90]:7–16

God's Favors and the Imperative to Help the Disadvantaged

The passage Sūrat al-Balad [90]:7–16 was revealed in the period when opponents of the Prophet in Mecca decided "to commit tyranny and excess against him,"

Maududi notes. The chapter points out "the true position of 'man' in the world." As Maududi makes clear, these verses explain that God has set two paths: the path of virtue and the path of vice; God has given humankind the ability to judge and to make a choice about which path to follow.

These verses address some of the claims people were making at the time and the motivations underlying their behaviors. According to Qutb, the human being had become "so conceited with what God has given him of power, ability, skill and prosperity that he behaves as if he is not accountable for what he does. He indulges in oppression, tyranny, victimization and exploitation, trying to acquire enormous wealth." However, Maududi notes, the verses say that God will hold people to account. Those who will be successful are those on the path of virtue. This path is steep and difficult, and it involves charity and unselfish love: "the freeing of a neck from bondage, or the feeding in a day of hunger of a nearly related orphan, or a poor man lying in the dust."

Sūrat al-Nisa' [4]:1–12

Protection of Orphans and Their Property and Inheritance

Sūrat al-Nisa', Qutb notes, is one of the longest Qur'anic chapters revealed in Medina. It comprises several discourses that were revealed on different occasions between the third and fifth years of the Prophet's presence in that town. It deals with moral and social reforms, Maududi points out, including the "right spirit for the observance of rules and regulations." In it, he notes, "the Muslims have been enjoined to show generosity to all around them and to be free from meanness, selfishness and stinginess of mind, because this is essential for the consolidation of the communities and helpful for the propagation of Islam."

As Qutb observes, the passage Q. 4:1–12 begins by recalling that all human beings have come from the same origin and are therefore closely related: "they all have one Lord and a single Creator, that they descend from the same origin and belong to one family." These ties of kinship establish the basis for the mutual obligation people have to one another for care, support, and compassion, and toward humanity as a "single whole." Ibn Kathir stresses that these verses set out the duties and legal provisions concerning orphans based on their protection as persons who are usually weak within the family and society. Therefore, orphans should be treated with justice and not taken advantage of. Moreover, as Ali mentions, women should have financial agency and a guaranteed portion of inheritance.[46]

The verses Q. 4:1–12 directly challenge existing practices from pre-Islamic Mecca and Medina, "where the rights of the weak in general, and orphans and women in particular, were either usurped or denied . . . altogether," says Qutb, including the marriage of orphans simply to take their property, the practice of taking multiple wives, and the failure to provide women with a personal right to a fair dowry. The verses emphasize justice and fair treatment. The final comment in the third verse, he notes, "refers to the purpose behind all these legal provisions. They all aim at maintaining fairness and avoiding injustice." The prescription of specific shares of inheritance for men and women aimed to ensure that women were given a designated share while recognizing the financial responsibilities that men carried for the household and family in society at that time.

Sūrat al-Nisa' [4]:36–39

The Need to Give and to Share and the Relationship between Giving and Faith

The essence of Islam is to serve God and do good to one's fellow creatures. As Ali points out, the first commandment is to worship God, which is followed by the prohibition to worship anyone other than Him.[47] Ibn Kathir notes that the passage Q. 4:36–39 goes on to command that kindness be extended to parents in particular and to relatives in general. It is God who taught human beings how to be kind and compassionate to one another. Qutb points out that these verses emphasize the importance of being kind to one's relatives before extending this concern to all those who need help in society or humanity at large. The instruction to be kind to parents, relatives, and other people fits most coherently with the Qur'anic view of social organization. For Maududi, it ensures that social security begins within the family before it is carried further to include the whole community. In addition to abhorring stinginess, Ibn Kathir reminds us that God does not condone the lavish spending of wealth so as to be seen by others.

Sūrat al-Tawba [9]:58–60

Compulsory Giving and Those Who Need to Be Primarily Supported

Revealed in Medina, Sūrat al-Tawba may be the very last Qur'anic revelation; certainly, it is among the last. For this reason, notes Qutb, "many scholars argue it contains final rulings on relations between the Muslim community and other people."

The term *sadaqat* (sing. *sadaqa*) can be understood to mean "offerings given for the sake of God," says Muhammad Asad.[48] This includes, he explains, "everything that a believer freely gives to another person, out of love or compassion, as well as what he is morally or legally obliged to give, without expecting any worldly return: that is, charitable gifts and deeds of every description . . . as well as the obligatory tax," *zakat*.

The people referred to at the beginning are the Muslim opponents of the Prophet (usually referred to as hypocrites) who disagreed with the distribution of zakat because they believed they were not being given their due share. They would accuse Prophet Muhammad of making unfair distributions, Maududi notes. This occurred when the payment of *zakat* was made an obligatory duty for all Muslims whose possessions exceeded the prescribed limits. As a result, Maududi explains, considerable wealth flowed into the hands of a single person: Prophet Muhammad. According to Qutb, the hypocrites (*munafiqun*) wanted to take as much as possible from this wealth. They did not make their claims because they were seeking justice but for "vested interests and ulterior motives." In Q. 9:58–60, says Maududi, this attitude is contrasted with the attitude of the believers, who felt that whatever God gave them was good and sufficient. He will certainly give His servants what will satisfy them.

Having established the right attitude a Muslim should have toward God and His Messenger, says Qutb, Q. 9:58–60 affirms that only God has the authority to decide on the distribution of *zakat*. This right does not belong to anyone else— not even to the Prophet. Only God may determine which groups of people are entitled to receive a share. The Prophet's role was only to execute what God had ruled. No one may add to or reduce these prescribed groups.

Sūrat al-Baqara [2]:275–79

Avoiding Riba and Injustice

Much of Sūrat al-Baraqa was revealed soon after Prophet Muhammad migrated from Mecca to Medina in 622 CE, Qutb asserts, noting that a common feature of the long Medinan chapters is that their verses were not revealed consecutively. For instance, several commentators consider verses 275–80, which ban *riba*, to have been revealed toward the end of the Prophet's mission, while the opening parts of the chapter were revealed early in the Medinan period. In any case the chapter outlines the principles and systems of Islam in several fields, Qutb points out, including the rules governing "spending, usury, lending and trade."

Technically, the notion of riba was most likely applied to the additional sum the creditor charged the debtor at a fixed rate on the principal he had lent. According to Maududi,

At the time of the revelation of the Qur'an, interest was charged in several ways. For instance, a person sold something and fixed a time-limit for the payment of its price, and if the buyer failed to pay it within the fixed period, he was allowed more time but had to pay an additional sum. Or a person lent a sum of money and asked the debtor to pay it back together with an agreed additional sum of money within a fixed period. Or a rate of interest was fixed for a specific period and if the principal along with the interest was not paid within that period, the rate of interest was enhanced for the extended period, and so on.

In the verses of the Qur'an on the topic, riba (often translated as usury or interest) is strongly and unequivocally condemned, notes Ali.[49] The subject of usury is connected with the subject of charity because "the former is morally the exact opposite of the latter: true charity consists in giving without an expectation of material gain," Asad explains, "whereas usury is based on an expectation of gain without any corresponding effort on the part of the lender." After mentioning those who "give charity, pay . . . [zakat] and spend on their relatives and families," says Ibn Kathir, the verses considered here refer to those who deal with usury and acquire people's money using such methods. Hence, they will receive punishment on the Day of Resurrection.

Q. 2:275–79 refer to an argument put forward by those who did not see a fundamental difference between profit and usury. As Maududi explains, they argued as follows: while "profit on capital is lawful in trade, why should the interest on money invested in loans be unlawful?" The primary difference between profit and interest, according to Maududi, is that the settlement of profit in trade between the buyer and the seller is made on equal terms: "The buyer purchases the article he needs and the seller gets profit for the time, labor and brains he employs in providing that article to the buyer. In contrast, in the case of interest, the debtor cannot settle the transaction on equal terms with the creditor because of his weaker position." While the trader charges his profit once, the moneylender charges interest repeatedly. Moreover, a person engaged in trade, industry, agriculture, and so on earns profit by spending time, labor, and intelligence, but the moneylender becomes the stronger partner in the earnings of the debtor without any risk or labor on his part. These practices were detrimental to society "morally and economically," Maududi stresses, whereas trade was not.

As Ibn Kathir points out, verses Q. 2:275–79 state that God destroys riba "either by removing this money from those who eat it, or by depriving them of the blessing and thus the benefit of their money." These verses also allow certain concessions for debtors. They present the case of faith and righteousness, highlighting the attributes of the community of believers and the foundations of the economic system. As Qutb stresses, the latter prohibits usury and institutes zakat, which involves "giving willingly, expecting nothing from any human being in return."

Sūrat al-Rum [30]:38–39

Giving to the Needy and the Indebted

Sūrat al-Rum is thought to have been revealed around the fifth year of the Prophet's mission in Mecca (615 CE). In the passage considered here (Q. 30:38–39), Ibn Kathir points out that the first verse affirms a Muslim's duty to respect and sustain the bonds of kinship and to give to the person who is in need and to the traveler who has needs on his/her journey. This is best for those who seek God's face; however, he explains, it does not mean that true success can be attained simply by rendering the rights of the needy. It means that those who do not recognize the rights of others will not attain true success.

The second verse (Q. 30:39) is probably the earliest condemnation of riba revealed in the Qur'an. It implies that riba does not increase wealth. The real increase comes from zakat. Some scholars argue that riba is prohibited due to the principle that any profit sought should come from people's own efforts, not from "exploiting other people or at their expense," as Ali puts it. However, he says, Q. 30:38–39 asks people to go beyond the simple negative stance of avoiding what is wrong by "spending of our own substance or resources or the utilization of our own talents and opportunities in the service of those who need them." If this is pursued, the reward will be multiplied significantly, not just what is deserved.[50]

Sūrat al-Baraqa [2]:177

Righteousness as Not about Meaningless Rituals but about Faith and Sharing One's Wealth

Ali notes in his commentary that Q. 2:177 gives a description of a "righteous and God-fearing" person. This person should obey God's instructions but also set his or her eyes on "the love of God and the love of his fellow-men." This verse affirms that faith should be true and sincere. It must be demonstrated in deeds of charity. People must also be good citizens and support social organization, and an individual's soul must be firm and unshaken in all circumstances. The Qur'an, he says, stresses the principle that mere compliance with outward forms does not fulfill the requirements of piety.[51]

In this regard, Ali continues, charity is valuable only when it proceeds from love. People have "graded" obligations: first to "our kith and kin" and then to "orphans (including any persons who are without support or help)," "people who are in real need but who never ask," "the stranger, who is entitled to laws of hospitality," "the people who ask and are entitled to ask, i.e . . . those who seek . . . assistance in some form or another," and "the slaves" (including helping them pursue their freedom).[52]

Sūrat al-Nur [24]:32–33

Support for Those Who Can Least Afford to Support Themselves, Such as Slaves

Maududi tells us that Sūrat al-Nur was revealed toward the middle of the Prophet's time in Medina, around year 627 or 628. This chapter was revealed to "strengthen the moral front" and "repair the cracks" that had arisen in the community after the attack concerning the Prophet's marriage to Zaynab and the second attack (the "slander") against 'A'isha, the Prophet's wife.

Concerning Q. 24:32–33, Ibn Kathir points out that this passage includes several "unambiguous rulings and firm commands," such as the exhortation to marry. These directives suggest, says Maududi, that "Muslims should ensure that none in the society should remain unmarried," even slave men and women "who are righteous." From an ethical and social point of view, Asad observes, the Qur'an prefers marriage to celibacy. However, Maududi stresses that "the owner whose slave does not show the right attitude nor seems to possess the necessary capability and temper to lead a reasonably happy married life" does not have to arrange the slave's marriage. Marriage can lead to wealth but not necessarily so. On the other hand, poverty does not mean a person should not marry.

Verses Q. 24:32–33 also affirm, notes Ali, that slaves could request "conditional manumission by a written deed fixing the amount required for manumission and allowing the slave meanwhile to earn money by lawful means."[53] Maududi explains that this involved "a deed of emancipation between the owner and the slave entitling the latter to earn his or her freedom after payment of an agreed sum of money in a certain period." In the Qur'anic context, Asad notes, this was a key method for slaves attaining their freedom. The verses also condemn those masters who force their female slaves to engage in prostitution.

Sūrat al-Nisa' [4]:75

The Need to Support the Weak and Oppressed by All Necessary Means

This verse, notes Qutb, appeals to the Muslims who were sensitive to "the cause of weaker men, women and children" being persecuted by the Meccan unbelievers. As Maududi points out, these vulnerable members of the community had stayed behind in Mecca without protection and safety. The verse, therefore (as Ibn Kathir explains), encourages believers to "perform Jihad in His [God's] cause and to strive hard to save the oppressed Muslims in Makkah, men, women and children who were restless because of having to remain there." It questions "how can believers hesitate to fight for God's cause" in this way, says Qutb, referring to the "vulnerable and heart-broken women and children" and the "defenseless elderly who are unable to defend their beliefs." The cause of God in this verse, Ali asserts, is justice: "the cause of the oppressed."[54]

Sūrat al-Nahl [16]:71

Financial Inequality

Maududi asserts that Sūrat al-Nahl [16] appears to have been revealed during the later years of the Prophet's time in Mecca. Verse 71, says Qutb, discusses the fact that people have different amounts of wealth instead of financial equality. It refers to this reality in Arabian society, he explains, using it to "dispel those myths that had their roots in the pagan beliefs of the Arabs. One such myth was their practice of allocating to false gods a share of the provisions of agricultural produce God gave them." The verse notes that the people who follow this practice do not give provisions to their slaves for the purpose of equality, yet they "give a portion of what God has granted them to false gods." In other words, Qutb stresses, "instead of expressing their thanks and gratitude to God who has given them these provisions, they associate partners with Him." However, commenting on Sūrat al-Nahl, Asad affirms that "the placing of one's dependents on an equal footing with oneself with regard to the basic necessities of life is a categorical demand of Islam." To fail to do this is to deny God's blessings.

Notes

1. Throughout this chapter, I draw heavily on two of my previously published writings on this topic: "Economics," in *Encyclopedia of the Qur'ān*, vol. 2, ed. Jane Dammen McAuliffe (Leiden: Brill, 2002); and *Islamic Banking and Interest: A Study of the Prohibition of Riba and Its Contemporary Interpretation* (Leiden: Brill, 1996). Except for instances in which I quote at length, these will not be cited further.

2. Syed Abul Ala Maududi, "The Economic Principles of Islam." Revised translation of a lecture given on March 2, 1948. Available at www.islam101.com/economy/economicsPrinciples.htm.

3. Jamail A. Kamlian, "Islam, Women and Gender Justice: A Discourse on the Traditional Islamic Practices among the Tausug in Southern Philippines," *Muslim World Journal of Human Rights* 2, no. 1 (2005): 7.

4. Saeed, "Economics," 5.

5. Timur Kuran, "On the Notion of Economic Justice in Contemporary Islamic Thought," *International Journal of Middle East Studies* 21, no. 2 (1989): 172.

6. Kuran, "Economic Justice," 172.

7. Kuran, "Economic Justice," 174.

8. Ahmed Saeed Imamuddin and Abdul Wahab Arain, "Principles of Islamic Economics in the Light of the Holy Qur'an and Sunnah," *International Journal of Humanities and Social Science Invention* 5, no. 5 (2016): 48.

9. Maududi, "Economic Principles."

10. Kuran, "Economic Justice," 174.

11. Asad Zaman and Junaid Qadir, "Putting Social Justice First: The Case of Islamic Economics," *Journal of Islamic Banking & Finance* 34, no. 4 (2017): 95.

12. M. Ökte and Savaş Kutluğhan, "Fundamentals of Islamic Economy and Finance: Theory and Practice," *Electronic Journal of Social Sciences* 9, no. 31 (2010): 185.

13. Zaman and Qadir, "Putting Social Justice First," 95.

14. M. Nusrate Aziz and Osman Bin Mohamad, "Islamic Social Business to Alleviate Poverty and Social Inequality," *International Journal of Social Economics* 43, no.6 (2016): 573–92, at 574.

15. Ökte and Kutluğhan, "Fundamentals of Islamic Economy," 185.

16. James Howard-Johnston, "The Life of the Prophet," in *Witnesses to a World Crisis: Historians and Histories of the Middle East in the Seventh Century* (Oxford: Oxford University Press, 2010), 399.

17. Fred McGraw Donner, "State and Society in Pre-Islamic Arabia," in *The Early Islamic Conquests* (Princeton, NJ: Princeton University Press, 1981), 15.

18. Donner, 28.

19. Howard-Johnston, "Life of the Prophet," 400.

20. Howard-Johnston, 402.

21. John L. Esposito, *Islam: The Straight Path* (New York: Oxford University Press, 1989), 12.

22. "A poor man in lying in the dust" is Maududi's turn of phrase. See his *tafsir* on Q. 90:7–16 in his *Tafhim al-Qur'an*, accessed September 24, 2019, https://www.english tafsir.com/.

23. Imamuddin and Arain, "Principles of Islamic Economics," 48.

24. Fazlur Rahman, "Riba and Interest," *Islamic Studies* 3 (1964): 1, 3.

25. Muhammad Umair, "Islam and the Distribution of Wealth," *Minhaj Al Qur'an*, February 25, 2016, https://www.minhaj.org/english/tid/36694/Islam-and-the-Distribution -of-Wealth-article-by-Muhammad-Umair.html.

26. Zaman and Qadir, "Putting Social Justice First," 95.

27. Esposito, *Islam*, 33.

28. Esposito, 10.

29. Sayyid Qutb, *Tafsir fi Zilal al-Quran* [*In the Shade of the Quran*], accessed September 21, 2019, https://tafsirzilal.wordpress.com/2012/06/05/english-language/.

30. Charles Tripp, *Islam and the Moral Economy: The Challenge of Capitalism* (Cambridge: Cambridge University Press, 2006), 128.

31. Tripp, 128.

32. Tripp, 128.

33. Kuran, "Economic Justice," 173.

34. Saeed, "Economics," 7.

35. Joe Bradford, "Charity and Zakāt," in *The [Oxford] Encyclopedia of Islam and Law*, Oxford Islamic Studies Online, accessed June 12, 2018, http://www.oxfordislamic studies.com.ezp.lib.unimelb.edu.au/article/opr/t349/e0030.

36. Bradford.

37. John L. Esposito, "Charity," in *The Islamic World: Past and Present*, ed. John L. Esposito (New York: Oxford University Press, 2004), 1:93.

38. Esposito, "Charity."

39. Bradford, "Charity and Zakāt."

40. Bradford. See also Saeed, "Economics," 7.

41. Maududi, *tafsir* of Surat al-Baqara in *Tafhim*. See https://www.englishtafsir.com/.

42. Abdullah Yusuf Ali, *Tafsir* of Surat al-Baqara [2]:275 in *The Holy Qur-ān: English Translation of the Meanings and Commentary*, rev. and ed. the Presidency of Islamic Researches, IFTA, Call and Guidance (Medina, Saudi Arabia: King Fahd Holy Quran Printing Complex, 1984), 126n324.

43. M. Raquibuz Zaman and Hormoz Movassaghi, "Interest-Free Islamic Banking: Ideals and Reality," *International Journal of Finance* 14, no. 4 (2002): 2429.

44. Masood Mashkoor, "The Meaning of Riba and Its Prohibition in Islam," *Research Journal of International Studies* 16 (2010): 59. See also Abdullah Saeed, "Ribā," in *Ency-*

clopaedia of Islam, 2nd ed., ed. P. Bearman, Th. Bianquis, C. E. Bosworth, E. van Donzel, and W. P. Heinrichs (Brill Online, 2011), https://referenceworks.brillonline.com/browse /encyclopaedia-of-islam-2.

45. For the remainder of this chapter, quotations and paraphrases of the *tafsir* of these four scholars are drawn from the following online editions: Ibn Kathir (1300–1373), *Tafsīr al-Qur'an al-'Aẓīm*, http://www.qtafsir.com; Sayyid Abul Ala Maududi, *Tafhim al-Qur'an* [*The Meaning of the Qur'an*], composed 1942–72, https://www.englishtafsir .com/; Sayyid Qutb, *Tafsir fi Zilal al-Qur'an* [*In the Shade of the Qur'an*], complete ed., composed 1951–65, https://tafsirzilal.wordpress.com/; and Abdullah Yusuf Ali, *The Holy Qur'an: English Translation of the Meanings and Commentary* (Lahore, 1934), https:// archive.org/details/TheHolyQuranEnglishTranslationoftheMeaningandCommentary. Since the online editions of the works of Ibn Kathir, Maududi, and Qutb are not paginated, quotations and paraphrases are not endnoted; quotations of Ali's *tafsir* are cited (page and note number) according to the version revised and edited by the Presidency of Islamic Researches, Ifta, Call and Guidance (Medina, Saudi Arabia: King Fahd Holy Quran Printing Complex, 1984).

46. Ali, *The Holy Qur-ān: English Translation of the Meanings and Commentary*, 209–10n516–19.

47. Ali, 221n550.

48. Muhammad Asad, *tafsir* of Surat al-Tawba in *The Message of the Qur'an* (Gibraltar, 1980), www.altafsir.com/.

49. Ali, 126n324.

50. Ali, 1189n3552.

51. Ali, 71n177–78.

52. Ali, 71n179.

53. Ali, 1014n2991.

54. Ali, 234n593.

Qur'an and Hadith Texts for Dialogue on Economic Inequality

In this chapter, we provide Qur'anic verses and hadiths selected for their usefulness to a deep discussion about Islamic notions of the nature of humanity and inequalities regarding gender, ethnicity, and religion. Qur'an passages are according to the translation by M. A. S. Abdel Haleem. They are presented here not in canonical order but in the order preferred for the facilitation of dialogue by the 2018 Building Bridges Seminar planners.

Sūrat al-Fajr [89]:14–20

¹⁴Your Lord is always watchful. ¹⁵[The nature of] man is that, when his Lord tries him through honour and blessings, he says, "My Lord has honoured me," ¹⁶but when He tries him through the restriction of his provision, he says, "My Lord has humiliated me." ¹⁷No indeed! You [people] do not honour orphans, ¹⁸you do not urge one another to feed the poor, ¹⁹you consume inheritance greedily, ²⁰and you love wealth with a passion.

Sūrat al-Balad [90]:7–16

⁷Does he think no one observes him? ⁸Did We not give him eyes, ⁹a tongue, lips, ¹⁰and point out to him the two clear ways [of good and evil]? ¹¹Yet he has not attempted the steep path. ¹²What will explain to you what the steep path is? ¹³It is to free a slave, ¹⁴to feed at a time of hunger ¹⁵an orphaned relative ¹⁶or a poor person in distress . . .

Sūrat al-Nisā' [4]:1–12

[1]People, be mindful of your Lord, who created you from a single soul, and from it created its mate, and from the pair of them spread countless men and women far and wide; be mindful of God, in whose name you make requests of one another. Beware of severing the ties of kinship: God is always watching over you. [2]Give orphans their property, do not replace [their] good things with bad, and do not consume their property with your own—a great sin. [3]If you fear that you will not deal fairly with orphan girls, you may marry whichever [other] women seem good to you, two, three, or four. If you fear that you cannot be equitable [to them], then marry only one, or your slave(s): that is more likely to make you avoid bias. [4]Give women their bridal gift upon marriage, though if they are happy to give up some of it for you, you may enjoy it with a clear conscience.

[5]Do not entrust your property to the feeble-minded. God has made it a means of support for you: make provision for them from it, clothe them, and address them kindly. [6]Test orphans until they reach marriageable age; then, if you find they have sound judgement, hand over their property to them. Do not consume it hastily before they come of age: if the guardian is well off he should abstain from the orphan's property, and if he is poor he should use only what is fair. When you give them their property, call witnesses in; but God takes full account of everything you do.

[7]Men shall have a share in what their parents and closest relatives leave, and women shall have a share in what their parents and closest relatives leave, whether the legacy be small or large: this is ordained by God. [8]If other relatives, orphans, or needy people are present at the distribution, give them something too, and speak kindly to them. [9]Let those who would fear for the future of their own helpless children, if they were to die, show the same concern [for orphans]; let them be mindful of God and speak out for justice. [10]Those who consume the property of orphans unjustly are actually swallowing fire into their own bellies: they will burn in the blazing Flame.

[11]Concerning your children, God commands you that a son should have the equivalent share of two daughters. If there are only daughters, two or more should share two-thirds of the inheritance, if one, she should have half. Parents inherit a sixth each if the deceased leaves children; if he leaves no children and his parents are his sole heirs, his mother has a third, unless he has brothers, in which case she has a sixth. [In all cases, the distribution comes] after payment of any bequests or debts. You cannot know which of your parents or your children is more beneficial to you: this is a law from God, and He is all knowing, all wise.

[12]You inherit half of what your wives leave, if they have no children; if they have children, you inherit a quarter. [In all cases, the distribution comes] after payment of any bequests or debts. If you have no children, your wives' share is a quarter; if you have children, your wives get an eighth. [In all cases, the

distribution comes] after payment of any bequests or debts. If a man or a woman dies leaving no children or parents, but a single brother or sister, he or she should take one-sixth of the inheritance; if there are more siblings, they share one-third between them. [In all cases, the distribution comes] after payment of any bequests or debts, with no harm done to anyone: this is a commandment from God: God is all knowing and benign to all.

Sūrat al-Nisa' [4]:36–39

36Worship God; join nothing with Him. Be good to your parents, to relatives, to orphans, to the needy, to neighbours near and far, to travellers in need, and to your slaves. God does not like arrogant, boastful people, 37who are miserly and order other people to be the same, hiding the bounty God has given them. We have prepared a humiliating torment for such ungrateful people. 38[Nor does He like those] who spend their wealth to show off, who do not believe in Him or the Last Day. Whoever has Satan as his companion has an evil companion! 39What harm would it do them to believe in God and the Last Day, and give charitably from the sustenance God has given them? God knows them well.

Sūrat al-Tawba [9]:58–60

58Some of them find fault with you [Prophet] regarding the distribution of alms: they are content if they are given a share, but angry if not. 59If only they would be content with what God and His Messenger have given them, and say, "God is enough for us—He will give us some of His bounty and so will His Messenger—to God alone we turn in hope." 60Alms are meant only for the poor, the needy, those who administer them, those whose hearts need winning over, to free slaves and help those in debt, for God's cause, and for travellers in need. This is ordained by God; God is all knowing and wise.

Sūrat al-Baqara [2]:275–280

275But those who take usury will rise up on the Day of Resurrection like someone tormented by Satan's touch. That is because they say, "Trade and usury are the same," but God has allowed trade and forbidden usury. Whoever, on receiving God's warning, stops taking usury may keep his past gains—God will be his judge—but whoever goes back to usury will be an inhabitant of the Fire, there to remain. 276God blights usury, but blesses charitable deeds with multiple increase: He does not love the ungrateful sinner. 277Those who believe, do good deeds, keep up the prayer, and pay the prescribed alms will have their reward with their Lord: no fear for them, nor will they grieve. [278]You who believe, beware of God: give up any outstanding dues from usury, if you are true believers. [279]If you do not, then be warned of war from God and His Messenger. You shall have your capital if you repent, and without suffering loss or causing others to suffer loss. [280]If the debtor is in difficulty, then delay things until matters become easier for him; still, if you were to write it off as an act of charity, that would be better for you, if only you knew.

Sūrat al-Rūm [30]:38–39

[38]So give their due to the near relative, the needy, and the wayfarer—that is best for those whose goal is God's approval: these are the ones who will prosper. [39]Whatever you lend out in usury to gain value through other people's wealth will not increase in God's eyes, but whatever you give in charity, in your desire for God's approval, will earn multiple rewards.

Sūrat al-Baqara [2]:177

Goodness does not consist in turning your face towards East or West. The truly good are those who believe in God and the Last Day, in the angels, the Scripture, and the prophets; who give away some of their wealth, however much they cherish it, to their relatives, to orphans, the needy, travellers and beggars, and to liberate those in bondage; those who keep up the prayer and pay the prescribed alms; who keep pledges whenever they make them; who are steadfast in misfortune, adversity, and times of danger. These are the ones who are true, and it is they who are aware of God.

Sūrat al-Nur [24]:32–33

[32]Marry off the single among you and those of your male and female slaves who are fit [for marriage]. If they are poor, God will provide for them from His bounty: God's bounty is infinite and He is all knowing. [33]Those who are unable to marry should keep chaste until God gives them enough out of His bounty. If any of your slaves wish to pay for their freedom, make a contract with them accordingly, if you know they have good in them, and give them some of the wealth God has given you. Do not force your slave-girls into prostitution, when they themselves wish to remain honourable, in your quest for the short-term gains of this world, although, if they are forced, God will be forgiving and merciful to them.

Hadith: Sunan Ibn Majah 3678

The Prophet said: "O God, bear witness that I have issued a declaration concerning the rights of the two weak ones: orphans and women."

Sūrat al-Nisa' [4]:75

What is wrong with you that you fight not in God's cause and for those oppressed men, women, and children who cry out, "Lord, rescue us from this town whose people are oppressors! By Your grace, give us a protector and give us a helper!"?

Sūrat al-Nahl [16]:71

God has given some of you more provision than others. Those who have been given more are unwilling to pass their provision on to the slaves they possess so that they become their equals in that matter. How can they refuse to acknowledge God's blessings?

Hadith: Al-Adab al-Mufrad 190

Sallam ibn 'Amr reported from one of the Companions that the Prophet, may Allah bless him and grant him peace, said, "Your slaves are your brothers, so treat them well. Ask for their help in what is too much for you and help them in what is too much for them."

PART FIVE

Possibilities and Obstacles toward a Common Ethic of Equality

Three Strands Leading
to the Edge

Considering the Possibility
of a Common Ethic of Equality

C. ROSALEE VELLOSO EWELL

I want to tell you two stories that I hope might help us together think about the possibilities and obstacles to a common ethic of equality. One story is very well known and comes from one of our sacred texts. The other story is a snapshot of a friendship in a contemporary, multicultural, and multireligious city. A better title for this essay is, I think, "Now What?" Or even, "Where Do We Go from Here?"

First Story

Now the serpent was more crafty than any other wild animal that the LORD God had made. He said to the woman, "Did God say, 'You shall not eat from any tree in the garden'?" [2]The woman said to the serpent, "We may eat of the fruit of the trees in the garden; [3]but God said, 'You shall not eat of the fruit of the tree that is in the middle of the garden, nor shall you touch it, or you shall die.'" [4]But the serpent said to the woman, "You will not die; [5]for God knows that when you eat of it your eyes will be opened, and you will be like God, knowing good and evil." [6]So when the woman saw that the tree was good for food, and that it was a delight to the eyes, and that the tree was to be desired to make one wise, she took of its fruit and ate; and she also gave some to her husband, who was with her, and he ate. [7]Then the eyes of both were opened, and they knew that they were naked; and they sewed fig leaves together and made loincloths for themselves.

[8]They heard the sound of the LORD God walking in the garden at the time of the evening breeze, and the man and his wife hid themselves from the presence of the LORD God among the trees of the garden. [9]But the LORD God called to the man, and said to him, "Where are you?" [10]He said, "I

heard the sound of you in the garden, and I was afraid, because I was naked; and I hid myself." [11]He said, "Who told you that you were naked? Have you eaten from the tree of which I commanded you not to eat?" (Gen. 3:1–11)[1]

You know the story: the man blames the woman who blames the serpent, and God pronounces punishment on them all. This bit of the text ends with these words:

[20]The man named his wife Eve, because she was the mother of all living. [21]And the LORD God made garments of skins for the man and for his wife, and clothed them. (Gen. 3:20–21)

So, the first time the concept of something like equality shows up in the Christian holy texts, the situation is not really very good. God's creation—man and woman—sought equality with God; they wanted to be like God, and that led to all sorts of disasters then and in all time since. I don't like the word "balance." It sounds too "average," too lukewarm and boring. But in this case, in this story, it was precisely the attempt at equality and the balance of power that disrupted the proper order between creator and creation, between the One God and all God had made.

The theme of the 2018 Building Bridges Seminar, "A World of Inequalities," functions mostly on the assumption that equality is a good thing and inequality is bad. That is, in order to enable the full flourishing of life, we must seek (peaceful) ways to fight against any inequality. This is not a bad assumption, but it demands that we consider very carefully how our sacred texts deal with the complexities and diversity of equality. Such texts can perhaps be resources for learning about living life in all its fullness without any mention of equality as the necessary framework for such a life.

The seminar examined the multiplicity of equalities and inequalities in the world. Even a short perusal of the other essays in this volume testifies to the wealth of research and knowledge on the many factors that either hinder or promote the flourishing of life. Yet the question remains, Is there a common thread that can be detected in this body of research and discussions, or are we simply left with a shopping list of issues without any clear way forward in terms of how such issues might be addressed? Put simply, have we come up with a common ethic of equality or identified challenges to such an ethic? I suggest that to answer this question we focus on three strands:

1. The textual strand: passages from the Qur'an, the Hadith, and the Bible
2. The readers' strand: us, or our religious communities, reading these texts
3. The contextual strand: the places where we are, our contexts—because equality or inequality might look very different if you're a wealthy mosque in Brazil or a poor church in Burundi

The Textual Strand

Christianity and Islam can support a common ethic of equality based on humanity's creation and origin in God. Read with generous eyes, say the scriptures of both Islam and Christianity, "remember your Lord who created you from a single soul . . . created countless men and women far and wide" (Q. 4:1) and "male and female, [God] created them . . . God saw . . . it was very good" (Gen. 1:27, 31). These texts and others like them give dignity and endow human beings, male and female, with the gift of life from God himself. The textual emphasis on life as a gift from God carries with it our duty not only to live such lives responsibly before God but to recognize that gift of life in others. That is part of how we live obediently toward God.

It is precisely in trying to reach beyond that gift, to have more than the gift God had given, that leads to the inequalities that follow from the first human sin. Remember your creator who created you good, it says in the Bible. We should aspire not to be equal to God but to be good as God's good creation.

While working with this textual strand, we might argue that compared to what was going on in the nations around them and the levels of oppression and inequalities in the societies out of which these sacred texts came, the texts are actually quite progressive. They suggest norms or methods of inclusion, acts of service that mitigate against the prevailing inequalities, which, when practiced by the faithful, exhibit generosity founded in obedience and respect for God.

The Readers' Strand

The readers' strand has to do with the fact that our religious communities over time and around the world read these texts. There are more challenges here for both Christians and Muslims because, as history would have it, these texts come to us mediated by and with centuries of interpretations done by educated, privileged (white) men. The cultural drift is always to other: to distance the one who doesn't look, talk, believe, or smell like me. That is what we do as humans. Notions of equality upset the powers and the status quo. This is a real challenge to any common ethic of equality because there are always questions around those who get to set the terms. An example in economic terms comes from my own part of the world: when I was growing up in Brazil in the 1970s, still under the military dictatorship, we were considered a "Third World" nation. In economic terms, the United States and Western Europe were the First World, the USSR and the other communist countries were the Second World, and we were Third. Well, the economy grew; the dictatorship ended around 1985; there was prosperity. We were so close to being First World, but no! They changed the terms, and we were relegated to "developing world"—or, in religious terms, "majority world."

So, while the texts in themselves might suggest practices and ways of life that are quite radical, that protect the vulnerable, that demand justice for the oppressed, there is a huge gulf between the texts themselves and how they get enacted in everyday life. Who gets to decide what development or justice look like in practice? Normally, it is those with the power; and they are also the ones most often responsible for the oppression and injustice in the first place.

The Contextual Strand

The third strand is closely related to the second one, but it brings us to our present context. To think of a common ethic of equality or of the challenges to such an ethic, we must take stock of where we are and who is reading these texts. We might say that from our texts it is clear that God is not pleased with oppression and with the exploitation of the victim; but living that out will look very different if you're a poor Christian minority community in India or an affluent church in Italy. Application of the laws of a same text will be different for these different contexts.

I think we can creatively and faithfully read our sacred texts to see generous, open readings that enable or favor equality, but I doubt that will make much difference to the lives of millions of faithful Muslims or Christians if such understandings of the texts do not address their daily struggles and issues. In addition to generous readings, there has to be some connection made between the readings and the lived experience of the people or community readings such texts. If we selectively interpret portions of the Qur'an or the Bible as reflective of the divine preference for equality and yet do not make the connections between such interpretations and quotidian life, such creative readings will be of little use in our struggle for equality.

The Edge

So what? Where do we go from here? In the natural sciences there is the concept of an "edge." In biodiversity terms, an edge might be between a field and a lake, or a forest and a river. Researchers have found that while there are typical forms of life that thrive in each separate ecosystem (in the field or in the lake), there are unique species that thrive only at the edge. They cannot survive in either separate ecosystem alone. Edges need tending; they need care and protection if they are not to be swallowed up by one or the other side. And they promote life. Niche species are made possible because of the edge. Could it be that part of what a dialogue like the Building Bridges Seminar makes possible is learning to live at the edges? Learning that, if left on our own, we might not be reading our sacred texts as well as we should and that it is through this interreligious encounter that God enables something new?

During the 2018 Building Bridges Seminar, among the texts studied was the New Testament story of Cornelius and Peter (Acts 10:28–48).[2] It reports on an incident that took place in an edge in which neither man was comfortable or at home. Peter had to go to Cornelius in order to learn the lessons God was trying to teach him. Had he not gone to Cornelius, Peter might not have heard all the words God wanted to say to him, nor would he have been used by God to bring about a radical new inclusion that surprised even Peter himself.

Peter is one ecosystem: the Jewish expression of God's people, who thinks he knows what it means to be a people constituted by the law and to live accordingly. Cornelius is the other ecosystem—the gentiles: the people outside God's promises. Each man can exist only as he is in his separate ecosystem. But they are interrupted, and in their encounter something new is made possible, something that surprises them both. In human ecology, that edge can be harmful and violent, or it can be beneficial and new.

The Building Bridges Seminar can be an edge. It is precisely in this encounter that we learn and see things anew in our sacred texts that challenge us to be more faithful and obedient to God's vision of human justice.

Second Story

In Birmingham, United Kingdom, where I live, we have neighbors about four houses down from ours: Mustafa and Zainab and their children. When we first moved to this neighborhood, my husband, Sam, was able to get permission from the town council to start a small community garden. That is how he met Mustafa, who wanted to know if he could plant some of his herbs from Gambia there. Thus, a friendship started between both men, and I got to know Zainab. When we are together, we learn about each other's faith, and we learn about ways we can collaborate and be better neighbors to those around us, together. Where we live, there is a lot of prejudice and just plain meanness toward people and children with mental disabilities. There is also a lot of poverty and debt. Together, Sam and Mustafa are trying to address some of these injustices by speaking in schools or with groups of teenagers in the local park, by talking with the local authorities, or by meeting with the faith communities of which the disabled person is a part. It is a powerful image to see them walking together, working together on behalf of the vulnerable, finding ways to get a microbusiness going, and so forth. They have not worked out all the theology, although each is very knowledgeable of his own tradition. They are tending to an edge and are willing to live at that edge where their unique collaborative voice is made possible. Alone, neither would have the impact that their joint voice has on behalf of the vulnerable and the poor.

Conclusion

I began this essay with a story from Genesis 3. Do you remember the last verse? "And the LORD God made garments of skins for the man and for his wife, and clothed them." I think God is still in the business of making new garments for us.

Part of that has to do with enabling us, together, in the variety of our contexts, to create and tend to the edges where new forms of life, new ways of inclusion and justice, are possible precisely because God has brought us together and wants to see us thrive in service to him.

Notes

1. In this chapter, all Bible quotations are according to the New Revised Standard Version.

2. For the text of this story, see the chapter "New Testament Texts for Dialogue on Inequalities" earlier in this volume.

Muslim-Christian Bridges

*Toward a Shared Theology
of Human Development?*

AZZA KARAM

Affirmations in the Christian-Muslim Textually Based
Readings and Dialogues on Inequality

Inequality is, fundamentally, a matter of power—power that, in turn, comes from access to resources. Given that equality is a permanent state of being, involving the production and distribution of the resources that we have, one of my top takeaways is a sense of both urgency and agency. We each have a role to play in perpetuating inequalities—and, in turn, we have some agency to effect changes in our own micro realities.

In fact, it would appear that, whether the text be Muslim or Christian, we are called upon as believers—indeed, we are obliged—to give of what we have: to give of our possessions (Luke 14:33), what we hold most dear; to share that which we cherish most (Q. 2:177); to urge one another to give. To serve, and thus to give, is therefore not a favor we do for those in distress, for the poor or hungry, including the enslaved, whom we are called upon to free. Nor is this merely a matter of a commandment to walk the "steep path"; it is how we know God.

In her essay earlier in this volume, Samia Huq takes us on a tour of one of the seemingly most difficult, long-standing, still living, globally contested terrains of inequality: gender.[1] Tracing the panorama of intersections over decades, if not centuries, she asserts that, while progress and religion are not antithetical, there is a need to question both notions of equality and religious traditions that are informed by the text and may often also abuse the text to serve several harmful traditional practices, many of which revolve around gender-based violence.

The 2018 Building Bridges Seminar discussions around gender—around each of the many features of inequality, actually—underscored how gendered dynamics of interaction, including ways of listening and conversing, can still require sensitivity by each and all. To my mind, a striking aspect of Huq's essay is her reference to the negotiation of intersecting realities of gender and religion. For many women and men, and for LGBTQ individuals especially, daily negotiation generates its own unique forms of hermeneutics. In some countries, too many pay dearly for their gender identities.

In reflecting upon Huq's essay, it occurs to me that we sometimes tend to speak of gender as though it could be a reality beyond religion. In other words, that gender dynamics take place even outside of religious considerations, spaces, or related discourses. Indeed, there are entire disciplines of study, and entire institutions—governmental and nongovernmental—that are dedicated to gender but do their work with nary a thought to religion. Yet I would contest whether we can even think of gender outside of the overarching framework of lived religion. The textual material studied during the 2018 Building Bridges Seminar (all of which is included in this volume) underscores, often powerfully, the fact that not only are the very definitions of "man" and "woman" inextricably connected to understandings of who we are in terms of social interaction, they are also inextricably connected to our understanding of the nature of the Divine Himself. They are likewise connected to our understanding of the words and lives of God's messengers/prophets/disciples, and even to our understanding of interpreters of divine words—most of whom have been men, century after century.

The seminar's very discussions of text, tradition, and lived realities of gender also demonstrated that even for us there exists a "no man's land" in which we (let's be honest) dared not tread or, at least, not tread too much or too deeply. This is the land where gender exists, lives, breathes beyond "man and woman"—gendered identities that included "others": LGBTQ. We left unsaid what this very religion-infused terrain has yet to come to terms with. And, in leaving this hybrid, living community of human beings out of our conversations, we may well have marginalized and excluded, may well have rendered unequal in our own discursive praxis, even as we spoke of inequalities.

In her essay, Elizabeth Phillips powerfully evokes another constantly painful reality of inequality: racism. Walking us through its persistence through multiple levels of consciousness, actions, manifestations, one of the many striking features of her narration is her elaboration of how "ontologies of 'whiteness' and 'blackness' are deeply woven into every fiber of the metaphysics of the modern West" and, from there, her assertion that "racism is metaphysical because it is ontological."[2] I found myself wondering about the racism rife in almost every single part of the world, including my own.

And I found myself also wondering whether it was only ontologies of Blackness that were woven into a part of the world or rather, whether racism could in fact be part of our very being. That is, is it almost our "default setting"? If so, would this perhaps explain why Jonathan Brown's excellent narration on slavery and economic exploitation inspired a reaction of distress in a number of seminar colleagues?[3] This also inspired animated plenary debates. Indeed, Brown's presentation gave us no choice but to ponder a question many of us, no matter how deeply we believe—indeed, precisely because of how deeply we believe—will ask, "How can God possibly . . . ?"

The question resonated with something François Kaboré shared in his insightful reflections on ethnicity and nationality in Africa.[4] Noting how higher religious diversity appeared to correlate with less inequalities, he spoke to how, in Traditional beliefs—and I paraphrase—God was so far . . . that there was a need for intermediaries; but somehow the intermediaries became god. Upon reflection, I wonder whether we approach the sacred text with such passion precisely because we are keen to avoid the intermediaries—precisely because we are hungry to understand how God could possibly allow, permit, enable, even just be party to a world riven with injustices that form deep crevices within the human soul. Because, after all, as Sunil Caleb reminded us in his own presentation, even the "good practices" we do have, which one would think should help to counter injustices, such as those of democracy, can, in fact—and do—strengthen what is arguably another molding of inequality (that is, the caste system) by virtue of how politicians will seek to mobilize and build supportive coalitions among and based on caste.[5]

And as we delved into the texts, we tempered our zeal to find answers and to understand them. We reminded one another to not impose our twenty-first-century morality onto hugely different contexts, to avoid the fallacy of applying a contemporary set of standards to analyze and evaluate texts that have emerged in another age and culture. Yet some of us were hungry to be shown how Muslim and Christian scriptures deemphasize inequality. Here we questioned each hermeneutical approach—even as we sought to interpret and understand the interpretations of the Word and endeavored to understand the meaning of the text, not in isolation from but in conversation with other texts.

What Does Inequality Look Like?

And it is through the conversations we have had with each other's texts, effectively, that I learned and wish to share a few reflections around our shared obligations, as believers, toward inequality. Before I do, let me state my position: I believe that it does not matter whether some inequalities are "good" and others are "bad"; inequalities are our normal—and they have always been. Gender, race, class, ethnicity, poverty, and arrogance are at once roots, drivers, and manifestations of inequalities. These are the "normal" aspects of inequality. And as one seminar participant rightly reminded us, we have made, in the last twenty years at least, massive strides to drastically cut down rates of poverty, illiteracy, child mortality, and several other major developmental challenges. However, we have not done away with inequality. Indeed, globally, all forms of inequality are on the rise and the gaps and rates and forms thereof are only likely to increase. So, what do our shared obligations look like? Let me share a few facts here.

Do We Think We Have No Slavery Today? If So, We Are Very Wrong!

A September 2017 report from the International Labour Organization (ILO) and Walk Free Foundation is laden with sobering statistics.[6] From it we learn that traffickers reap profits of roughly $150 billion annually. Of this total, commercial sexual exploitation garners $99 billion; construction, manufacturing, mining, and utilities, $34 billion; agriculture (including forestry and fishing), $9 billion. Private households that make use of domestic workers under forced-labor conditions save some $8 billion by avoiding payment of proper wages. An estimated 24.9 million persons are, in fact, trapped in modern-day slavery. Of trafficking victims around the world, 71 percent are women and girls; 29 percent are men and boys. Some 15.4 million victims (75 percent) are aged eighteen or older, with the number of children under the age of eighteen estimated at 5.5 million (25 percent). Of these nearly 25 million trafficking victims, 4.8 million (19 percent) were sexually exploited, 16 million (64 percent) were exploited for labor, and 4.1 million (17 percent) were exploited in state-imposed forced labor.

Forced labor takes place in many different industries. According to the ILO, victims spend an average of twenty months in forced labor. Of the 16 million trafficking victims exploited for labor, 47 percent work in construction, manufacturing, mining, or hospitality; 24 percent are domestic workers; and 11 percent work in agriculture. The majority of forced laborers (62 percent the global total) come from the Asia-Pacific region; 23 percent come from Africa. Of the global total of persons trafficked for forced labor, only 9 percent come from Europe and Central Asia; the Americas contribute only 5 percent, and the Arab States, 1 percent. But behind these small percentages are more than 3 million enslaved individuals.

Violence against Women Is Rampant

Do we think our sacred texts are clear about violence against women? If so, why is it, then, that an estimated 35 percent of women worldwide have experienced either physical or sexual intimate partner violence or sexual violence by a non-partner at some point in their lives? However, some national studies show that up to 70 percent of women have experienced physical or sexual violence from an intimate partner in their lifetime. Worldwide, almost 750 million women and girls alive today were married before their eighteenth birthday. Child marriage is more common in West and Central Africa, where over four in ten girls were married before age eighteen, and about one in seven were married or in union before age fifteen. Child marriage often results in early pregnancy and social isolation, interrupts schooling, limits the girl's opportunities, and increases her risk of experiencing domestic violence.

Access to Water: Another Inequality

A somewhat "new" concern—which was not on the Building Bridges Seminar's 2018 agenda—has to do with climate change implications, some of which will lead to another basic inequality: access to water. A 2017 World Bank report, *Turbulent Waters: Pursuing Water Security in Fragile Contexts*, describes what happens when institutions in fragile countries fail to manage the range of challenges related to water.[7] (The estimation is that 2 billion lives are affected by fragility; by 2030 virtually half of all the world's poor will live that way.) When water insecurity repeatedly affects populations, it can act as a risk multiplier, fueling the perception that institutions and governments are "not doing enough," exacerbating existing grievances, creating new risks, and deepening inequities. In turn, this contributes to destabilizing already fragile contexts, aggravating the challenges of water management, and perpetuating a vicious cycle of water insecurity and fragility. As Bezen Balamir Coşkun states in the *NATO Review*, "To head off water's potential for conflict and radicalism, disadvantaged groups need to be assured that they have access to the resources they need to live. Both states and international organisations have a role to play. Enhanced security demands increasingly that *water resources be obtained cooperatively, rather than competitively.*"[8]

What We Miss: Building Bridges
toward a Shared Theology for Human Development

One of the prominent lessons learned by international development practitioners, foreign policy experts, multilateral institutions, and even, increasingly, business corporations is that legislation and political commitments alone, while necessary, are by no means sufficient for this "cooperation" that is required. Many have awoken, over the last decade in particular, to the influence of religious actors. Leaders, institutions, faith-inspired community initiatives, and even transnationally active faith-based development and humanitarian nongovernmental organizations (NGOs) are increasingly identified as "agents of change." These are the actors who—through pulpits or pews; in internally displaced person shelters or refugee camps; in clinics, schools, hospitals, and hospices; or by backing political parties and politicians—can shift attitudes and behaviors and can change norms.

Some of us have sought to "engage" them. And a whole new industry—nay, a business—around this "engagement" is fast developing. But far from resulting in a more nuanced appreciation of collaboration and cooperation or a more concerted effort to change attitudes, mind-sets, and cultures, I see some major pitfalls. These grow ever larger as more and more governments begin to see value in faith-based engagement and seek to instrumentalize the faith-based actors for their specific national interest agendas, all while touting sustainable human development and the global common good.

However, rather than moving us toward scaling up the work to address the above, by providing support to faith-based entities and enabling the international and regional development and humanitarian organizations to work more and better, Western donor governments are giving each other money to host conferences at which faith-based NGOs are convened in a seemingly endless series of meetings. And rather than action lists featuring global challenges such as those noted above, specific Western national interests are slowly but surely making their way onto the to-do lists for these religious organizations.

What are these national interests making their way on the agenda of religious leaders and NGOs? What are the indications of where funds are being directed?

- Counterterrorism—thinly veiled as countering or preventing violent extremism
- Seeking to reduce the flow of migration in western Europe and North America (particularly into the United States)
- Defending the freedom of religion and belief for Christian minorities in the Muslim-majority countries

I contend, and emphatically so, that marshaling religious leaders and religious NGOs—many of which are vested in serving the basic needs of their communities (nutrition, water, sanitation, education, health, etc.)—and seeking to mobilize them to work for the specific agendas above is, at best, a disservice to the cause of strategic cooperation. Not only will this form of engagement derail the important collaborative work needed to address human trafficking, gender-based violence, and the disaster that is water shortage, but it will politically compromise many of these faith-based organizations vis-à-vis certain non-Western governments. Furthermore, it will eventually delegitimize many religious leaders vis-à-vis their respective communities—for they are simply too busy running from one conference to another.

Moreover, in this evolving circus of "religious engagement," the voices of enlightened religious leaders tend to be relatively muted. Where and when they are invited, they reflect political or institutional positions; they are invariably male and affirming of the status quo within their respective political regimes and institutional spaces. They are rarely the champions of all the disenfranchised. These are the very religious leaders who are prepared to "be quiet" about the most difficult issues that feed into the marginalization of certain humans.

Totally absent in this fray is any form of what several in the Building Bridges Seminar have called "mutual theological hospitality." Indeed, to a believer like me, heavily involved and invested in this form of religious engagement, the cacophony of religious voices and instrumentalization initiatives drowns any likelihood of even a basic hermeneutical reasoning of either text or tradition grounded in and mutually instructive to the actual lived realities of religion.

But why should that matter, you may ask? It matters because without the theologically informed conversations between the text, tradition, and praxis, what is ultimately being built is a Trojan Horse (entitled religion or religious engagement). And we know what transpired with that story. Suffice it to say, our already fragile abodes of peace, and ever-increasing abodes of war, can ill afford it.

Amartya Sen, winner of the 1998 Nobel Prize in Economics, argues that economic development entails a set of linked freedoms, noting therein political freedoms and transparency in relations between people, among other forms of freedom. If we are to work with what seminar colleague Sherman Jackson has called the "good-faith commitment to what is possible," seeking to build a bridge between believers in an attempt to deal with the ever-present reality of inequalities, injustice, and disempowerment, then we need to understand how and what the theologies of these freedoms might look like and what they will entail.[9] And then we need to make sure these theologies can inform the so-called religious engagement for sustainable human development.

Notes

1. See Samia Huq, "Gender and Islam: Obstacles and Possibilities," in this volume.

2. See Elizabeth Phillips, "The Problem of Race in Christianity," in this volume.

3. During the 2018 seminar, Brown's presentation on slavery was given extemporaneously. His formal essay on the topic, "Slavery: Source of Theological Tension," is in the present volume.

4. See François Kaboré, "Nationality and Ethnicity in West Africa: An Economic and Religious Perspective on Inequalities," in this volume.

5. See Sunil Caleb, "Caste and Social Class in the Christian and Islamic Communities of South Asia," in this volume.

6. This section of my essay is an adaptation of *Global Estimates of Modern Slavery: Forced Labour and Forced Marriage* (Geneva, 2017), an original work by the International Labour Office (ILO), Walk Free Foundation, and International Organization for Migration (IOM). The views and opinions expressed in the adaptation are solely the author's and are not endorsed by the ILO, Walk Free Foundation, or IOM. To download the full report, see https://www.ilo.org/global/publications/books/WCMS_575479/lang --en/index.htm. The 2017 report is summarized by Human Rights First in their fact sheet, "Human Trafficking by the Numbers," https://www.humanrightsfirst.org/resource/human -trafficking-numbers.

7. Claudia W. Sadoff, Edoardo Borgomeo, and Dominick de Waal, *Turbulent Waters: Pursuing Water Security in Fragile Contexts* (Washington, DC: World Bank, 2017), http://hdl.handle.net/10986/26207.

8. Bezen Balamir Coşkun, "More than Water Wars: Water and International Security," *NATO Review*, Winter 2007, https://www.nato.int/docu/review/2007/issue4/english /analysis5.html; emphasis added.

9. See Sherman Jackson, "Islam and the Challenge of Sociopolitical Equality: The Contribution of Religious Creed," in this volume.

PART SIX

Reflections

Considering Inequalities as Scholars of Faith

Reflections on Bridge-Building in Sarajevo

LUCINDA MOSHER

As stated in the introduction to this volume, when the Building Bridges Seminar convenes, its goals are always to gain better understanding of each other's tradition, to wrestle with theological complexities, and to improve the quality of our disagreements. The Seminar's structure facilitates this by conducting most of its work in closed session and by insisting that, in reporting on seminar conversations, the "Chatham House Rule" be observed: remarks by participants are quoted or paraphrased without attribution. In 2018 achieving those goals was enabled by the city of Sarajevo itself: its warm welcome; its determination to make history lessons visible; and its coffee-shop culture's provision of additional venues for conversation beyond our shared meals, our plenaries, and our small-group sessions. One newcomer to the Seminar said that "small group discussion was the highlight of my experience in Sarajevo," speaking as well for many colleagues. "Our small-group time allowed the assigned Biblical and Quranic texts to ground our discussions closer to our religious experience and traditions." For every convening, four discussion circles are established and remain consistent throughout the week. Each day is opened and closed with a robust plenary conversation. However, because the topics and concerns of plenary and small groups often provide fodder for discussions over meals, the line between formal and informal seminar exchanges may be blurry.

With all of this in mind, the purpose of this chapter is to convey a sense of the seventeenth seminar's many conversations[1]—the topics of which ranged from economic theories (including Islamic finance) to new forms of social enterprise (such as "impact investing"), theology of work, charity, scriptural mandates to care for widows and orphans, religious freedom, the village as the norm, the importance of listening to the oppressed and attending to their priorities, and more. We shall concentrate on six: hermeneutics, election, slavery, the possibility of a common ethic, the metaphor of "the edge," and the metaphor of "the bridge."

Hermeneutics

While the overarching theme of Building Bridges 2018 was "a world of inequalities," most participants felt the need to begin their small-group work by giving some attention to the nature and status of Christian and Muslim sacred texts—how believers understand, experience, struggle with, navigate, and reinterpret them. "Hermeneutics is essential to both Christians and Muslims," one Christian noted. "Both communities need 'hermeneutical protections.' But what exactly are we protecting? Surely the Word of God needs no protecting!" Perhaps the Word of God does need protecting, mused another Christian. "Our focus on texts is a risky one. We are listeners for the Word. The Word cannot be limited to the text. The risk is to think that the Word of God has been heard once for all." In a similar vein, one Muslim reminded his colleagues that "scripture will not translate itself into reality. Only we do that! But we must not do it on a whim. We need a hermeneutic that does not take us out of the conversation." Toward the end of the seminar, one small group considered the extent to which philosophical principles rather than hermeneutical principles were brought to bear in order to reinterpret. Justice and equality are subjective, someone noted. What does it mean to treat people equally? How do we come up with a definition of equality that does not penalize some and privilege others? Are we in fact in a position to talk about a common vision? How might we solidify a common commitment? Thus the need for hermeneutics.

"For me as a Christian, it was illuminating to revisit familiar biblical texts in this context—to share my own interpretational struggles; to discuss the meaning of the Abrahamic blessing in Genesis 12 or the call to take care of 'the poor and the alien' in Leviticus 19," reported a first-timer at the Building Bridges Seminar. He continued,

> Wrestling with themes of exclusivity and inclusivity before and with Muslim scholars stretched my own thinking about what we read out of—and sometimes, into—our sacred texts, as well as what we bring to them. At various moments, intrareligious disagreements within our group showed us how complicated this practice of scripture reasoning is—and caused me to also reflect on my own intrareligious engagements with Christian colleagues. While as scholars we have the theological, historical, and exegetical tools to unpack the meaning of our scriptures, yet there's still the reality of internal disagreements and external cultural (or even religiopolitical) pressures that may highjack how texts are used for dominating agendas.

The Building Bridges Seminar's small-group method allows for a safe space for enriching dialogue. Yet, at times, we still had uncomfortable confrontations. Those moments helped us to take note of our own blind spots or surprised us with interpretations and insights that cause us to review—and even revise—our perspective on the theme of inequality.

"Texts and their authoritative readings are an inheritance that we have received after extensive processes of commission, omission, and the reading-lenses of commentary," asserted one of the Muslim scholars:

Those texts and lenses were undoubtedly compiled and used as vehicles of social control, including through exclusive claims to universal creedal validity. Putting on my economist lens, I can agree with Adam Smith that a free market for religion provides for a greater variety of religious flavors catering to different preferences, and thus enhance religiosity (and per-chance morality). However, as his overtly less religious friend David Hume had already argued, religious competition erodes the credibility of each religious narrative for its adherents, and thus invites demonization of other narratives to retain and gain market share (and thus social control). Such is the checkered, but mostly dark, history of Christianity and Islam, which has shaped our texts and how we read them. Building horizontal-social bridges between the two faith communities thus requires either demolish-ing some vertical-temporal bridges with our traditions, or at least some ingenious reconstruction thereof.

Closely related to methods and principles of scriptural interpretation is the matter of authority—a topic to which all four small groups moved quickly during the first round of study. One group asked, who gets to define what is moral? Many of the initial presentations had offered binary choices. Left uncomfortable as a result, one group raised awareness of the need for a "third way." Another group noted how often the consideration of one moral issue results in the need to bring in other moral issues. They offered "prudence" as a means of evaluation and prioritization. "Prudence is a moral strategy," one Christian asserted. "It is not antithetical to morality. The term has been corrupted by modern politics; but classically, it was related to wisdom."

From hermeneutics, apologetics is but a small step—and throughout the week, noted a Muslim scholar, "both Muslim and Christian apologetics were on full display." This was particularly evident during close reading of scripture relating to the issue of gender inequality. In the end, he says, "we reached no conclusions, and failed to fortify any temporal bridges to tradition. Rather, we were merely content with having pointed out that some verses were non-discriminatory, and (at best) agreeing to disagree on how to read the other verses today."

Election

Close reading of Genesis 12:1–4, in which God says to Abram, "I will make of you a great nation, and I will bless you," inspired two groups to talk at length about inequality's relation to divine election. The term has various interpretations among Christians, one participant explained. "A supersessionist would say that the election of Abraham is superseded by Christ. Roman Catholics and mainline Protestants have explicitly rejected supersessionism, speaking rather of parallel elections—parallel covenants between God and humanity." In the Bible, one Christian noted, divine election often turns expectation on its head. "In so many biblical examples, we see God choosing the unlikely." In another group, discussion of the question of election was linked to the notion of being children of God and, from there, to matters of charity and service to humanity—but also to the need for balance between power and dependency.

A Muslim noted that prophets were "elected." His group examined Islamic notions of election in light of Q. 2:47 ("Children of Israel, remember how I blessed you and favoured you over other people") and Q. 28:5 ("But We wished to favour those who were oppressed in that land, to make them leaders, the ones to survive"). A Christian wondered about the place of such verses in the Muslim imagination regarding the land. Several Muslims noted that, whereas Christians may see election as unconditional, the Qur'an speaks of conditional election. As one explained, "election is not 'determined'; rather, it is earned and can be lost."

Slavery

For one of the Christians new to the Building Bridges Seminar, a striking feature of plenary and small-group discussions was the proximity of political interpretations.

> The recurring themes around slavery were a case in point. We were grappling with the historic (and contemporary) realities of unequal class and status versus core principles about the equality of all human beings in both theology and broad ethical understandings that underpin human rights. So, what does it all mean when gender inequalities are raw and immediate? What does it mean when labor standards and realities are not far removed from slavery? We were left perhaps more challenged to confront the issues around inequality that are, at the level of reality, one of the contemporary world's most urgent and complex ethical and practical challenges.

Indeed, while each "inequality" generated lively discussions during the seminar, the topic of slavery was most provocative. "How did God allow it ever?" The question was raised repeatedly by Muslims and Christians alike. A Muslim asked,

"What are we to do with the fact that the Prophet did not condemn something we now consider reprehensible?" Here followed a complex intrareligious exchange.

In summarizing his experience of the conversations around the topic of slavery, one Muslim had this to say:

> On the issue of social class, all participants were happy to express their antipathy to the existence of a permanent underclass, including in the extreme form of slavery. The usual mix of apologetics ensued ("but the traditions also encouraged freeing slaves," "true freedom is of the spirit," and the like). However, the most shocking moments in the seminar for me took the form of attempts to forge an apologetic narrative on slavery that compared some modern forms of economic subordination (including of salaried employees) to the historical abomination of human slavery. Pragmatic apologetics were perfectly familiar and understandable in this regard (slavery was a fact of life, production technologies were limited, and so on), suggesting that various degrees of tolerance or benign neglect for the institution of slavery by revered religious figures was understandable as a matter of economic necessity. What I found disturbing was the extension of apologetics discourse almost to the point of defending the historical institution, beyond the necessary historical evil characterization. For me, this was evidence of a vertical-temporal bridge that must be demolished: reverence for the texts and the past to the point of questioning our true moral stance as educated modern human beings.

Woven into the seminar's examination of the topic of slavery was the consideration of its interconnection with other inequalities, such as race and class (or caste). Particular attention was given to the impact of gender on slavery—the additional layers of consequences when the slave is a woman. From these conversations emerged the theme of freedom. A Christian noted the centrality of that concept to the New Testament, where it is theologically complicated. How is freedom to be defined? A Muslim emphasized the need to be clearer about the kind of freedom we are talking about. That point was well received. "Freedom: Christian and Muslim Perspectives" would be the theme of Building Bridges 2019.[2]

The Possibility of a Common Ethic

Stimulating consideration of the possibilities for and the obstacles to a common ethic of equality were complex questions such as, Do fundamental theological differences preclude a shared ethic? Does error have rights? Is one vision of human society as good as another? Might there be kinds of inequality that are acceptable, even necessary? If there be a common ethic, who gets to set its terms?

Who gets to say what interpretation is valid? One small group concluded that a common ethic is impossible without intrareligious work first. Furthermore, if we are to be truly helpful to the poor, we must hear their priorities. When we look from too far up, we miss our actual priority.

Another group determined that, rather than picking up on distinctions negatively, Christians and Muslims are trying to understand one another. "There is a common ethic," one participant insisted; "but what can we do to prevent calamities? How can we show that a bridge for others exists, especially when public media try to destroy such bridges?" We may have to settle for ethical commitment, someone suggested.

A Christian noted that just before United Nations Climate Change Conference (Paris, December 2015) several forceful, faith-based statements were issued. Among them were *Laudato si'* from the Vatican; *Hindu Declaration on Climate Change* from the Bhumi Project at the Oxford Centre for Hindu Studies was another, as was the international *Islamic Declaration on Climate Change*; and the pan-Buddhist statement, *The Time to Act Is Now: A Buddhist Declaration on Climate Change*.[3] "These are concrete examples of convergence," he asserted. This led to an in-depth consideration of "common ethic" versus "common commitment" versus convergence. "Coming up with a common ethic is too constrictive," said one Muslim. "It would be better 'to get to know one another'—as Q. 49:13 suggests; that is a better project. If convergence happens naturally, that would be interesting. The possibilities for it are many."

In weighing the difference between cooperation and establishment of a common ethic, someone recalled points made by Azza Karam in her lecture, about the effectiveness of the influence of religious actors.[4] "Religious actors can indeed shift attitudes," she had stressed; however, she had also underscored the consequences of instrumentalization of faith-based engagement for state gain rather than common good: containing violent extremism becomes all the more difficult. Religion and freedom of belief may continue to be defended—but only in certain parts of the world; rather than enjoying mutual theological hospitality, we find ourselves assaulted by religious discord. With all of this in mind, a Christian asserted that the question of fundamental, theological shared ethic will start with a life-giving, life-affirming God. "The hermeneutical principle of life-giving God means that to be on the side of the oppressed is to be on the side of God," he said. A colleague concurred that that God is never pleased with oppression of the vulnerable, adding that scriptural laws may stand firm—but application of the same law will differ according to context.

In assessing cooperation versus competition, one group wondered, What leads to improvement? Another group discussed the spectrum between "giving up everything" (as suggested in the gospels) versus the consolidation of resources (as recommended in Acts) versus the notion of "balance" (advocated in Corinthians). Group members wondered how each of these approaches actually works out in life. In any case, one member summarized, "all three norms suggest a community of radical interdependence." Indeed, a Muslim noted, "religion tries to mitigate the bad effects of society's inequalities. This has happened over and over again in history. We need to consider how to understand our religions, not as revolutionary, but as mitigating forces."

The Metaphor of the Edge

In her presentation on possibilities for and obstacles to a common ethic of equality," Rosalee Velloso Ewell had made much of the phenomenon of "the edge effect."[5] The edge is life-giving, she had stressed; it enables a certain kind of life. Aware of this, we need to learn to live at the edge and to practice patience at both the micro and macro levels. Her point: the Building Bridges Seminar is a kind of *edge*. He seminar colleagues latched on to this notion readily, proclaiming this metaphor's importance and developing it at length.

"Our focus on the 'edge' calls to mind the definition and role of translators," one woman noted. "Especially in a war zone, their occupation puts them at grave risk—as they have no choice but to straddle boundaries. Immigrants and refugees provide another example of living on the edge." Others responded with calls for understanding—both of the individual situation and what is happening at a global scale. One of the Muslims cataloged "a few hard facts" so that the seminar might hear "what lived inequality might sound like."

Later another Muslim acknowledged that the seminar had thus "poignantly been made aware of the plenitude of problems—and we're supposed to do something about it." Missing from the discussion, he suggested, had been a consideration of "the economy of moral outrage, the need to prioritize what we are enraged about. We can't just be outraged at everything!" Furthermore, he pointed out, "inequalities contradict each other. Fixing one will create another." Moreover, "there is a hierarchy of inequalities." Indeed, another had observed how "many inequalities are our norms." Yet, a Christian insisted, "We are not talking about a zero-sum game. There are indeed levels of suffering; but there is also a superabundant God. No individual can address all of these inequalities adequately, but a community might."

"In the Next World," another Christian noted, "we are all equal. So, why is This World so unequal? We need to be termites and moles undermining corrupt societal structures, creating just, inclusive communities in their place." A Muslim concurred, suggesting that, as an alternative to the status quo, we make more effort to take care of those close to us—that we "reconstitute relationships at the local level." Relatedly, a Christian urged, "Let's disentangle 'markets' from 'capitalism.' Small and mid-sized enterprises work quite well. Practice often works better than theory. Small and mid-sized enterprises ask: How do I build a fantastic product? How do I build a happy community? In the current system, alternatives already exist."

For one Muslim, this discussion of the "edge" called to mind historian Richard Bulliet's assertion that the history of Islam is best considered from the edge rather than from the center "because, in truth, the edge ultimately creates the center."[6] A Christian found the notion of the "edge" appealing because the edge "is a creative place." From the vantage points both of economics and theological hospitality, "What we think at the macro level can't happen unless there is change at the micro level," he stressed. "The edge phenomenon is part of both Christianity and Islam," he continued. Both traditions began on the edge and became corrupted as they moved away from it. "Both traditions have been instrumentalized to preserve the status quo." He wondered, "What would it take for us to learn together? To be creative together in the edge?"

The Metaphor of the Bridge

Unsurprisingly, given the Seminar's name—plus the fact that the Miljacka River, which divides the city of Sarajevo, is spanned multiple times—the "bridge" metaphor was a recurrent theme during the 2018 discussions. Speaking to this reality of multiple bridges, one Muslim pointed out that dilemmas may indeed have more than two sides: "Part of the function of a bridge is to cross over liminal space. Therefore, we build a bridge from edge to center." During the closing plenary, it was suggested that bridge-builders stand, of necessity, at the edges of their respective traditions—but with nonetheless solid footings therein, building bridges toward one another. One Christian put it this way:

> Ivo Andric, a Nobel Prize winner from Bosnia and Herzegovina, wrote that bridges are worthy of our attention, because they show the place where humankind encountered an obstacle and did not stop before it, but overcame and bridged it the way humankind could, according to understanding, taste, and circumstances. All bridges, according to Andric, must overcome and bridge something: disorder, death, or the lack of meaning. For everything is a transition, he continued, a bridge whose ends fade away into the infinity and toward which all earthly bridges are nothing but mere playthings, pale symbols. And all our hopes are on the other side. The very essence of this Seminar is found in this basic human, academic, religious desire to overcome the obstacle encountered.

Perhaps, another Christian suggested, we are standing together in front of an obstacle, ready to go beyond it together.

The agenda for this seminar had been especially ambitious, given the number of topics explored: inequality on the basis of gender, race, nationality/ethnicity, religious identity, caste/class, or slavery as well as discrepancies of income and wealth. Yet, even after many hours of close reading and well-focused discussion, one of the Christian participants was moved to call for further interrogation of the very concepts of equality and inequality. "We must go back to core principles," she asserted. In evaluating his own experience of the seminar, one Muslim noted,

> The common characteristic of all participants was expertise in bridge-building in a particular sense: everyone at the workshop seemed to be committed in their own thought and personal conduct to bridging the gulf between their religious traditions and modern lives. The focus on reading together English translations of some selected canonical texts (Biblical and Qur'anic) provided multiple opportunities to learn from others' experiences in building vertical-time bridges in their own traditions and personal lives, and, in the process, to give birth to friendships that fortify and extend existing horizontal-social bridges between the two communities of faith.

Notes

1. This essay is informed primarily by notes taken throughout the convening by members of the Building Bridges Seminar staff and assisting scribes. The lengthy quotations are excerpts from postseminar reflection pieces submitted by several attendees during the summer of 2018. In keeping with our observance of the Chatham Rule, these contributors are not named; however, we are most grateful for their carefully considered input.

2. It has become the custom of the Seminar's leadership to spend part of the closing plenary brainstorming possible themes for the next convening. The actual choice of theme is announced some months later.

3. For the full text of *Laudato si'* in English, see http://w2.vatican.va/content/fran cesco/en/encyclicals/documents/papa-francesco_20150524_enciclica-laudato-si.html. For the text of the *Hindu Declaration on Climate Change*, see http://www.hinduclimatedecla ration2015.org/. For the *Islamic Declaration on Climate Change*, see https://www.islamic -relief.org/muslim-leaders-deliver-islamic-climate-change-declaration/. For the full text of *The Time to Act Is Now: A Buddhist Declaration on Climate Change* (May 14, 2015), see http://fore.yale.edu/files/Buddhist_Climate_Change_Statement_5-14-15.pdf.

4. See Karam's essay in this volume.

5. See Ewell's essay in this volume.

6. Richard Bulliett, *Islam: The View from the Edge* (New York: Columbia University Press, 1994), 12.

Subject Index

Note: A separate index follows for Scriptural Citations.

Aaron, 98
Abbasids, 15, 153
abolition of slavery, 12, 30, 56, 57, 85
Abraham, 55, 95–96, 99, 108, 220
Abrahamic tradition: equality as concept within, 14; slavery within, 83–84, 86
Abu Dharr, 152
Abu Huraira (Muhammad's companion), 165
Abu-Lughod, Lila, 14, 44
Abu Zayd, Nasr Hamid, 159
Adam and Eve, 10, 87, 127, 146, 151, 163, 164, 171, 201–4. See also creation
adultery, 71
Africa: child marriage in, 210; democracy in, 31; economic growth in, 59; forced labor from, 210; growth without jobs in, 59; religious map of, 64. See also specific regions and countries
African Development Bank's Economic Outlook on Africa (2018), 59
Afro-pessimism, 55–56
agency: antiracist resources of Christian scripture and tradition, 57; to deal with inequalities, 207; of women, 42, 183
Ahaz (king of Judah), 98
Ahl al-Fatra, 87
Ahmad Baba, 85
Ahmed, Leila, 43
'A'isha (Muhammad's wife), 156, 165, 188
Ajlafs (converted Muslims in India), 80
Ali, Abdullah Yusuf, 180, 181–84, 186–88
"All Things Bright and Beautiful" (hymn), 79
Al-Muhajiroun, 47
alterity, 46–48, 208
Ambedkar, Bhimrao, 78
American Revolution, 15
Ammonites, 95, 111
Amr Osman, 153
Anas b. Malik (Muhammad's companion), 165, 167

ancient Near East: chattel slavery in, 104; community leadership role of women in, 94; competition for resources and armed conflict in, 95; cross-cultural influences in, 98, 99, 104–5, 122; patriarchy in, 12. See also Arabian seventh-century society; Israelites; specific peoples, kingdoms, and regions
Andric, Ivo, 224
Andronicus (early Christian), 144
Anjum, Ovamir, 2, 7
antimodernity, 16
Apollos (church leader in Ephesus), 126
apologetics, 219, 221
Aquila, 144
Aquinas, Thomas, 25, 26–27
Arabian seventh-century society, 155–60; Meccan context (610–622 CE), 174–76; Medinan context (622–32 CE), 176–79; slavery in, 178; women in Meccan and Medinan societies, 155–56, 160, 177–78
archaeological excavations of ancient Israelite sites, 99
Aristotle, 26, 27, 134n15
Asad, Muhammad, 181, 184, 186, 188, 189
Ashrafs (Muslims in India), 80
Asia-Pacific region: forced labor from, 210. See also specific regions and countries
Assyrian empire, 96–97, 119
Athaliah (ruler in Judah), 94
atonement theology, 129
Augustine (saint), 28, 86
authoritarianism, 31

Baal (Canaanite deity), 98
Baba, Ahmad, 85
Babylonian empire, 96–97
Babylonian exile, 97
Bangladesh: marriage age for girls in, 39; piety among educated, urban women in, 41; resisting Arabization of Islam in, 48; Sufism in, 47

banking system in conflict with *riba* prohibition, 180–81
Barlas, Asma, 43, 159
Baul mystics, 48
Bedouin Arabs, 95
Belgium as African colonial power, 63
Berlin Conference (1884–85) to divide Africa into colonies, 63–64
Bismarck, Otto von, 63
Black Americans, 23, 56, 117–18
Black Lives Matter movement, 70
Blackness, 56, 208; of Jesus, 57
Black theology, 57, 58n7
Boaz, 98, 103, 111
Boko Haram, 43
Bracton, Henry de, 28
Brahmins (priestly caste), 78, 80
Brazil as "Third World" or "developing" nation, 203
the "bridge" metaphor, 224–25
Britain. *See* United Kingdom
brotherhood/sisterhood, 173–74
Brown, Jonathan, 2, 83, 208–9
Buddhism, 222
Building Bridges Seminar (Sarajevo 2018), 1–4, 217–18
Bulliet, Richard, 224
Burkina Faso, 61–65

Caleb, Sunil, 2, 77, 209
Canaan (Ham's son), 55
Canaanites and land of Canaan, 96, 98; apportionment of land among Israelite tribes, 99; continuing conflicts with Israelites, 105n7
Canada, Al-Fatiha Foundation for LGBTQ Muslims in, 47
capability approach of Sen, 61, 77
capitalism, 8, 12, 17, 223
Carson, D. A., 133n6
Carter, Stephen, 71
Case, Anne, 23
caste and social class (India), 77–81, 209; among Christians, 79–80; caste distinguished from class, 79; definition of caste, 78; definition of class, 78; honor as part of maintaining, 78; among Muslims, 80–81; power behind, 77–78, 209; ritual as well as legal creation of caste distinction, 78. *See also* India
Chad, 67n4
charity: need to give and relationship between giving and faith, 184, 187, 195, 196; Qur'anic

rules from Meccan period on, 175, 176; Qur'anic rules from Medinan period on, 177, 179–80; shared Christian-Muslim value, 207; usury's relationship to, 186–87; *zakat* and *sadaqa*, 11, 179–80, 184–85, 186
chattel slavery, 28, 104, 105, 106n15
chauvinisms, 122
cheating, 108, 109, 125, 176, 177
children. *See* family; orphans, protection of
Christian-Muslim relations: competition within, 219; developing common ethic of equality in, 3, 201–6, 221–23; shared affirmations, 207–13
Church of South India, 80
citizenship, 61
Civil Rights movement (US), 56, 57
class inequality, 23, 77–81, 152, 166. *See also* caste and social class; economic equality/inequality; poverty; the wealthy
climate change, 211
colonialism and imperialism, 17, 49, 54, 56, 69
common destiny, 32
common ethic of equality, 3, 201–6, 221–23
communist persecution of religions, 29, 31
community: ability to address inequalities, 223; antiracist resources of Christian scripture and tradition, 57; brotherhood/sisterhood and mutual responsibility, 173–74; God's organization of human beings into, 151–52; male leadership in Old Testament, 94. *See also* cooperation
compassion: failure to uphold teachings of, 7; God teaching humans to show, 184; as translation of *rahma*, 7, 9
conscience, 26; right to freedom of conscience, 28–29, 71
conservatism, 7; gender roles and, 39, 41–43, 45
Constantine (Roman emperor), 79
contractual duties, 177
cooperation, 211, 222–23; the "bridge" metaphor, 224–25. *See also* the "edge" metaphor
Cornelius (Gentile), 117, 121–22, 131, 142–43, 204–5
corruption, 101, 106n13, 182, 223
Coşkun, Bezen Balamir, 211
Côte d'Ivoire, 62–65, 67n1
counterterrorism, 212
creation: in image of God, 25, 28, 30, 31–32, 93; of man and woman in Genesis, 93–94, 105, 107, 127, 131, 201–4; of man and woman in Qur'an's creation story, 155, 159, 163–64, 171, 194; not meant to be equal to God, 203

cultural differences. *See* ethnic equality/inequality; ethnicity
cultural-political intersections: in intrareligious discussions, 218; Islam and, 45, 48
Cushites (Ethiopians or Nubians), 98, 105n9
Cyrus (Persian king), 97, 105n8

Dalai Lama, 30
Dalits, 77, 78–79, 80
Daniel, 98
Dardīr, Aḥmad al-, 72
David, 55, 98, 111–12
Deaton, Angus, 23
Deborah (prophet), 94
debt slavery, 86–87, 103, 105, 106n15, 178
Declaration of Independence, 117
Deeb, Lara, 43
de las Casas, Bartolomé, 58n4
democracy: Catholicism's role in advancing, 21, 30–31, 35n35; Hinduism's role in advancing, 31; Islam's role in advancing, 31; Orthodoxy's role in advancing, 31; Protestantism's role in advancing, 21, 31; in sub-Saharan Africa, 65; voting in, 27
de Nobili, Roberto, 80
deprivation theory, 8
dietary laws, 121, 123, 129, 132, 135n24, 143, 168
dignity, 22–32; conferred by God, 151, 203; gender equality and, 155; in Qur'anic texts, 171; social progress and, 41
Dioula people, 63, 65
disabled persons, outreach to, 205
divine election, 96, 97, 108, 220
divine will: impartiality of, 131, 134n19, 136n51; New Testament's view of equality and, 132, 143–44; poverty as contrary to, 102–3; Qur'anic view of equality and, 153
divorce, 11, 44, 98, 156–57
domestic workers under forced-labor conditions, 210
dowry and bride-gifts, 156, 168, 177, 183–84

East Asia: decrease of poverty in, 22; "missing women" in, 24
Eastern Orthodox, 31
'ebed, translation of, 83
economic equality/inequality, 3, 8, 11–12, 22; access to resources, 173; brotherhood/sisterhood and mutual responsibility, 173–74; challenge to overcome, 32, 209; clarification of concept, 60; decrease between countries,

22; fairness in economic transactions, 173; gender and socioeconomic disadvantages in Qur'anic texts, 155–57; increase within countries, 22; justice in economic transactions, 172–73, 176–77; mitigation measures, 11–12, 209; in New Testament, 120, 122, 136n48; in New Testament's self-sacrifice of Jesus Christ, 129–30, 144–45; in Old Testament, 99–103, 105, 114; pagan practice of allocating agricultural share to false gods, 189; in Qur'anic texts, 171–91; ritual friendship in Hellenistic society, 120–21. *See also* charity; class inequality; poverty; the wealthy
the "edge" metaphor, 204–6, 223–24
Edomites, 95, 105n6, 111
egalitarianism, 15, 79, 80, 84, 118, 121, 126, 131
Egypt: influence on Israel's theologians, 98; "Instruction of Amen-em-ope," 98; Israelites as slaves in, 104, 110; Joseph in (Old Testament), 104; piety movement in, 42–43
Eike von Repgow, 83
elopement, 39
Emon, Anver M., 74n2
empowerment: disempowerment, 213; lack expressed in inability to benefit from opportunities, 61; of Muslim allies against neoliberalism, 17
English Standard Version Translation Oversight Committee, 83
Enlightenment, 41, 69
Epaenetus (first Christian conversion in Asia), 144
Ephesus, role of women in, 126–28
equality: Aquinas on, 26–27; arithmetic, 26–27, 31; in Christian tradition, 24–26, 31; context determines actual application of the religious texts on, 204, 209; developing common ethic of, 3, 201–6, 221–23; elusive meaning of, 218; identical treatment not required, 26; inclusion based on, 32; intrareligious engagements discussing, 218, 222; justice and, 26–27; learning to live at the "edges" of interreligious encounter, 204–6, 223–24; as modern concept, 69; modern Muslim responses, 15–16; modern secular ideologies and, 16; New Testament use of term *"isotés,"* 130; proportional, 27, 28, 137n53, 171; in Qur'anic texts, 9, 151–61; rejection of particular teachings of Qur'an and hadith, 15; religious actors, role as

equality *(continued)*
    "agents of change" for, 211–13, 222; as reli-
    gious value, 66; of respect, 72; in today's
    Christian living tradition, 32–33, 137n53.
    See also cooperation; New Testament on
    equality/inequality; *specific types*
Esau, 95
Esther, 98
ethics and morality: definition of morality,
    219; developing common ethic of equality,
    3, 201–6, 221–23; modern views, 16; natural
    law–based conviction of ethical responsibil-
    ities, 25; prudence compared to morality,
    73, 219; of reciprocity in Qur'an, 89n12;
    about slavery, 84–85
ethnic equality/inequality, 3, 12; *imitatio Christi*
    concept and, 129–30; in New Testament,
    118–20, 121, 131, 132; in Old Testament,
    95–99, 110–11, 122; in Qur'anic texts, 152,
    159, 164
ethnicity: difference from nationality, 61–62;
    as social construct, 62; in West Africa,
    59–67, 209. *See also* ethnic equality/
    inequality
Evangelicals, 56
Ewell, C. Rosalee Velloso, 3, 201, 223
Ewell, Sam, 205
exclusion, 32, 69, 72, 110–11, 128, 218. *See also*
    types of inequality
Exodus, 104
Ezra, 98

fairness, 9, 66, 136n48, 155–57, 173, 178, 184.
    See also justice
family: both parents responsible for raising
    children in Old Testament, 94, 95; child
    custody, 11; domination of heterosexual
    and nuclear family, 39–40; father's respon-
    sibility to support children, 157; of God
    through Jesus Christ, 130, 140; household
    codes in New Testament, 122–23, 124–26,
    135n30, 145–46; reform of family law, 44;
    respect and kindness for parents, 167, 184,
    195; sanctity of, 39. *See also* orphans,
    protection of
fascist persecution of religions, 29, 31
Al-Fatiha Foundation, 47
Fatima (Muhammad's daughter), 166
feminism, 42; Islamic Feminism, 43–44
fideism, 16
Fiorenza, Elisabeth Schüssler, 125
Flavius Josephus, 105n2, 105n6

forced-labor conditions in contemporary world,
    210, 221
forgiveness, 2, 7, 10, 129, 143, 155, 166
fragile countries, access to water in, 211
France, as African colonial power, 63
Francis (pope), 32
freedom, 8; antiracist resources of Christian
    scripture and tradition, 57; political free-
    doms and transparency as part of set of
    linked freedoms, 213; as sign of divine
    image, 26; social progress and, 41; types of,
    221; of women in context of marriage, 159.
    See also manumission of slaves
free market, 12, 33, 219
French Revolution, 15
friendship, 120–21, 134n15
fundamentalists' definition of gender roles,
    42, 43

al-Gamā'ah al-Islāmīyah (Islamic Brother-
    hood), 73
Gandhi, Mohandas, 30
gender roles and inequality, 3, 8, 10–11, 12,
    39–52, 207; age for girls to marry in Bangla-
    desh, 39; apologetics and, 219; biblical
    Hebrew as gendered language, 95; charis-
    matic leaders and biblical prophets, 94,
    115–16; complementary roles of men and
    women, 40, 43–46; conservatism of Islam
    and, 41–43; demands for gender equality, 14;
    early syncretistic Islam and equal gender
    relations, 48; Eve's (woman's) susceptibility
    to deception and, 127, 131; female obedience
    to male and punishment for disobedience,
    10, 42; gender-based violence, 207, 210;
    gender fluidity, 46; gender justice, 43, 45;
    imitatio Christi concept and, 129–30;
    male-headed family, 41–42; monarchs and
    community leadership in biblical period, 94;
    in New Testament, 118–20, 122, 126–29, 131,
    132, 143–44; in Old Testament, 93–95, 105,
    114, 134n10; only men who provide for their
    wives can have privilege of superiority over
    their wives, 44, 168; poverty and, 23–24;
    qiwama (authority of men over women),
    158–59; in Qur'anic texts, 155–59, 166–67,
    171, 177–78; religious reform focusing on
    women and femininities, 45; religious
    stances on gender, 48–49, 207–8; social
    progress and, 40–41, 207–8; "Western
    woman" image and, 43; womanism, 57, 58n7.
    See also inheritance rights

Gentiles: in New Testament, 120–23, 130, 131, 134n12, 142–43, 204–5; in Old Testament, 97–98, 105. *See also* non-Israelites in Old Testament

Germany as African colonial power, 63

Ghana, 62, 63

globalization, 47, 212

Global Muslim Women's Shura Council, 44

glossolalia, 120, 141, 165

God. *See* creation; divine election; divine will; poverty

God-consciousness (*taqwa*), 10, 152, 173, 176

God's love, 25

gō'ēl (next-of-kin) as method to control land, 103

Good Samaritan parable, 128, 139–40

Greek culture: chauvinism in, 122; influence on Muslim social structure, 153; morality and household structure in, 125–26

Gregory of Nyssa, 83, 88n5

Gregory XVI (pope), 28–29

Hadith: Al-Adab al-Mufrad, 167, 197; al-Bukhari, 165, 167, 168; Jami' al-Tirmidhi, 165–66; Muslim, 165; Prophet's Farewell Sermon, 165; Sunan Ibn Majah, 197

Ham (Noah's son), 54–55

Hammon, Jupiter, 117–18, 132–33, 137n54

Ḥanafīs, 18n6, 71, 74nn4–5

Haustafeln. *See* household codes in New Testament

Hays, Christopher M., 3, 117

heretics, treatment of, 28

hermeneutics, 218–19, 225. *See also* New Testament; Old Testament; Qur'an

hierarchical inequality, 11, 13, 18n4; believers vs. non-believers, 153; family, clan, and tribe, 12; gender hierarchy, 42, 129. *See also* caste and social class; patriarchy

Hinduism, 8, 31, 49, 78, 222

Hizbollah, 43

Hollenbach, David, 2, 21, 71

Holy Spirit: Cornelius's conversion and, 122, 142–43; egalitarian unity in, 121, 143; glossolalia and, 120, 141

homosexuality, 46–48

honesty, 172, 173

honor as part of maintaining social class, 78

honor killings, 44

Hoppe, Leslie J., 3, 93

household codes in New Testament, 122–23, 124–26, 135n30, 145–46

Huldah (prophet), 94, 115–16

human rights: Christian promotion of, 21, 29–31; equal dignity and, 30; separation of Muslim women from their own cultures and, 44. *See also* poverty; slavery

Hume, David, 219

Huq, Samia, 2, 39, 207–8

hypermasculinity, 43

hypocrites who criticized Muhammad about distribution of wealth, 184–85, 195

Ibn Kathir, 181, 182–84, 186, 188

Ibn Taymiyya, 11

idolatry, 98–99

Imaan (UK-based group), 47

IMF (International Monetary Fund), 59

IMI (Inclusive Mosque Initiative), 46

immigration, 70, 212, 223

imperialism. *See* colonialism and imperialism

Inclusive Mosque Initiative (IMI), 46

indentured slaves. *See* debt slavery

India, 77–81; Ajlafs (converted Muslims), 80; Ashrafs (Muslims) and class hierarchy in, 80–81; *avarna* (people without caste), 78; castes in, 78–79; Catholic missionaries in, 80; Christians maintaining caste system in, 80; Dalits ("Untouchable" castes) in, 77–80; democracy in, 31; *varnas* (four caste orders), 78. *See also* caste and social class; Hinduism

individualism, 8, 14

Indonesia, democracy in, 31

industrialization, 16

inequality: as challenge for contemporary Christians, 21–35, 209, 224; as challenge for contemporary Islam, 7–19, 209, 224; changing norms of, role of religious actors in, 211–13, 222; in Christian tradition, 28–29; as concept, 13–15, 207; concerted organization and struggle for change, 78; contradiction created by fixing one in creating another, 223; divine election and, 220; envy in relation to, 24; as injustice, 16; mitigating forces, 11–12, 209, 223; needing to hear what "lived inequality" sounds like, 223; nobility based on piety and faith as permissible, 9–10, 18n4; recognized as norm in nature and society, 13, 171, 209, 223; ubiquity of, 1, 209; water, access to, 211. *See also* cooperation; New Testament on equality/inequality; *specific types of inequality* inheritance rights: division of estate, 157, 194–95; of orphans, 183–84; patriarchal, 95, 177, 194; prebendal system replacing family-based system of inheritance, 100; *sadaqa*, limits on, 179–80; of women, 10–12, 157, 183, 194

injustice: as construct determined by the major powers, 204; context determines actual application of the religious texts on, 204; inequality as, 16; Muslims as victims and as perpetrators of, 7, 8; premodern tradition's view of, 16

intellect, 25–26

International Labour Organization (ILO) report on forced labor (2017), 210, 213n6

International Monetary Fund, 59

intersectionality: antiracist resources of Christian scripture and tradition, 57. *See also* cultural-political intersections; the "edge" metaphor

Iranian Revolution, 43

Isaianic tradition, 96, 97–98

Ishmael (Abraham's son), 95

Isidore of Seville, 86

ISIS, 18, 43

Islamic finance. *See* money lending

Islamic history, legal or doctrinal effect of, 73

Islamic State of Iraq and Syria (ISIS), 18, 43

Israelites (ancient Israel): agrarian economy, 99–100; as chosen people of God, 96, 97, 108, 220; ethnic/religious inequality and, 95–99; gender equality/inequality and, 93–95; land distribution and ownership, 100–103; poverty and, 101–2; prebendal system of governance, 100, 106n12; slavery and, 104; socioeconomic inequality and, 99–103

Italy, as African colonial power, 63

Jackson, Sherman A., 2, 69, 213

al-Jamāʿah al-Islāmīyah (Islamic Brotherhood), 73

James, 128

Janissaries, 83

Japheth (Noah's son), 54–55

Jeremiah (prophet), 94

Jesse (father of David), 112

Jesus Christ: Blackness of, 57; family of, 130, 140; freeing of the oppressed, 56; identifying himself as the Messiah, 119; impartiality of, 136n51; redemption offered in, 25; Samaritan woman at the well and, 118–19, 140–41; self-sacrificial death and *imitatio Christi*, 129–30, 144–45; slavery and, 55; superses-

sionist view of Christ superseding Abraham, 56, 220

Jews, anti-Semitism and persecution of, 29, 134n12

Job, 98

jobs: forced-labor conditions in contemporary world, 210; growth without jobs in, 59; upper class/caste forcing lower class/caste to do unpleasant and demeaning jobs, 77

John (apostle), 129

John XXIII (pope): *Pacem in terris* (encyclical), 31

John Hyrcanus I (Hasmonean king), 105n6

John Paul II (pope), 28, 29, 30, 34–35n31

Joseph (Old Testament), 104

Joshua, 55, 96, 105n7

Josiah (biblical king), 94

jubilee years, 103, 108–9

Judah, kingdom of, 96–97, 105n1, 105n8

Junia (leader of a house church), 126, 132, 144

justice: "the cause of the oppressed," 188; elusive meaning of, 8–9, 218; equality and, 26–27; failure to uphold teachings of, 7, 8; gender justice, 43, 45; inheritance shares, distribution of, 184; Qurʾanic call for, 9, 172–73, 176–77; as religious value, 66

Kaʿba (Meccan pagan shrine), 174

Kaboré, François Pazisnewende, 2, 59, 209

kāfirs, 75n9. *See also* unbelievers

Kant, Immanuel, 25

Karam, Azza, 3, 207, 222

Kenrick, Francis, 28

Keturah (Abraham's wife), 95

Khadija (Muhammad's wife), 156

Kharijites, 15

King, Martin Luther, Jr., 30

Kshatriyas (rulers and warriors caste), 78, 80

Kugle, Scott, 46

Kuran, Timur, 173

Kuwait, democracy in, 31

Kuznets's curve, 60

Lalon Fakir, 48, 51n32

land ownership. *See* property

language diversity. *See* glossolalia

Latin America, democracy in, 30

law and legal norms, 13; consent of majority to, 73–74; Israelites influenced by laws of other cultures of ancient Near East, 98; reforms of, 44, 45; slavery and, 86–87

Lebanon, women joining Hizbollah in, 43

Levites, 106n11, 110

LGBTQ persons, 46–48, 208

liberalism: democratic equality and, 9; denial of religious roots in, 14; as modern Western construct, 72; outcome inequality as result of, 13; progressivist interpretation of Qur'an and hadith texts, 8, 15. *See also* Enlightenment; neoliberalism

life expectancy, 23

lived religion, 40

living traditions and equality, 29–32, 137n53

Locke, John, 72

Longenecker, Richard, 123

Lot, 46, 95, 108

love: Christian love, 34n17; God's love, 25; of neighbor, 128–29, 139–40

Lugo, Juan de, 28

Luke (apostle), 120, 128, 134n15

Luther, Martin, 79

Macedonians, 129, 144

MacIntyre, Alasdair, 14, 16

Madigan, Daniel A., 1

Mahmood, Saba, 42, 44–45

"Make America Great Again," 70

Mali, 62–64

Mamluks, 153

manumission of slaves, 12, 87, 94, 103, 106n16, 109, 110, 124, 175, 178, 188, 193, 196, 197

Manusmriti, 78

marriage, 10, 11; age for girls to marry in Bangladesh, 39; child marriage (worldwide statistics), 210; dowry and bride-gifts, 156, 168, 177, 183–84; heterosexual monogamous unions as dominant form, 40; law of Levirate marriage, 95; Musawah seeking to shift construction of, 44; New Testament on relationship between husband and wife, 125, 129, 131, 136n37, 136n52; Old Testament warning against Jewish men marrying non-Jewish wives, 98, 112; orphans, marrying for financial gain, 178, 183, 194; Qur'an on number of women a man could marry, 178; Qur'an on relationship between husband and wife, 152, 156–57, 166, 168; Qur'an's encouragement of, 188, 196; widows, protection of, 122, 177, 178–79, 217. *See also* polygamy

Martin, Ralph, 130

Marxism, 78

Mashkoor, Masood, 180

Maududi, Sayyid Abul Ala, 172, 173, 175, 180, 181, 182–90

Mecca. *See* Arabian seventh-century society

Medina. *See* Arabian seventh-century society

Mehmed IV (Ottoman sultan), 83

men: all prophets in Qur'an as, 11; forms of masculinity, 46; political equality of, 14. *See also* patriarchy

mercy, 7, 9

Mernissi, Fatima, 43

Mesopotamian empires. *See* ancient Near East

Middle East: Islamist reform ideas from, 48; most economically unequal region in the world, 23; views on justice, accountability, and rights, 18. *See also* ancient Near East

Midianites, 95, 98

militant Islamists' definition of gender roles, 42

Miriam (prophet), 94, 98, 115

missionaries, 54, 80

Moabites, 95, 98, 111

modernity, threat of losing traditions in, 49, 72

monarchy and government bureaucracy during biblical period: economic effects of, 100–103, 115; gender roles and inequality, 94

money lending, 11, 109, 111, 165, 178, 185–86; prohibition of *riba*, 180–81, 185–86, 187, 195–96

monotheism, 14, 15, 17, 69, 132, 167, 183, 202

morality. *See* ethics and morality

Moses, 98, 104, 119, 164

Mosher, Lucinda, 4, 217

Mosse people and Mosse Empire, 61–65, 67n6

Movassaghi, Hormoz, 180

Mughals, 81

Muhammad: criticized for his distribution of wealth, 185, 195; on execution as punishment, 70–71; farewell sermon, 165; on justice and compassion, 7; on Mecca's inequal economic society, 174; on poverty, 11; Quraysh tribe of, 152; on racial inequality, 152; on slavery, 84, 86–87; on women's equality, 155

Murray, John Courtney, 35n31

Musawah, 44; Global Life Stories Project, 45

Muslims. *See* Christian-Muslim relations; Muhammad; Qur'an

mutual theological hospitality, 212

Naboth's vineyard, 106n13

Nahum (prophet), 97

Naomi, 103, 111–12

nationality and ethnicity: difference between, 61–62; as social constructs, 62; in West Africa, 59–67. *See also* ethnic equality/ inequality
natural law, 25
natural order as divine, 13
Nehemiah, 98
neoliberalism, 8, 17
Newman, John Henry, 29
New Testament on equality/inequality, 117–37, 133n4; conversion of the first Gentile, 121–22, 131, 142–43; created order, 131, 136n45; dietary and calendrical disputes, 123; equality in people of God, proclaimed by Paul, 122–23, 134n12; family of Christ, 130, 140; Good Samaritan, 128, 139–40; household codes, 122–23, 124–26, 145–46; imitation of Christ (*imitatio Christi*), 129–30; impartiality of God, 131, 134n19, 136n51; love of neighbor, 128–29, 139–40; Pentecost and birth of Jerusalem community, 120–21; repeating from Ten Commandments, 128; Samaritan woman at the well, 118–19, 140–41; slavery teachings by Paul, 123–24, 126, 130, 132, 146–47; women to be subordinate to men, 126–28, 131, 132
NGOs (nongovernmental organizations), 211–12
Nicolaus of Antioch, 121, 134n17
Niger, 64
Nigeria, 62
Noadiah (prophet), 94
Noah, 54–55, 107–8
nobility in piety and faith, 9–10, 18n4, 176
nongovernmental organizations (NGOs), 211–12
non-Israelites in Old Testament, 97–99, 104
non-Muslims: equality with Muslims in areas of public domain, 73, 154; fair treatment by Muslims, 154; legal restrictions on, 70–71; military service by, 74, 154; permitted to follow their own religions, 70–71, 154; slavery and, 87; superiority of Islamic believers over, 152–54, 164–65, 168; tax (*jizya*) paid by, 70, 74, 154, 168
Noonan, John T., 28–29
North Africa, Christianity and Islam in, 64

Obadiah (prophet), 97
Obed (grandfather of David), 112
obscurantism, 16
Old Testament: Christian churches' differences on what books constitute, 93; ethnic/reli-

gious inequality in, 95–99, 105, 110–14; gender equality/inequality in, 93–95, 105; inequality in, 93–106; "patriarch" terminology not used in, 95; on slavery, 85, 86, 103–4, 105, 114; socioeconomic inequality in, 99–103, 105, 108–9, 114, 131. *See also* Israelites
Onesimus (runaway slave), 123–24, 130, 146–47
oppression and the oppressed: caste system, 80; as construct determined by the major powers, 204; context determines actual application of the religious texts on, 204; freeing of the oppressed, 56; God as life-giving and on side of the oppressed, 222; need to support weak against, 188, 197, 222; Qur'an showing oppression of Muslim slaves, 85; race as construct and, 53; in story of Lot and city of Sodom, 46–47; uprising of German peasants (sixteenth century), 79. *See also* poverty
orphans, protection of, 85, 110, 122, 175, 177, 178, 183–84, 187, 193–97, 217
Ottoman slave armies, 153
outcome inequality, 13

pagans, 85–89, 135, 174, 189
Page, Sarah-Jane, 47
Pastuns, 80–81
patriarchy: ancient household codes and, 125–26; in ancient Near East culture, 12; Christianity and, 50n3; Hebrew Bible not using term, 95; inheritance rights and, 95, 177, 194; love-patriarchalism, 126; *Men in Charge: Rethinking Authority in Muslim Legal Tradition*, 44; Paul's affirmation of, 122, 125–26; women's negotiations within, 42. *See also* gender roles and inequality
Paul (saint), 28, 31–32, 79, 84, 118, 122–26, 128–31, 134n20, 135n35
Paul VI (pope), on lack of development of poorer countries, 33n9
Pentecost, 120–21, 141–42
Perez's descendants, 112
perpetuation of inequalities, 2, 3, 207, 211
Persian Muslims, 152, 153
Peter (apostle), 120, 121–22, 131, 141, 142–43, 204–5
Philemon, Paul's writing about runaway slave to, 123–24, 130, 146–47
Philippines, democracy in, 30
Phillips, Elizabeth, 2, 53, 208

Philo of Alexandria, 86
Philpott, Daniel, 30–31
Phoebe (church deacon), 144
piety: among educated, urban women in Bangladesh, 41; fulfillment of requirements of, 187, 196; piety movement in Egypt, 42–43. *See also* nobility in piety and faith; ritual purity and piety
pluralism, 46, 70
Poland, democracy in, 30
politics: faith-based engagement of, 211–12; leadership dominated by men in Old Testament, 94; leadership dominated by men in Qur'anic texts, 155–56; political equality of men, 14; political freedoms and transparency as part of set of linked freedoms, 213. *See also* power
polygamy, 10, 40, 178, 183
Portugal: as African colonial power, 63; democracy in, 30
poverty, 11, 12, 17; in Africa, 59; of biblical-era Israelites, 99–101, 108–9, 114–15; call to take care of the poor, 218; exclusion of the poor, 32, 181; extreme poverty, 22, 23; fragile countries, access to water in, 211; gender inequality and, 23–24; increase in number of poor people, 22; listening to the poor, 222; oppression of poor people by caste system, 79–80; racial inequality and, 173; reduction of, 24, 209; relationship of the poor with God, 106n14, 108, 134n19, 168, 182, 193; as result of inequality, 32, 101–3, 106n14; sacrifice of Christ in becoming poor, 129; wealthier Christians looking down on poorer Christians, 79; wealthier Christians sharing with poorer Christians, 121, 132; wealthier landowners' treatment of the poor in ancient Israel, 101–2; wealthier Muslims sharing with poorer Muslims, 175–76, 177, 182, 193, 197; *zakat* and *sadaqa* requirements on Muslims, 179–80, 184–85, 186. *See also* charity; economic equality/inequality
power: behind caste and social class, 77–78; countries with power who determine the norms for oppression and injustice, 204; inequality as matter of, 207; need to balance between power and dependency, 220; power theory, 8
prebendal system of governance, 100, 106n12
premodern Islam, 16
primitive tribes, hierarchy within, 13–14
primogeniture, 127, 136n45

Prisca/Priscilla, 126, 132, 144
profit vs. usury, 186
progressivists: gender roles and, 45; responses to equality issues, 15
property: *gōʾēl* (next-of-kin) as method to control land, 103; inequality in, 12, 102; land, in light of Qur'anic texts, 220; land ownership and economic inequality in biblical period, 99–103, 105; right to own, 12. *See also* inheritance rights; slavery
the Prophet. *See* Muhammad
prophethood: election of prophets, 220; women's role in, 94, 115–16. *See also specific prophet by name*
prostitution of female slaves, 188, 196
Protestantism, 31; Reformation, 79
prudence, 73, 219
punishment: criminal sentencing, 27; execution as, 70–71, 74n5; in Hereafter, 168, 176, 182, 186; husband's discipline of his wife, 10, 42; slavery as, 86–88, 104; of slaves, 12, 124
purity, 18n4, 79, 129. *See also* ritual purity and piety

Qadir, Junaid, 177
Qaraḍāwī, Shaykh Yūsuf al-, 73–74
Qarāfī, Shihāb al-Dīn al-, 73
Qays b. Sa'd b. (Muhammad's companion), 168
qiwama (authority of men over women), 158–59
Qoheleth, book of, 98
Quakers, 56
Quraysh (Meccan tribe), 85, 152, 175
al-Qurtubi, 158
Qur'an: Arabian seventh-century society reflected in, 155–60, 174–79; class inequality in, 152, 166; divine election in, 220; economic equality/inequality in, 171–91; gender equality in, 155–59, 166–67, 171; inheritance rights in, 157; marriage in, 156–57; Mecca's importance in, 175; Prophet's farewell sermon, 165; *qiwama* (authority of men over women) in, 158–59; racial equality in, 151–53, 164–65; religious equality in, 153–54, 164–65, 167–69; slavery in, 85, 152–53, 165, 171, 177, 178; wealth as legitimate goal in, 173; wealth distribution in, 174
Qutb, Sayyid, 178, 181, 182–86, 188–89

racial equality/inequality, 12, 23, 53–58, 208–9; Afro-pessimism and, 55–56; antiracist movements in Christianity, 56; antiracist resources of Christian scripture and tradition, 57;

racial equality/inequality *(continued)*
  assumption nonwhiteness is deficient, 54;
  collusion of Western Christianity in, 54;
  history of "race" and racism, 57nn1–2; missionaries and, 54; in New Testament, 118–20,
  122; in Qur'anic texts, 151–53, 164–65; race
  as social construct, 53, 54–55, 62; slavery
  and segregation in America, 54–55, 56,
  117–18; white supremacy, 55. *See also* Blackness; slavery; whiteness
Rahman, Fazlur, 159, 176, 181
Rawls, John, 67n3
al-Razi, 158
redemption, 16, 25
reformists: gender roles, definition of, 44, 45;
  responses to equality issues, 15
religious authenticity, 48
religious engagement in contemporary world
  problems, 207–13, 218–19
religious equality/inequality, 3, 12; denial of
  religious freedom to non-Christians, 28–29,
  30; description of concept, 60–61; in New
  Testament, 128; in Old Testament, 95–99;
  in Qur'anic texts, 153–54, 167–69
religious freedom, 28–31, 71, 212, 219
religious practice: ancient Near East cultures'
  influence on Israelites, 98–99; contributing
  to inequality, 209; covenant of Israelites
  extended to all who obey, 97, 113–14; creed's
  claim to universal validity, 219; creed's contribution to sociopolitical equality, 69–74,
  213; diversity within a given religion, 40;
  New Testament views on, 128, 132, 143–44;
  refusal by Israelites to use images, 98–99; of
  Samaritans, 119. *See also* religious equality/
  inequality
religious wars, 28–29
repentance, 165, 173, 196
respect, 25–26, 30, 44, 72, 78, 123, 126, 146,
  167, 186, 203
Revival of the Religious Sciences of al-Ghazali,
  85
Riḍā, Rashīd, 75n9
righteousness, 102, 114, 115, 186, 187
Rig Veda, 78
ritual friendship, 120–21
ritual purity and piety, 119, 121, 122, 123, 129
Roman culture: debt slavery in, 86; human
  status as freedom in, 86; morality and household structure in, 125–26; slave status
  transferred through mother in, 88

Romania, democracy in, 31
Ruth, 98, 103, 111

sabbatical years, 103, 106n16, 109–10
Sadat, Anwar, 73
Saeed, Abdullah, 3, 151, 171
Safra Project, 47
Sahl b. Hanif (Muhammad's companion), 168
Sallam ibn 'Amr, 197
Salman al-Farisi, 84
Salome Alexandra (queen of Judah), 105n2
Samaritans, 133n7; ritualized friendship to
  include, 121; superiority of Jews to, 128;
  woman at the well, 118–19, 140–41. *See also*
  Good Samaritan parable
Sarkar, Tanika, 49
Saudi Arabia, 17–18
Sayyads, 80
Second Vatican Council (1962–65), 25–26,
  28–31, 35n31
secularism, 8, 14, 17, 41; family model favored
  in, 40
Sen, Amartya, 23–24, 61, 77, 213
Senegal, 62–64
Serbia, democracy in, 31
sexism. *See* gender roles and inequality; patriarchy
sexual diversity, 46, 47
sexual exploitation and sex-trafficking, 210
sexual orientation, 46–47. *See also* LGBTQ
  persons
Shah, Timothy, 30–31
Shaikh, Sadiya, 45
sharia, 13, 86–88
Shaykhs, 80
Shem (Noah's son), 54–55
Shudras (laborers caste), 78, 80
Shu'ubiyya movement, 152
Sisters in Islam, 44
slavery, 12–13, 28, 30, 54–55, 83–89, 208–9,
  220–21; in America, 54–55, 56, 117–18;
  apologetics and, 221; Arabic dictionary entry
  for, 84; chattel slavery, 28, 104, 105, 106n15;
  contemporary types of forced labor, 210,
  221; conversion of American slaves to Christianity, 117–18; conversion of slave by Paul,
  123–24, 130, 146–47; conversion of slaves to
  Christianity or Islam, 86; debt slavery,
  86–87, 103, 105, 106n15, 178; diminishing
  hierarchy around, 84; *doulos,* translation of,
  83; *'ebed,* translation of, 83; gender equality

when gaining freedom, 94, 103; Gregory of Nyssa in opposition to, 83; just/fair treatment of slaves, 55, 84, 126, 131, 146, 178, 195, 197; legal tradition of, 86–87; marriage of slaves, 188; New Testament on, 117–18, 123–24, 126, 130, 132, 146–47; Old Testament on, 85, 86, 103–4, 105, 108–10, 114; prostitution of female slaves, 188, 196; as punishment, 86–88, 104; Qur'an on, 85, 152–53, 165, 171, 177, 178, 195, 220–21; Qur'an use of "the slaves of God," 83; sexual exploitation and sex-trafficking in contemporary world, 210; slave status passed through mother, 88; theological justification for, 86–88, 220–21; theological vs. moral views of, 84–85, 104, 220. *See also* abolition of slavery; manumission of slaves

Smith, Adam, 219

social activism, 15, 56; religious actors, role as "agents of change," 211–13, 222

social equality/inequality, 8; moral good of sociopolitical equality, 14; in New Testament, 120, 122; in Qur'anic texts, 152. *See also* caste and social class; economic equality/inequality; poverty; the wealthy

social hierarchy. *See* caste and social class; hierarchical inequality; patriarchy

socioeconomic inequality. *See* economic equality/inequality

sociopolitical equality/inequality: ambiguity of concept, 74; moral good of, 14; Muslim reactions to calls to banish, 72; qualified in actual application, 26, 71; reconciling Muslim scripture and Tradition with, 73–74; religious creed's contribution, 69–74; state of society and, 69–70; West Africa's nationality and ethnicity in relation to, 65, 66t. *See also* caste and social class

Sodom, 46

sodomy, 46–47

solidarity, 15, 41, 57

Solomon, 55, 98, 104, 112, 115

South Africa: Al-Fatiha Foundation for LGBTQ Muslims in, 47; apartheid in, 27; gay imams in, 47; precolonial period, 62; Zulus in, 64

South Asia: caste and social class in, 77–81; "missing women" in, 24; Sufism revival in, 47. *See also* caste and social class; *specific countries*

South Korea, democracy in, 31

Soviet Union, demise of, 30

Spain: as African colonial power, 63; Al-Fatiha Foundation for LGBTQ Muslims in, 47; democracy in, 30

Stoicism, 86

sub-Saharan Africa: Christianity in, 64; democracy in, 65; extreme poverty in, 22

Sufism: revival in West and Muslim-majority countries, 47–48, 51n31; traditions and gender discrimination, 45

Sunni: male superiority to women, 158; tradition and racial equality, 152

Syrian Christians, 80

Tabataba'i, Muhammad Husayn, 158

Taheb (messiah expected by Samaritans), 119

Tammuz (deity), 98

taqwa (God-consciousness), 10, 152, 173, 176

Ten Commandments, 55, 128

Thales of Miletus, 122

theft, 12, 165–66

Theissen, Gerd, 126

Timothy, Paul's letter to, 126

Toft, Monica Duffy, 30–31

tolerance, 46, 48

trade and trade networks, 12, 155, 174–75, 186, 195

tradition: everyday responses to, 40; multiple authorities on, 41; sociopolitical inequality accepted as norm, 71

traditionalists: gender roles, definition of, 42; responses to equality issues, 16

transcendence, 26

translators living in war zones, 223

Troeltsch, Ernst, 126

Turkey, 17

Tutu, Desmond, 30

unbelievers, 34, 69, 72, 85, 188

United Kingdom: as African colonial power, 63; Al-Fatiha Foundation for LGBTQ Muslims in, 47; citizenship in, 61; cross-cultural and interfaith initiative in, 205

United Nations, 31; Climate Change Conference (2015), 222; Sustainable Development Goals, 22

United States: Al-Fatiha Foundation for LGBTQ Muslims in, 47; citizenship in, 61; class inequality within, 23; gay imams in, 47; increasing inequality within, 23; inequality in, compared to Western Europe, 23; racial inequality within, 23; slavery in, 117–18 universalism: argumentative, 49; creed's claim to universal validity, 219; in New Testament, 120–22, 132, 141–45; in Old Testament, 96–98, 112–14

Usama b. Zaid (Muhammad's companion), 166

US Catholic Bishops on exclusion of the poor, 32

usury, prohibition of. *See* money lending

Vaishya (artisans, merchants, farmers caste), 78

Vatican II. *See* Second Vatican Council

veiling, 44

violence and threats: in ancient Near East, 95–97; to existence of Israelites, 96–99; gender-based violence, 207, 210; to Muslims, 154, 188; religious wars, 28–29, 168; war zones, translators living in, 223

virtue: mercy and compassion as more important than justice, 9; modern secular ideologies and, 16; path of virtue vs. path of vice, 175, 183; sexual virtue, 119–20; slavery and, 86–87

voting, 26–27

Wadud, Amina, 159

wages: depressed wages, in caste and social class systems, 77; equality in, 27; fairness in, 173

Wahhabis, 17

Walk Free Foundation report on forced labor (2017), 210, 213n6

Walzer, Michael, 27

water, access to, 211

the wealthy: conspicuous spending, 173, 184, 195; God as giver of wealth, 175, 182; not to exploit the vulnerable, 172, 182–83; ritual friendship in Hellenistic society, 120–21; wealth and corruption of morals, 17; wealth as legitimate goal, 173; wealth distribution, 174, 179, 182. *See also* economic equality/inequality; poverty

Weber, Max, 78

Welchman, Lynn, 50n11

well-being, 24, 30, 41, 172

West Africa, nationality and ethnicity in, 59–67, 209; access to education and, 65; Berlin Conference (1884–85) and division into colonies, 63–64, 67n8; challenges of nation-building, 62–64; colonial administration's collaboration with Christians, 65; economic inequality as concept, 60; precolonial period, 62–63, 63t; religious inequality as concept, 60–61; religious map, 64; sociopolitical fragmentation and inequality related to, 65, 66t

Wheatley, Phillis, 133

whiteness, 53, 54, 56, 208

white supremacy, 55

widows, protection of, 122, 177, 178–79, 217

wisdom: human wisdom reflecting God's wisdom, 25; prudence and, 219

Wolof people, 63, 64

womanism, 57, 58n7

women: age for girls to marry in Bangladesh, 39; agency of, 42, 183; aligning role with virtuous community, 39; as charismatic leaders and biblical prophets, 94, 115–16; effects of child marriage on, 210; Jewish religious leaders and teachers restricted from speaking with (New Testament), 119–20, 134n10; in Meccan and Medinan societies, 155–56, 160, 177–78; "missing women," 23–24, 156, 166; as monarchs in biblical era, 94; mosques, women-led and women-run, 46; prostitution of female slaves, 188, 196; silence of, 126–27; violence against, 207, 210; as witnesses, 11, 159, 166–67. *See also* gender roles and inequality; inheritance rights

Woodhead, Linda, 48

Word of God, 29, 118, 218. *See also* New Testament; Old Testament; Qur'an

World Bank, 22, 59; Doing Business (2018), 59; *Turbulent Waters: Pursuing Water Security in Fragile Contexts* (2017), 211

worship. *See* religious practice

worth of persons, 25

YHWH, 56, 97, 99

Yip, Andrew, 47

Zaman, Asad, 177

Zaman, M. Raquibuz, 180

Zanj revolt, 152

Zaynab (Muhammad's wife), 188

Zedekiah (king of Judah), 103

Zipporah (Moses's wife), 98, 105n9

Zoroastrians, 71

Zulu people, 62, 64

Scriptural Citation Index

Bible

Genesis *1:27*, 24–25, 203
Genesis *1:31*, 203
Genesis *1–3*, 127, 131
Genesis *1–11*, 98
Genesis *1:27*, 93, 107
Genesis *2*, 131
Genesis *2:7–24*, 131
Genesis *2:18*, 107
Genesis *2:18–22*, 93
Genesis *2:21–22*, 107
Genesis *2:24*, 131
Genesis *3:1–11*, 201–2
Genesis *3:1–19*, 131
Genesis *3:16*, 136n52
Genesis *3:20–21*, 202
Genesis *3:21*, 205
Genesis *9*, 54–55
Genesis *9:2*, 135n35
Genesis *9:8–11*, 107–8
Genesis *9:25*, 55
Genesis *9:26–27*, 55
Genesis *10*, 54–55
Genesis *12*, 55, 218
Genesis *12:1–4*, 108, 220
Genesis *12:3*, 96
Genesis *19:17*, 95
Genesis *19:38*, 95
Genesis *24*, 55
Genesis *25:1–4*, 95
Genesis *25:12–15*, 95
Genesis *25:19–20*, 95
Genesis *25:25*, 95
Genesis *36:8*, 95
Genesis *37:27–28*, 104
Genesis *41:37–45*, 104
Genesis *43:18*, 104
Exodus *1:11–14*, 104
Exodus *2:16–22*, 98
Exodus *12:40*, 104
Exodus *13:3*, 104
Exodus *15:20*, 94

Exodus *15:20–21*, 115
Exodus *20*, 55
Exodus *20:8–10*, 94
Exodus *20:12*, 94
Exodus *21:20–21*, 86
Exodus *38:8*, 94
Leviticus *12:8*, 129
Leviticus *19*, 218
Leviticus *19:9*, 100
Leviticus *19:9–10*, 108
Leviticus *19:13*, 108
Leviticus *19:18*, 128
Leviticus *25*, 55
Leviticus *25:4–5*, 106n16
Leviticus *25:8–17*, 108–9
Leviticus *25:13–17*, 103
Leviticus *25:35–46*, 108–9
Leviticus *25:43*, 86
Leviticus *25:44–46*, 104
Leviticus *25:46*, 86
Leviticus *25:47–49*, 103
Numbers *12:1*, 98
Numbers *12:10*, 98
Numbers *20–21*, 106n11
Deuteronomy *2:4–5*, 95
Deuteronomy *5*, 55
Deuteronomy *5:14*, 94
Deuteronomy *5:16*, 94
Deuteronomy *6:5*, 128
Deuteronomy *10:9*, 106n11
Deuteronomy *10:17*, 121–22
Deuteronomy *10:18*, 122, 131
Deuteronomy *14:2*, 96
Deuteronomy *15*, 106n16
Deuteronomy *15:1*, 103
Deuteronomy *15:1–18*, 109–10
Deuteronomy *15:4–5*, 102
Deuteronomy *15:12*, 94, 95
Deuteronomy *15:14*, 103
Deuteronomy *15:15*, 85, 94
Deuteronomy *15:17b*, 95, 103
Deuteronomy *16:11–12*, 94, 110

Deuteronomy 16:12, 85
Deuteronomy 16:14, 94
Deuteronomy 17:20, 95
Deuteronomy 18:1, 106n11
Deuteronomy 18:18–22, 119
Deuteronomy 20:11–14, 104
Deuteronomy 21:18–21, 94
Deuteronomy 23:1–8, 110–11, 116n1
Deuteronomy 23:3, 95
Deuteronomy 23:7, 95
Deuteronomy 23:19–20, 111, 116n2
Deuteronomy 24:19–20, 100
Deuteronomy 25:5–10, 95
Deuteronomy 26:5a–9, 104
Joshua 5:13–12:24, 96
Joshua 9, 55
Joshua 13:1–21:45, 99
Judges 1:28, 55
Judges 4:4, 94
Ruth 1:16–17, 111
Ruth 4:1–4, 103
Ruth 4:13–22, 111–12
1 Samuel 2:22, 94
1 Samuel 8:10–18, 104
1 Samuel 8:11, 100
1 Samuel 8:14, 100
2 Samuel 20, 55
1 Kings 9, 55
1 Kings 9:20–22, 104
1 Kings 10:2–5, 104
1 Kings 11, 98
1 Kings 21:1–29, 106n13
2 Kings 4:1, 103
2 Kings 11:1–21, 94
2 Kings 16:10–16, 98
2 Kings 17:23–24, 119
2 Kings 22:13, 94
2 Kings 22:14, 94, 115–16
2 Kings 22:15, 94
2 Chronicles 19:7, 134n19
2 Chronicles 34:22, 94
2 Chronicles 36:22–23, 105n8
Ezra 1:2–4, 105n8
Ezra 10:1–44, 98
Nehemiah 5:3–5, 103
Nehemiah 6:14, 94
Nehemiah 13:22–27, 98
Nehemiah 13:23–27, 112
Job 34:19, 134n19
Psalm 29, 98
Psalm 72:1–4, 102, 115

Psalm 82:1–14, 134n19
Psalm 115:3–8, 98–99
Psalm 140:12, 102
Proverbs 10:1, 94
Proverbs 10:4, 100
Proverbs 12:9, 104
Proverbs 21:17, 100
Proverbs 22:7, 104
Proverbs 22:17–24:34, 98
Proverbs 24:30–34, 100
Proverbs 29:19, 104
Proverbs 29:21, 104
Isaiah 2:2–4, 96, 112–13
Isaiah 5:8, 101
Isaiah 5:23, 101
Isaiah 8:3, 94
Isaiah 13–23, 97
Isaiah 40–55, 97
Isaiah 40–66, 98
Isaiah 41:8–9, 97
Isaiah 42:1, 97
Isaiah 45:1, 97
Isaiah 56–66, 97
Isaiah 56:1–8, 113–14
Isaiah 56:6–7, 97
Isaiah 66:20, 98
Jeremiah 5:27, 101
Jeremiah 22:13–17, 101, 114
Jeremiah 34:8–22, 103
Jeremiah 46–51, 97
Ezekiel 8:14, 98
Ezekiel 25–32, 97
Ezekiel 45:9, 101
Daniel 1:16, 135n24
Joel 2:28–29, 114
Joel 2:28–32, 120, 141–42
Amos 1:2–2:16, 97
Amos 2:6, 103
Amos 2:6–7a, 115
Amos 3:9, 101
Amos 4:1–2, 101
Amos 5:7, 101
Amos 8:6, 103
Obadiah, 97
Micah 2:9, 103
Micah 3:9–11, 101
Nahum, 97
Habakkuk 2:9, 101
Zephaniah 2:3, 106n14
Zephaniah 2:4–15, 97
Malachi 3:5, 101

2 Maccabees 5:27, 135n24
Matthew 12:50, 130
Matthew 22:16, 136n51
Matthew 22:34–40, 128
Matthew 23:31–33, 134n12
Matthew 28:19, 120
Mark 7:15, 123
Mark 7:27, 120
Mark 10:5–6, 134n13
Mark 12:14, 136n51
Mark 12:28–34, 128
Luke 2:23–24, 129
Luke 4, 56
Luke 9:23, 129
Luke 9:58, 129
Luke 10:25–37, 139–40
Luke 10:27, 128
Luke 14:25–27, 140
Luke 14:26, 130
Luke 14:27, 129
Luke 14:33, 140, 207
Luke 20:21, 136n51
John 4, 127–28, 132
John 4:4–27, 118–20, 140–41
John 4:9, 119
John 4:14, 119
John 4:22, 119
John 4:23, 119
John 4:25–26, 119
John 4:27, 119
John 8:37–39, 134n12
John 8:44–47, 134n12
John 10:14–16, 129
John 12:20–23, 129
John 12:20–32, 120
John 12:32, 129
Acts 1:8, 120
Acts 2, 120–21, 127, 132
Acts 2:1–18, 141
Acts 2:9–11, 120
Acts 2:17–18, 120
Acts 2:21, 141–42
Acts 2:42–47, 142
Acts 2:44–45, 120
Acts 4, 132
Acts 4:32–35, 142
Acts 6:5, 121
Acts 10, 127–28
Acts 10–11, 121–22, 132
Acts 10:28, 121
Acts 10:28–48, 142–43, 204–5

Acts 10:34, 131
Acts 10:34–35, 117, 121
Acts 10:36–43, 122
Acts 17:26, 31–32
Acts 18:26, 126
Romans 2:11, 131
Romans 13:9–10, 128
Romans 14, 123, 128, 132, 135n24
Romans 14:1–6, 143
Romans 14:2, 123
Romans 14:4–6, 123
Romans 14:5, 123
Romans 14:13–23, 143–44
Romans 14:14, 123
Romans 14:15, 123, 129
Romans 14:20–23, 123
Romans 14:21, 130
Romans 16:1–7, 144
Romans 16:7, 126
1 Corinthians 2:3, 135n35
1 Corinthians 7, 55, 134n20
1 Corinthians 10, 135n24
1 Corinthians 11, 79
2 Corinthians 7:15, 135n35
2 Corinthians 8, 129–30, 132
2 Corinthians 8:1–15, 144–45
2 Corinthians 8:2–5, 129
2 Corinthians 8:9, 129
2 Corinthians 8:13–14, 130
Galatians 2:6, 131
Galatians 3, 122–23, 124–26, 128
Galatians 3:16, 130
Galatians 3:26–29, 122, 130, 134n12, 145
Galatians 3:27–28, 56–57
Galatians 3:28, 117, 122, 130
Galatians 3:29, 130
Galatians 5:14, 128
Ephesians 1:4, 125
Ephesians 2:11–22, 129
Ephesians 2:14, 57
Ephesians 5–6, 124–26, 128
Ephesians 5:21, 124, 125
Ephesians 5:21–6:9, 145–46
Ephesians 5:22, 117, 125
Ephesians 5:23, 125
Ephesians 5:25, 125
Ephesians 5:25–26, 129
Ephesians 5:28, 125
Ephesians 5:28–31, 131
Ephesians 5:33, 125
Ephesians 6, 117–18

Ephesians 6:5, 117, 125
Ephesians 6:6, 125
Ephesians 6:9, 84, 126, 131
Philippians 2:12, 135n35
Colossians 3, 55
Colossians 3:11, 134n20
Colossians 3:25, 136n51
1 Thessalonians 2:14–16, 134n12
1 Timothy 2, 126–28, 131
1 Timothy 2:8–15, 126, 146
1 Timothy 2:11–12, 126
1 Timothy 2:11–15, 131
1 Timothy 2:13–14, 127
1 Timothy 6, 55
1 Timothy 6:3–10, 127
Philemon, 128
Philemon 2:5, 129
Philemon 2:8, 129
Philemon 10, 123
Philemon 10–16, 146–47
Philemon 11, 124
Philemon 13, 124
Philemon 16, 124, 130
Hebrews 9–10, 129
James 2:8, 128
1 Peter 1:17, 131
Revelation 2:6, 134n17
Revelation 2:9, 134n12
Revelation 2:15, 134n17
Revelation 3:9, 134n12

Qur'an

Al-Baqara [2]:47, 167, 220
Al-Baqara [2]:62, 167
Al-Baqara [2]:177, 187, 196, 207
Al-Baqara [2]:228, 10, 155, 158
Al-Baqara [2]:231, 157
Al-Baqara [2]:237, 156
Al-Baqara [2]:253, 18n4
Al-Baqara [2]:256, 153, 167
Al-Baqara [2]:275–79, 185–86
Al-Baqara [2]:275–80, 195–96
Al-Baqara [2]:282, 11, 167
Āl 'Imran [3]:92, 176
Āl 'Imran [3]:104, 153
Āl 'Imran [3]:130, 180
Al-Nisa' [4]:1, 49, 151, 155, 203
Al-Nisa' [4]:1–12, 178, 183–84, 194–95
Al-Nisa' [4]:4, 156
Al-Nisa' [4]:7, 157
Al-Nisa' [4]:11, 157

Al-Nisa' [4]:12, 179
Al-Nisa' [4]:19, 156
Al-Nisa' [4]:20–21, 156
Al-Nisa' [4]:24, 156
Al-Nisa' [4]:32, 11
Al-Nisa' [4]:34, 10, 11, 41–42, 44, 49, 156, 158
Al-Nisa' [4]:35, 157
Al-Nisa' [4]:36–37, 177
Al-Nisa' [4]:36–39, 184, 195
Al-Nisa' [4]:75, 188, 197
Al-Nisa' [4]:135, 9
Al-Ma'ida [5]:2, 9
Al-Ma'ida [5]:5, 168
Al-Ma'ida [5]:19, 87
Al-Ma'ida [5]:32, 14
Al-Ma'ida [5]:55–58, 168
Al-An'am [6]:165, 164
Al-A'raf [7]:10–15, 164
Al-A'raf [7]:11, 151
Al-A'raf [7]:156, 9
Al-A'raf [7]:172, 151
Al-Anfal [8]:26, 85
Al-Tawba [9]:28–29, 168
Al-Tawba [9]:29, 154
Al-Tawba [9]:58–60, 184–85, 195
Al-Tawba [9]:72, 155
Ibrahim [14]:35, 153
Al-Hijr [15]:26–30, 163
Al-Hijr [15]:29, 151
Al-Nahl [16]:57–61, 166
Al-Nahl [16]:71, 86, 175, 188–89, 197
Al-Isra' [17]:15, 87, 153
Al-Isra' [17]:23–24, 167
Al-Isra' [17]:24, 89n12
Al-Isra' [17]:70, 151, 163
Al-Kahf [18]:29, 153
Ta Ha [20]:121, 10
Al-Nur [24]:32–33, 178, 187–88, 196
Al-Nur [24]:51–54, 153
Al-Nur [24]:55, 153
Al-Shu'ara' [26]:22, 85
Al-Qasas [28]:4, 85
Al-Qasas [28]:4–6, 164
Al-Qasas [28]:5, 220
Al-Qasas [28]:38–42, 164
Al-'Ankabut [29]:46, 154
Al-Rum [30]:21, 157, 166
Al-Rum [30]:22, 165
Al-Rum [30]:38–39, 186–87, 196
Al-Rum [30]:39, 180
Al-Sajda [32]:18, 168

Al-Ahzab [33]:35, 10, 155, 166
Al-Ahzab [33]:71, 153
Fatir [35]:19–22, 169
Saad [38]:72, 151
Al-Zumar [39]:32–35, 153
Al-Zumar [39]:61, 153
Ghafir [40]:9, 153
Al-Zukhruf [43]:32, 86
Al-Hujurat [49]:11, 152
Al-Hujurat [49]:11–13, 164–65
Al-Hujurat [49]:13, 10, 152, 222
Al-Hujurat [49]:14, 153
Al-Dhariyat [51]:56, 153
Al-Najm [53]:32, 18n4

Al-Mujadala [58]:1, 166
Al-Hashr [59]:20, 169
Al-Taghabun [64]:3, 151
Al-Talaq [65]:6–7, 157
Al-Mulk [67]:2, 153
Al-Qalam [69]:34, 176
Al-Mudaththir [74]:43–44, 176
Al-Takwir [81]:8–9, 156
Al-Takwir [81]:9, 156
Al-Fajr [89]:14–20, 175, 182, 193
Al-Fajr [89]:17–20, 176
Al-Shams [90]:7–16, 175, 182–83, 190n22, 193
Al-Tin [95]:4, 151
Al-Tin [95]:4–6, 163

About the Editor

Dr. Lucinda Allen Mosher, rapporteur of the Building Bridges Seminar, is faculty associate in interfaith studies at Hartford Seminary and an affiliate of its Macdonald Center for the Study of Islam and Christian-Muslim Relations. Concurrently, she is senior editor of the Journal of Interreligious Studies, president of NeighborFaith Consultancy LLC, and fellow emerita of the Center for Anglican Communion Studies at Virginia Theological Seminary. Mosher is the author or editor of more than a dozen books and many essays on multifaith matters. She received her doctorate in theology from General Theological Seminary in New York City.